COMPUTING FOR ORDINARY MORTALS

COMPUTING FOR
ORDINARY MORTALS

Robert St. Amant

Hand-drawn illustrations by

Stefano Imbert

OXFORD
UNIVERSITY PRESS

OXFORD
UNIVERSITY PRESS

Oxford University Press is a department of the University of Oxford.
It furthers the University's objective of excellence in research,
scholarship, and education by publishing worldwide.

Oxford   New York
Auckland   Cape Town   Dar es Salaam   Hong Kong   Karachi
Kuala Lumpur   Madrid   Melbourne   Mexico City   Nairobi
New Delhi   Shanghai   Taipei   Toronto

With offices in
Argentina   Austria   Brazil   Chile   Czech Republic   France   Greece
Guatemala   Hungary   Italy   Japan   Poland   Portugal   Singapore
South Korea   Switzerland   Thailand   Turkey   Ukraine   Vietnam

Oxford is a registered trade mark of Oxford University Press in the UK
and certain other countries.

Published in the United States of America by
Oxford University Press
198 Madison Avenue, New York, NY 10016

Library of Congress Cataloging-in-Publication Data
St. Amant, Robert.
Computing for ordinary mortals / Robert St. Amant; hand drawn
illustrations by Stefano Imbert.
p. cm.
Includes bibliographical references and index.
ISBN: 978–0–19–977530–9 (hardback: alk. paper)   1. Computer science.   I. Title.
QA76.S7375 2013
004—dc23
2012015125

3 5 7 9 8 6 4
Printed in the United States of America
on acid-free paper

CONTENTS

INTRODUCTION

My house is filled with computers. Across the room I can see a digital video recorder and a gaming console; my mobile phone is somewhere else in the house, probably not too far from the electronic book reader and portable music player that I'm always misplacing. Computers are embedded in my dishwasher, microwave, and other kitchen appliances; they're also in my washing machine and clothes dryer. At the moment, I'm writing this book on my laptop computer. I'll take a break shortly to read email from friends who are scattered across the continent, and later I'll probably surf the Web, which connects me with other computers in every part of the world—I can even watch live images from cameras in Antarctica.

All this might have been impressive a few decades ago, but I could be describing the average household in almost any developed country today. We can use computers to do work, to play games, to simplify our lives in any number of different ways. Thousands of people assemble their own computer systems, and millions of people write software to give their systems new capabilities. Sometimes it seems as if computers can do almost anything we can imagine.

But that's not all there is to computing. The really interesting part is the ideas behind the technology. They're powerful ideas, the foundations for everything that computers do. They're so general that they can also give us insight into our own daily activities, how we interact with other people, and in some cases even what's going on in our heads. Computing is all around us. That's what this book is about.

We'll start off with an overview of basic concepts in computing—computers are machines, though different in a few important ways from other kinds of machines. From that point we'll follow two different threads through the fabric of computing.

One thread is practical. We'll consider how the architecture of a computer (it's a more dynamic architecture than that of a building) makes it possible for computers to be efficient. We'll see how to write down instructions so that a computer can accomplish specific tasks (programming), how the computer manages those tasks as it runs (in its operating system), and how computers can communicate with each other (over a network).

The other thread is theoretical. Computers are physical machines, but they process information—in the abstract, they're machines for solving problems. We'll look into the nature of computing itself, to see what can be computed and how easily it can be done.

We'll wrap up with the human side of computing, from two different perspectives. Artificial intelligence explores the possibility that computers might eventually be capable of human-level intelligence. Human–computer interaction is about the ways in which computers can enrich our lives—and the ways they fall short. Computing is a very human activity, at its core.

I've written this book for readers curious about what lies beneath the everyday use of computers. You might be a high school senior who wonders whether computer science would be a good major in college, or a blogger who thinks, "I work with computers every day, but I don't really understand them." You might simply enjoy reading science magazines and the science supplement in the Sunday newspaper.

The topics I've included cover the entire range of computing, those typically studied by college students majoring in computer science. A few hours of reading won't make you a computer scientist (I've left out the messy technical details), but you'll come away knowing how to think about computers and computing. It should be an interesting journey. You may come to see the world in a different way.

COMPUTING FOR ORDINARY MORTALS

## Chapter 1

Getting Started

Most of my friends and colleagues in computer science are happy to talk about their work.[1] I'm the same way. Of course, we have to tailor our explanations to the background of the person we're talking to. I might tell a new colleague, "I'm interested in cognitive models for human–computer interaction." In contrast, I was once talking to my 5-year-old nephew about what I do as a college professor, and he went away with the impression that I'm just like his kindergarten teacher, but with older students.

Often, my colleagues and I are trying to share our sense of what's interesting—even exciting—about the field of computing. What problems do we find compelling? How do we go about solving them? Why is any of it important?

Good explanations rarely need to get down to mathematics or the complexities of programming. Instead, they focus on ideas. Computing isn't only (or even mostly) about hardware and software; it's about the ideas *behind* the technology.[2] Some of these ideas are incremental, tiny additions to what we already know; others are powerful enough to change the world.

Here are a few examples from the history of computing—all within my own lifetime.

Back in 1963, using a typical computer was not all that different from punching keys on a fancy typewriter.[3] Ivan Sutherland, then a 25-year-old Ph.D. student at the Massachusetts Institute of Technology, observed that people were essentially "writing letters" to computers. Sutherland was something of a prodigy; in high school he'd learned to program a computer, the Simon, when there were fewer than a thousand such "personal" computers in the world. His new idea was a drawing system he called Sketchpad. Using Sketchpad, people could interact with a computer through a graphical user interface, by pointing with a light pen to create architectural and engineering diagrams, artistic drawings, and animations. Today's Apple Macintosh and Microsoft Windows would look very different, if they existed at all, without Sketchpad's influence.

Around the same time, on the other side of the continent, Doug Engelbart was directing the new Augmentation Research Center at the Stanford Research Institute. Engelbart had a grand vision of computers: they would "augment the human intellect," partly by automating routine tasks, and partly by making it easier for people to work with each other. In 1968 he and his colleagues made public the oNLine System (NLS), in what later came to be known as the mother of all demos. They demonstrated video conferencing, windows containing text and graphics, shared word processing documents, and an invention they called a mouse—new ideas for how people could interact with and through computers.

Closer to the present, in 1989, we find Tim Berners-Lee working in Geneva, Switzerland, at CERN (*Conseil Européen pour la Recherche Nucléaire*, or the European Council for Nuclear Research). At 34, Berners-Lee had long experience with computers; he'd built simple components from scratch while in primary school in the 1960s. (He comments that "if you have enough time and enough power and enough nails, you could actually build a whole computer out of nails.") At CERN, Berners-Lee proposed a new information management system to help thousands of physicists share their work with each other. He called it the World Wide Web. Today, the Web lets billions of people explore more than a trillion documents, interactive experiences, sound files, and videos, making connections with each other and with every kind of information we can imagine.

Each of these innovations was a tour de force, given the technology of the time. The first prototype of Engelbart's mouse was built with a wooden housing and metal gears. Sutherland established the field of interactive graphics working on a computer that stored less information than one of today's digital Christmas tree ornaments.[4]

More important, though, were the ideas behind these systems:

- *We can represent and interact with visual models of the real world, inside a computer.* Once we have an idea that this is possible, we can also imagine video games and virtual reality systems that expand the boundaries of our everyday experience.
- *We can work (and play) with people elsewhere in the world, through computers, as if they were in the same room.* Now we can think about telecommuting, online multiplayer games, online social networks, even romantic entanglements with people we've never met in person.
- *People and organizations can produce information that anyone can access over a global information network.* Now think about reading, shopping, banking, and blogging online; think Google.

Today, Sketchpad, NLS, and the World Wide Web are viewed as milestones in computing, especially interactive computing, because they made it possible for us to see computers and the real world in new ways. They gave us insight. This is the single most important thing about computing, as Richard Hamming, an influential mathematician and computer scientist, pointed out in 1962:

The purpose of computing is insight, not numbers.[5]

In the rest of this book we'll see more of these insights.

WHAT IS COMPUTING?

If this book were about biology, you'd probably expect to find a definition of the field in the introduction: "Biology is the study of living organisms." Or in a book about physics: "Physics is the study of matter and energy."

We can define computing along similar lines, but first we need to think about the nature of such definitions. They're just placeholders, and the definitions of physics and biology work because we already have good intuitions about those subjects.[6] We might not understand life, matter, or energy in scientific terms, but we all experience physics from the moment we wake in the morning to the moment we fall asleep at night, and we're intimately familiar with biology, being biological organisms ourselves. Most people don't have the same natural intuitions about computers and computing, though, which makes it difficult to offer a short definition that makes immediate, intuitive sense.

Let's fill in some of the blanks. You may have a computer sitting on your desk. If you've ever opened up its case, you know what its *hardware* looks like. You probably saw green circuit boards studded with dark-gray silicon chips and other bits of electronics, looking much like a satellite photo of a major city and hardly less complex.

If you've used that computer, you've interacted with its *software*. Software includes applications for reading email, composing reports, exploring the World Wide Web, playing games—in fact, everything a computer does from the moment you turn it on is carried out by software.

Computer architecture is the study of how the different components of a computer's hardware can be organized. Like the architecture of a building, a computer's architecture is designed to support the activities inside. In a computer, these are computations rather than human activities, but they still need to respect logical, physical, and even economic constraints.

Building software systems that make computers do useful things is mainly the concern of *programming* and *software engineering*. Dozens or even hundreds of people might work on a complex software system over its lifetime, contributing at the most detailed level ("What should the computer do when such-and-such happens?") and at higher levels ("How can we organize our activities to meet a November deadline for our next software release?"). Producing dependable software means understanding constraints on all the levels.

Computing also has a more abstract side, which is harder to describe in terms of how computers behave or what people do with computers. But a story should help to illustrate.

You've been abducted by aliens. "It's not really an abduction," one of the aliens tells you. "We'd just like to borrow some of your time." The alien asks you to call him Bob—he says you wouldn't be able to pronounce his real name. You discover that these aliens are not the kind that views humanity as a food source; they're about to announce themselves to the world, but they want to know how humans are likely to react to the news. Bob offers you a choice. He can bring you back home immediately, or he can give you a guided tour of his spaceship, answering your questions. You take the tour.

As you start walking, you ask, "Do all aliens speak such good English?"

Bob shows his teeth, which you take for a smile. "No, it's not like in the movies. I've had to study English for years. But of course I have my own language. Listen." Bob purses his lips, and you hear a series of hums, clicks, and high-pitched whistles. "There. That's the beginning of my favorite…song, you'd probably call it."

A singing, English-speaking alien hardly seems threatening, but you're still unsure. "Seriously, you're not going to conquer the Earth?"

"Not at all. We'll ask you to join our federation, which has a few thousand other members. We've accomplished great things through cooperation—and it's much more civilized than conquest."

"Does that mean you'll be sharing your knowledge with us?"

"Of course! We actually have a lot to learn from each other. It will take some work, though. There are so many different ways to organize what we know. For instance… " It turns out that Bob likes the human concept of "games" but is still puzzled by it; you spend some time discussing the idea with him. A new question comes to mind.

"Are you smarter than us humans?"

"That's a hard question," he says. "How do you measure intelligence? We've met people on one planet who can't count higher than three without help, and yet even their children can name thousands of different colors. And they're fun to talk to. It might be that there are different kinds of intelligence."

Eventually you reach the end of the tour. "Any last questions?" asks Bob.

You think for a moment. "What's it like to be an alien?"

"Oops—time's up." Bob and his alien spaceship fade away, and you find yourself at home again, safe and sound.

What are we to make of your alien visitation? If we look at your questions and Bob's answers, we can learn something about the abstract side of computing.

Your first question is about *communication*. In computing, communication is about the challenges of transferring information reliably between a computer's hardware components, its software systems, and even computers that might be thousands of miles away from each other. The information typically isn't expressed in ordinary English, but there are some similarities between the structure of human languages and of languages for computer communication.

Next up is *coordination*. In some situations, as with processing on a single computer, it makes sense for activities to be coordinated by a single master controller, which can allocate resources for different tasks. As systems grow larger, however, looser coordination schemes become more practical. Early work to create the Internet, which connects hundreds of millions of computers together, aimed at "federations" of different networks.

Sharing knowledge is one aspect of *information management*. Information comes in different forms, including text, drawings and photos, audio and video. Computers need to store large amounts of such information and make it available, quickly and efficiently, when needed.

Your question about intelligence is a difficult one. What would nonhuman intelligence look like? *Artificial intelligence* studies different aspects of intelligent human behavior—we make decisions based on what we know, we learn from experience, we interact with other people and with the world—and searches for ways to turn these into computations.

Your last, unanswered question matches a fundamental question in the *theory of computing*: What is computation? The answer will help us understand what can be computed, in principle and in practice.

I've told a fanciful story to illustrate the abstract side of computing, but a more ordinary analogy would have worked just as well. Understanding most complex systems in the real world means breaking them down along similar lines. On a large scale, businesses and governments are all about communication, coordination, and making intelligent decisions based on available information; researchers at think tanks and universities spend their careers developing theories to explain these kinds of organizations.

On a smaller scale (of size, not complexity), we understand how our own brains work by asking similar questions about how information is stored, how different regions of the brain coordinate and communicate with each other, how decisions are made, and how all this can be explained by biological or mathematical theory.

I've based my outline of the field on the work of computer scientist Peter Denning.[7] Denning divides the principles of computing into three categories: *design* (which covers hardware and software systems), *practice* (which includes the work of computing professionals who envision, build, and manage such systems), and *mechanics* (which encompasses the abstract concepts illustrated in my story). Concepts flow constantly from one category into another, making computing a rich ecosystem of ideas.

With slightly better intuitions in place, let's return to definitions. We could say that computing is about all of these things, but remember that a definition is just a short placeholder:

> *The field of computing studies the major phenomena surrounding computers.*[8]

We'll spend the rest of the book exploring the specifics of these "major phenomena" and finding out what "computers" are.

HOW TO THINK ABOUT COMPUTING

Some aspects of computing are variations on the ways we deal with familiar situations in our lives. For example, when you call different departments of a shipping company to find out why your package hasn't been delivered, you're *debugging*, something that programmers do to track down errors in computer software. A good debugging strategy, either for lost packages or misbehaving programs, is to figure out the last point at which everything was going as expected—your package in a known location or the program at a known point in its processing—and then to explore the possibilities for what might have gone wrong.

Or think about writing down a shopping list in case you forget what you need at the store. You're using *secondary storage* to keep the same information in two places. A paper list is more permanent than a list kept in your head (in my head, at any rate—I tend to be absentminded when I shop). Computers also use secondary storage, often in the form of a disk drive, for a similar reason.

Every area of computing contains such specialized concepts. Debugging is part of programming, and secondary storage is a computer architecture concept. A few concepts, though, are much more general, cutting across all areas of computing. Here's a story to illustrate one.

> *Clark is an administrative assistant at an old-fashioned company that has resisted the attractions of computing. The company keeps paper records, and Clark is in charge of filing for his department.*
>
> *His boss comes in one day with an armful of manila folders, and says, "We're taking over the Antique Alternators account. Would you please file these?" Clark looks at his metal filing cabinets and sighs. They're not entirely full, but he'd have to move thick stacks of folders between the drawers to make room among the "A" folders in the top drawer, at least an hour of dusty work.*
>
> *He has a better idea. He labels a new folder "Antique Alternators" and puts it in the top drawer in the right place. In the folder he inserts a note, "Look in the bottom drawer of Cabinet 6." He puts all the company's files in that bottom drawer.*
>
> *A few weeks later, when Clark's boss asks for a document from the Antique Alternators account, Clark first opens the "A" drawer and then goes to Cabinet 6, following his earlier instructions. It takes him an extra step to find the document, but he's saved himself a good deal of work in the long run.*

Computer scientists have a term for what Clark has done: *indirection*. When Clark is looking for information, he doesn't immediately find it where it should be; instead he finds a "pointer" to where it actually is. Indirection means dealing with a pointer, a name, or some other handle for an item of information, rather than working directly with the information itself.

This gives Clark quite a bit of flexibility. For example, if the Antique Alternators company changes its name to Elderly Engines, Clark still doesn't have to move its folders; he just adds a new folder in the "E" drawer with a note that points to Cabinet 6. He now has two different ways to refer to the physical files, and he can handle paperwork that comes in under either company name.

This might eventually get complicated for Clark if he repeated his filing cabinet trick for other accounts, but computers are very good at keeping track of such information.

The use of indirection is a core strategy in computing. How important is it? There's a famous aphorism in computing: *Any problem in computer science can be solved with another level of indirection.*[9] This is an exaggeration, but it suggests that indirection is *very* important.

The document icons you see on your computer display are indirect references to information kept in secondary storage on your computer; the arrangement of icons on the screen doesn't need to match how the information is managed internally. Have you ever noticed that when you're dragging a document from one folder to another, it takes about the same amount of time whether the document is very small or very large? That's because you're not moving the information itself, but only changing indirect references to it. Further, the Web address you click on in a browser is an indirect reference to information that might be stored on another computer halfway across the world, but you don't need to know this to use the Web. Programmers rely on indirection in practically every program they write, and it's a deep part of the mathematics and logic of computing.

Indirection is widespread outside computing as well. I can forward the telephone in my office to my mobile phone, so that calls to my office number reach me wherever I go. Or when I'm planning a complicated trip, I'll talk to my travel agent, who knows the ins and outs of making flight reservations. She usually finds a better deal than I can, and much faster. Indirection lets us delegate responsibilities to those best able to handle them. There are potential drawbacks, though. If you've ever reached a wrong number on the phone or heard the message, "This number is no longer in service," you've discovered that indirection can break down. And if you've ever tried to register a complaint with a company and been transferred from one person to another, moving more and more slowly through protective layers of management, you've found that indirection serves some people better than others. The concept of indirection turns out to be important in real life—it gives us a way to think about how the world works.

When we use terms like debugging, secondary storage, and indirection, we're doing more than applying technical jargon to ordinary situations. We're recognizing a natural correspondence between those situations and what's known about the theory and practices of computing. This is part of what's sometimes called *computational thinking*.[10]

Computational thinking doesn't mean thinking like a computer, any more than mathematical thinking means acting like a calculator, or musical thinking means pretending to be a musical instrument. Rather, it's about understanding concepts in computing that have proved their value and applying them to new problems and situations—even some that might not involve computers at all.

In the rest of this book, we'll examine more ideas like those above. We'll make sense of them, standing on their own and in connection with the real world. I'll illustrate the ideas with examples and a good number of stories.

Why stories? Because stories help us understand the world and our place in it. They're used in politics (personal interest stories), in religion (parables and moral lessons), and even in the sciences (Maxwell's demon and Einstein's elevator are famous thought experiments in physics).[11]

I'm taking a slight risk in drawing analogies between people and computers. I've tried to be careful with my stories, by explaining what's relevant and important in each analogy.

For example, in popular science publications, it's not uncommon to find something like this: *Your mind works a lot like a computer. Your brain puts information it judges to be important into "files." When you remember something, you pull up a file.* (This is from an informal introduction to memory, published by the National Institutes for Health.) Unfortunately, the analogy isn't very good. Not that it's *wrong*—by nature, analogies are never literally true—but it can mislead us in some ways. Can I copy or delete a memory in the same way that I deal with a computer file? Should I consider backing up my memories in case I get in some kind of accident? These would be nice abilities to have, but they're not very realistic.

If we apply the analogy in the reverse direction, it also breaks down. There are so many ways that a computer is *not* like your mind, most of the inferences we might draw are wrong. Do I need to remind my computer of some minor thing I typed in last week? If I'm talking to an automated system on the telephone and I answer a question with "Whatever" or "Make it so" instead of "Yes," should I expect to be understood? If I accidentally instruct my computer to delete all the email messages I've ever received from my boss, will it tell me that this would be a bad idea? The answer to all of these questions is "Probably not."

But stories are worth the risk. Stories about people tend to be much more interesting than stories about machines, so I'll draw parallels between the abstract ideas of computing and more familiar activities: calling people on the telephone, sending a package through the post, counting fish, chaperoning children, and so forth. I hope that when you read each story, you'll have a small "Aha!" moment and be able to tie the general idea to your own experience. Thinking about everyday activities (even imaginary ones) should make it easier to understand computing and, conversely, thinking about computing should give useful insights into those everyday activities.

Let's get started.

FURTHER READING

The emphasis in this chapter is on computing concepts, rather than skills. Surprisingly few other books, aside from those written for professional computer scientists, have such a focus. All of the following make for good reading:

Blown to Bits: Your Life, Liberty, and Happiness after the Digital Explosion, by Hal Abelson, Ken Ledeen, and Harry Lewis (Addison Wesley, 2008)
Computer Science Unplugged, by Mike Fellows, Tim Bell, and Ian Witten (lulu. com, 2002)

The Pattern on the Stone: The Simple Ideas that Make Computers Work, by W. Daniel Hillis (Basic Books, 1999)

D is for Digital: What a well-informed person should know about computers and communications, by Brian W. Kernighan (CreateSpace, 2012)

Code: The Hidden Language of Computer Hardware and Software, by Charles Petzold (Microsoft Press, 2010)

Out of their Minds: The Lives and Discoveries of 15 Great Computer Scientists, by Dennis Shasha and Cathy Lazere (Springer, 1995)

"What is computation?" by Ian Horswill, in *ACM XRDS* 18, 3 (March 2012), pp. 8–14

If you've taken courses in computer science, then all of the concepts in this chapter and the rest of the book will be familiar. I've selected topics from the curriculum guidelines developed by the Association for Computing Machinery (ACM), which can be found in the Computing Curricula Computer Science Volume, written by the Interim Review Task Force in 2008. I've also been guided by *Being Fluent with Information Technology*, by the Committee on Information Technology Literacy, National Research Council (National Academies Press, 1999).

## Chapter 2

From Mechanical to Electronic Computers

Computers are machines, but they seem different from many of the other machines around us, like kitchen blenders or soda dispensers.

What's the difference?

It's not that computers are full of electronics rather than mechanical parts; some simple computers are entirely mechanical. And saying that a computer is a machine that processes information instead of chopping vegetables or turning pocket change into bottled drinks isn't really a satisfying explanation. To see what makes a computer a computer, we'll take a short tour through history, starting with one of its simpler ancestors: the loom.

JACQUARD AND THE DRAW LOOM

As I sit typing on my laptop, I can see one of my wife's looms in the corner of the room. It's a beautiful example of a pre-industrial machine, all polished oak, leather cording, and silvery metal fittings. If you were sitting at the loom, you'd see hundreds of threads stretching from front to back, passing through a comb-like "reed" and a pair of harnesses. These threads—imagine that they're numbered in order—form what's called the warp. One harness controls all the odd threads, the other all the even threads, and each harness is tied to a foot treadle.

When you press one treadle, it separates the odd threads from the even threads, creating an opening. You pass a device called a shuttle, which trails a weft thread behind it, through the opening and across the warp. You then let up the treadle so that the warp lies flat again, you pull back on the reed to force the weft thread straight, and you've finished one row. You move on to the next row. Back and forth with the shuttle, row by row, odd threads then even threads . . . you're weaving, and eventually you'll hold in your hands a piece of plain-woven cloth.

This may not sound very much like computing, but here's the connection. If you could take a snapshot of the ends of the warp threads after each step in the weaving process, you'd see something like this: threads all down, then alternating threads up, then threads all down again, and so forth (Figs. 2.1 and 2.2).

We can think of each of these snapshots as a different *state* of the loom, and we can describe these states as specific patterns of ups and downs in the threads. Each step, by changing the positions of some of the threads, takes the loom from one of its states to the next.

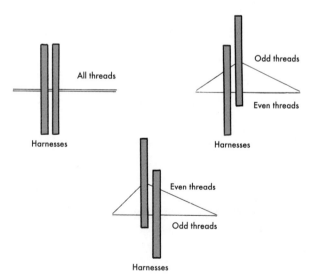

Figure 2.1. Pressing a treadle causes alternate warp threads to be raised.

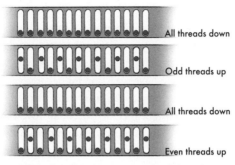

Figure 2.2. At different times, different patterns of threads are raised.

A computer works in a similar way, but at a different scale and speed. Instead of hundreds of threads being moved up or down by harnesses, a computer has trillions of internal elements that can be turned on or off, and the system moves between different states billions of times a second. This, by the way, is why we say that computers are *binary* machines; the patterns describing its states are made up of on–off elements ("binary" means "coming in twos," as in a binary star system). On the loom, different up–down binary patterns create different kinds of woven cloth; in a computer, different on–off binary patterns produce all of its complex behavior.

Now, we might imagine taking snapshots of any machine, or for that matter any process at all, and calling the collection a set of states. Computers and looms are different from many other kinds of machines, though. Their states are all we need to pay attention to. That is, if we were to compare one snapshot and the next, it wouldn't matter how much time had passed or anything else that had happened between the two shots; we can predict the results the machine will produce just by looking at its states. For contrast, imagine a waterwheel on an old mill, another nice pre-industrial machine. No matter how closely we space our snapshots of the wheel, we'll be missing parts of its continuous motion and all the complexity of the water flowing under and over it. Thinking of a waterwheel as a state-based machine can be only a very rough approximation.

Computers are different. They're designed so that, in principle, their step-by-step transitions between states are all that matters in understanding how they work. We therefore say that computers (and looms) are *discrete,* rather than continuous, systems.[1]

Looms and weaving have another important lesson for us. To see how, imagine living sometime in the late 1700s. If you were a French aristocrat of the era, you'd have a passion for decorative patterned silk. Making this silk was enormously labor-intensive, as with many luxury goods—a fine brocade might include dozens of roses, for example, a thousand threads to the inch, every row showing a slightly different pattern in the warp threads. Ordinary looms like the one in my living room weren't enough to handle this complexity. The work could be done only by expert artisans with a draw loom.

Weaving with a draw loom was a two-person job. The master weaver would stand at one end of the loom, and his helper—a drawboy—would sit within or on top of the frame of the loom. The master weaver would tell the drawboy to raise specific threads for a single row in a pattern to be woven. The drawboy would draw up those threads, the master weaver would throw the shuttle, and they'd continue to the next row. Weavers managed to produce just one inch of silk per day in this way.

Joseph-Marie Jacquard, the son of a silk weaver, invented a replacement for the draw loom and revolutionized the weaving industry.[2] He became an inventor late in life, after inheriting and spending a fortune, fighting on both sides during the French Revolution, and finally retiring due to war injuries. His engineering work soon brought him patents and prizes. (Though not all of his inventions were received equally well, as recorded in an early biography: "[A]ccording to the arbitrary fashion of the time, he and his machine were placed under arrest and conveyed to Paris, where the invention was submitted to inspectors, upon whose report a gold medal was awarded to him."[3])

In a Jacquard loom, the raising or lowering of threads is controlled by spring-loaded rods, rather than a human drawboy.[4] Pushing on the ends of some rods but not others creates different patterns in the warp threads. We might imagine pushing the rods with our fingers, as if playing a church organ, but Jacquard had a different solution: punch cards, which are stiff pieces of paper with holes punched in some locations but not others. When a card is put in place on a panel, the blank locations push on a specific pattern of rod-ends and the holes let the others through. The cards themselves are linked together, so that by pressing a foot pedal, a weaver can advance the cards and put each one in place against the panel, throwing the shuttle at each step (Fig. 2.3).

Jacquard's design gave weavers a tremendous boost in productivity. One person using his loom for a day could do as much as a master weaver and drawboy working for a month.

The Jacquard loom is still a discrete system, moving from one state to another, and the holes and blanks in each punch card match the binary pattern in the warp threads for each row of the cloth. The innovation in the Jacquard loom, aside from its engineering design, has to do with another essential concept in computing: *control*. Think about the dexterity, the knowledge, and even the communication skills that the master weaver and drawboy relied on to do their jobs. In the Jacquard loom, most of this is replaced by machinery. Control is no longer external to the machine, in the dynamic decisions made by human beings, but part of the machine itself.

In a computer, control is the "what happens next" in its processing. Computers can be programmed to carry out a sequence of steps without supervision. While human control is usually needed in the beginning, to set up a task, the computer is capable of following through on its own. We'll talk about exactly how this is done in later chapters, but for now, it's enough to recognize that this is largely what makes computers so powerful in practice.

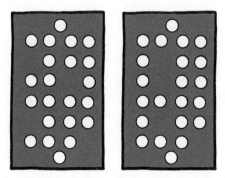

Figure 2.3. The holes and blank spaces in a punch card govern the raising and lowering of threads.

Let's stop for a moment to put all these ideas in perspective. When we talk about the states of a discrete system and how it is controlled, we're applying a core strategy in computing: finding and applying *abstractions* that give us a better understanding of the system. Abstractions strip away details so that we can focus on the important, general aspects of a system. In the first chapter I gave one definition of computing, but I might have said instead that computing is the study of abstract models of the structure and control of discrete processing systems.[5]

It's important to realize that abstractions are never a perfect match for the real world. They're idealizations. For example, I've described looms as discrete systems, but I've left out certain realities—threads might need to be untangled, parts might break, and so forth. Sometimes a computer will break down or misbehave in its own electronic way. These sorts of problems aren't part of our abstraction. Still, a step-by-step description fits the processes of weaving and computing well, even if it's only an approximation of reality.

Similarly, in talking about control in the Jacquard loom, we might wonder whether we should think of the loom having one controller that uses different sets of punch cards to produce different patterns, or rather many possible controllers—a new one for each new set of punch cards. We might wonder whether we can include the master weaver, who decides when the cards should be advanced, as part of the controller. We could pose analogous questions about computers—when I press a key on the keyboard or click a mouse button, am *I* part of its controller?

Fortunately, control is a flexible abstraction; all of these interpretations are plausible. Even if the boundary between the controller and other parts of a machine (or its users) isn't precise, it's enough to recognize that the machine *has* a control component that's largely automatic.

It's natural to think that we're losing something when we describe a system at a high level of abstraction, paying attention to some of its properties and ignoring others. This is definitely true. But there's a different way to think about this that's just as valid. George Box, a modern statistician, puts it this way:

All models are wrong. Some models are useful.[6]

Whenever we describe anything at all, we emphasize some details and leave out others, for convenience or clarity. What we *do* decide to put into our description is what makes it useful.

A MECHANICAL COMPUTER

With this conceptual background in mind, let's return to Jacquard's time. The next major step in the intellectual history of computing was taken by the British mathematician Charles Babbage. Babbage was a polymath, interested in astronomy, ophthalmology, cryptography, and technology, as well as in mathematics. He held the Lucasian Chair of Mathematics at Cambridge, the same chair held at different times by Isaac Newton and Stephen Hawking.

When Babbage learned about the Jacquard loom, he had been working for several years on a project to build a mechanical calculating machine. The loom was an inspiration to him. He wrote, "The Jacquard loom is capable of weaving any design that the imagination of man may conceive."[7]

It was the early 1800s, the beginning of the Industrial Revolution. A great demand for information,[8] in the form of numbers, had sprung up among scientists, engineers, financiers, land surveyors, military planners, ships' navigators—everyone who wanted to explain patterns in the world or make predictions about the future in some precise way. Tables of numbers were needed. In Babbage's time, such tables could be produced only by teams of human "computers" who carried out mathematical calculations by hand, in a long, tedious, and error-prone process. A single adding mistake, or even a transcription error, might lead to lost ships, falling bridges, or worse.

Babbage proposed that a machine could calculate the numbers, to remove human error from the process. He designed a machine to do this: the Difference Engine. He later designed a successor, the Difference Engine No. 2, and an even more ambitious machine for general-purpose computing, the Analytical Engine.

I won't go into great detail about the physical construction of these machines; their designs are so complex that a complete, working model of a Difference Engine wasn't built until the 1990s, as a historical exercise taken on by the London Science Museum. Imagine a Victorian clockwork device standing eight feet tall, consisting of column after column of well-oiled brass gears, linked together by axles and racks, activated and controlled by lugs and studs and barrels. On the turn of a crank, the gears revolve to show numbers etched on their circumference, answering the question that the machine's attendants have given it. (Another Difference Engine was later completed, but a working Analytical Engine has never been built.)

But wait—how can a machine be said to calculate or compute anything at all? How can it even represent numbers? Some of the possibilities that Babbage saw around him are still commonplace today: clocks whose hands measure the hours of the day, gauges for measuring pressure, dials that can be turned to specific settings. If a machine's internal gears (or rods or levers or springs or electrical voltages) are put into stable positions that can be reliably distinguished from each other, we can think of the different arrangements as different numbers. And if these internal settings are linked together in appropriate ways, such as the movement of one gear causing another to turn at a faster or slower rate, then the machine can handle one of the basics of calculation: counting.

The concept we're relying on here is *encoding*, or turning one representation of an item of information—a number, but also a letter, symbol, or even a sound or picture—into a different but equivalent representation. Going in the reverse direction is called *decoding*.

Encoding and decoding are technical terms for something that we do automatically in our everyday lives. For example, I can look at a clock face showing the Roman numeral IV and decode this to produce the number 4. If I'm keeping track of an amount by counting on my fingers, I encode each additional item as a raised finger, and I decode the total by translating all of the fingers I've raised back into a number.

Babbage applied this idea in the design of his machines. The Analytical Engine contains thousands of figure-wheels, gears marked with the ten digits on their circumference. The position of each figure-wheel represents a particular one-digit number. Five figure-wheels in a row, then, can represent a five-digit number, with one figure-wheel representing the ones digit, the next the tens digit, the next the hundreds digit, and so forth. The figure-wheels are linked to each other so that when ratchets are released and gears are meshed, their actions give us the familiar operations of addition, subtraction, and so forth. What's 2 + 2? What's 45 × 34? The Analytical Engine calculates the answers, literally like clockwork.

The numbers for a problem are given to the Analytical Engine on punch cards, one number per card. Here we can see some of the power of the idea of encoding. Say we have a problem we'd like to solve that involves a specific number. We encode this number on a punch card, in a pattern of holes on the card. Once this card is fed into the Analytical Engine, that pattern is further encoded into positions of its gears. As long as the translation for each encoding stage is consistent and reliable, we can say that the machine internally represents the number.

Babbage took the idea of encoding a step further. He realized that, just as we can encode numbers on punch cards, we can encode *instructions* on punch cards, to specify actions the machine should take in dealing with the numbers. Two punch cards might hold the same pattern, one representing a specific number, the other a specific instruction; it's a matter of how the pattern is interpreted.

If encoding instructions the same way we encode numbers seems implausible, remember a line of poetry that most American schoolchildren learn: "One if by land, and two if by sea." Paul Revere's message is more than just, "Oh, by the way, this is how the British are coming." It's the less poetic message, "Of the two courses of defense we've worked out, carry out the first plan if you see one lantern light, the second plan if you see two lantern lights." In other words, Revere's message depends on a particular encoding of actions. The case with the Analytical Engine is similar—even if it's designed to handle instructions for mathematics rather than military actions.

Babbage's Analytical Engine processes both numbers and instructions on punch cards.[9] It's capable not only of carrying out a sequence of instructions, but also of "deciding" (based on the numbers it receives as input and its internal computations) whether to carry out specific instructions or not. For example, imagine a punch-card sequence of instructions that adds 1 to the value of a given figure-wheel. We might feed the Analytical Engine a large set of number cards, each representing the age of a different person, and tell it, via additional instruction and number cards, to count the people who are over the age of 65. The Analytical Engine could run back and forth through its cards, selectively adding 1 to its figure-wheel counter only when appropriate. This is a simple example, but there are strong similarities between the way the Analytical Engine solves this problem and the way most computers of today would solve it.

Now that we know roughly how the Analytical Engine works, we can see how control fits into the architecture of the machine.[10] Babbage named the two most important parts of the Analytical Engine the mill and the store. The mill is given a set of numbers and a set of instructions representing a problem; the store is used to record intermediate results produced by the mill as it steps through its computations toward a solution. Problems for the mill to solve are encoded for input through a card reader, whose counterpart we saw in the Jacquard loom; solutions generated by the mill would be visible on figure-wheels or even as output to a printer. Control, as a discrete process, is managed by the mill and the card reader working together.

Some of Babbage's contemporaries recognized the potential of the machine, even though it was never built. Ada Lovelace, a mathematician who corresponded with Babbage, wrote, "there is no finite line of demarcation which limits the powers of the Analytical Engine."[11] Lovelace wrote the first program for the Analytical Engine, and her enthusiasm for computing is echoed by thousands of programmers today.

How high can you count on your fingers? You'll probably say, "Ten." If I told you that computer scientists can count to over a thousand on their fingers, you'd probably suspect that there's a trick involved. Here's the trick: We pay attention to which fingers are being raised.

If you put both hands on a tabletop, you can think of your fingers as representing "places," with your left pinkie being the highest place, your right pinkie the lowest place. When all your fingers are down, that's 0. When all your fingers are down except for your right pinkie, that's 1. How do we get to 2? If you recall learning to add two numbers in elementary school, the phrase "Remember to carry the 1" should seem familiar. This happens if you're adding two digits in a column and the result is higher than 9; you need to add an extra 1 in the column to the left.

We'll do the same thing in counting on our fingers. We want to add 1 to the right pinkie, but we can't represent a number higher than 1 on a single finger. So we lower the right pinkie (giving a 0 in that place) and raise the right ring finger (carrying the 1). This pattern, with all the fingers lowered except the right ring finger, gives us 2. To get to 3, we raise the right pinkie again. Essentially we're adding 1 to a number, repeatedly, just as we would with "ordinary" numbers, except that instead of being able to get all the way to 9 in a single place, we can only go as high as 1. Any higher, and we have to carry a 1 to the next place.

This is a binary rather than decimal counting scheme. Why is it that we use ten different digits in everyday counting? If we realize that "digit" can mean either 0, 1, 2,…9, or one of our fingers, the answer becomes obvious: We count to ten because we have ten fingers. For a decimal number, we can talk about the ones place (the rightmost digit), the tens place (the next digit to the left), the hundreds place, and so forth. Each place represents units that are ten times as great as the units in the place to the right. In binary the basic pattern of representation is the same, except that each place is just two times more than the place to its right. With ten fingers for ten binary places, we can count from zero to $2 \times 2 \times 2 \times 2 \times 2 \times 2 \times 2 \times 2 \times 2 \times 2$, or 1,023.

Modern computers do arithmetic in binary, for technological reasons. If you want to represent a single digit by a voltage level, it's easier and more reliable if you only need to test whether the voltage is above or below some threshold (a one or a zero) than having to test for ten different possible voltages. By analogy, it's easier to see whether a standard light bulb is on or off than to look at a light attached to a dimmer switch and estimate which of ten different brightnesses the light has.

So if you ever hear someone say, "In a computer, everything is just ones and zeroes," you know what that means.

ELECTRONIC COMPUTERS

Let's jump forward about a century, to the 1940s, when the first electronic computers were being built. Our stop here will be short.

In 1945, mathematician John von Neumann was working on the EDVAC (Electronic Discrete Variable Automatic Computer) project, directed by J. Presper Eckert and John Mauchly at the University of Pennsylvania. Von Neumann described a design for general-purpose computers in the influential "First Draft of a Report on the EDVAC."[12]

Part of this draft, in what came to be called the *von Neumann architecture*, is a reasonable description of most general-purpose computers today.

The von Neumann architecture is a modern version of the organization we saw in the Analytical Engine. Von Neumann identified five components in a general-purpose computer:

- *Input devices*, which transfer data and instructions to the computer from some external source (such as a reader for punch cards or magnetic tape—today we might use a keyboard or touch pad)
- A *memory*, to record this information as well as intermediate results of computations
- A *controller*, in charge of sequencing computations
- An *arithmetic/logic* component, which actually carries out the computations, and
- *Output devices* that make results available to the operator of the computer (such as a printer, or today a visual display).

Today, the controller and the arithmetic/logic unit are now usually treated together as the *central processing unit*, or CPU. There's a clear family resemblance to Babbage's machine.

Von Neumann didn't include a diagram of this architecture in his report, but it would have looked something like Figure 2.4.[13]

An important concept is apparent in this diagram: *modularity*. Modularity is a familiar aspect of today's world; in fact, the words "modular" and "modern" share the same Latin root. We tend to think of a modular system as having standardized parts that can be easily assembled, like modular furniture or modular housing.

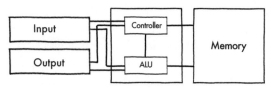

Figure 2.4. The von Neumann architecture includes input and output, memory, a controller, and an arithmetic/logic unit.

The concept of modularity goes deeper in computing. A modular design breaks down a complex system into functional parts, each with its own clear responsibility (in this case, input, output, storage, or processing), which interact with each other in relatively simple ways.[14]

Modularity helps reduce complexity in two ways. First, when we're considering a system at some level of abstraction, we only have to think about *what* its components do, rather than *how* they do it. Second, if we decide to examine some component in more detail, we can consider it in isolation from all the other components; ideally, each will have its own modular structure, as we see with the CPU.

Modularity is part of the way we understand the everyday world. We live in homes with separate rooms for sleeping, eating, cooking, and so forth; we break up the hours of the day into morning, afternoon, evening, and night; some of us work for large organizations that have separate departments with different responsibilities. It shouldn't be surprising that the same kind of modularity contributes to the design of computer systems, from Babbage's designs to von Neumann's architecture.

Von Neumann also gave us one of the first detailed accounts of what "control" means for a computer. It's surprisingly simple. Unlike the Analytical Engine, modern computers don't need to shuffle through cards to carry out instructions to process data. Instead, a set of instructions, called a *program*, is loaded into the memory component, where the controller can access the instructions more quickly and directly. As von Neumann described it, the controller needs to handle just four basic types of instructions. On reading an instruction from memory, the controller can

- Direct the arithmetic/logic unit to carry out some piece of arithmetic or logic
- Transfer data from one place to another
- Prepare for the next instruction to be read, potentially from a different place in memory
- Send a directive to an input or output device

Remarkably, that's enough to handle the enormous range of tasks that we expect of modern computers, from computing tables of numbers to handling the exchange of electronic mail messages across the world, to producing the special effects we see in action movies and video games. Of course, computers of the 1940s were not fast enough to do very much—there's more computational power in the mobile phone in my pocket right now than in the EDVAC—but today's computers work in a very similar way.

One last historical note is worth our attention. In his draft, von Neumann emphasized conceptual relationships he saw between the computer and the human nervous system. He referred to the functional components in his computer organization as "organs." The "memory organ" of the computer corresponds to the relevant parts of the human brain, while the computer's "input organs" and "output organs" are analogous to sensory and motor neurons.

These were early days in the new field of cognitive science; today we have much better models of some kinds of human thought. Just how far can we extend the capabilities of computers? We're still finding out.

COMPUTING TODAY

In this brief tour, we've visited only a few of the prominent historical figures and moments in computing. There are many more. For example, I haven't yet mentioned Herman Hollerith, whose work on tabulating census data with the help of punch cards led to the founding of the company IBM; I've skipped over Alan Turing and Alonzo Church, who established the mathematical foundations of computing; I've left out Grace Hopper, who became one of the very first software engineers *and* a rear admiral in the U.S. Navy. Further, my descriptions of the Jacquard loom, the Analytical Engine, and the EDVAC are quite a bit simpler than the actual machines—it's hard to understand the details without a degree in mechanical or electronic engineering. Still, we've covered some important basics.

Computers are ultimately machines. They all share the ability to store and process information, but they may be constructed from wooden and metal parts, from vacuum tubes, from transistors, or from some other yet-to-be-invented technology. A group of computer science students in the Netherlands has even built a working computer from Lego blocks.[15]

We have a basic understanding of the organization of modern computers, and we've seen elements of the same organization in some historical machines. More importantly, we've learned a few of the central concepts in computing, including the encoding and decoding of information in different forms, discrete processes, control, and modularity as a tool for reducing complexity. These are more than just concepts; they're the basis for powerful strategies in computing that help us understand and solve difficult problems. They also shape our everyday lives in ways that may be surprising because we take them so much for granted.

Encoded information surrounds us. When you're driving your car through an intersection, you're paying attention to an encoded instruction from the traffic signal: green means go and red means stop (yellow is open to interpretation). Symbols on road signs give warnings—even the writing itself on the signs is an encoding. A customized ringtone on your mobile phone can tell you who is calling before you glance at the display. There are often many different ways to express information, and people often choose or even invent a special encoding because it works better than others. It may be faster, more efficient, or simply a better match for the information to be processed or communicated.

Thinking of a complicated process in terms of discrete steps or stages is also a useful and common strategy. We follow step-by-step instructions for filling out forms, for learning some kinds of hobbies, even for cooking. Sometimes, when I'm assembling a complicated toy, following badly written instructions, I'll get stuck halfway through because the process *isn't* divided into stages, and I don't know what to do next—looking at the partly assembled piece, I can't even tell what it's supposed to be. (Is this piece the toy robot's foot? Oh, it's the head...) When a process is broken down into appropriate, discrete pieces, it can become easier to understand, easier to tell whether progress is being made, and easier to recover from problems.

Control, in combination with discrete processes, is a subtle concept. Take the labor-saving devices we have in our homes: dishwashers, washing machines, clothes dryers, and so forth. (Although we don't think of these as robots, they really are.) One of the lessons our historical overview teaches us is that sometimes it pays to simplify a system so that it can be controlled more easily. Jacquard didn't try to build human-sized robots to replace the master weaver and drawboy; he identified a few of their actions and decisions that could be handled by the technology of the time.

Some tasks can be redesigned so that simple controllers can manage them. Our modern machines do work that we'd otherwise have to do by hand, but that's not the only way they assist us. When I put a dish of food in a microwave oven, I don't have to watch through the window as it cooks, to make sure it doesn't burn. Instead, I set the timer and turn my attention to something else. All of the machines I've mentioned are designed to control a complicated process in discrete stages, and if I'm aware of those stages, I can do better things with my time, without constantly monitoring what's happening.

Finally, modularity helps us understand systems of all kinds, large and small. Every American schoolchild is taught that the U.S. government has an executive, a legislative, and a judicial branch, along with the basics of how these branches interact. That's a better description than a list of all the thousands of organizations and offices within the government.

Or imagine if you asked me to explain how a car works, and I said, "Cars have airbags and batteries and brakes and bumpers..." Even if you like Dr. Seuss, you haven't learned much from what I've told you. A better explanation would be that a car is a four-wheeled vehicle for moving people around on roads, driven by an engine. In this answer, I've named the main parts and at least suggested how they work together.

Modularity is often part of our physical environment as well. In my building at work, my colleagues and I have our own offices; in my office I have computing books on my bookshelves, organized by category; within each book the topics are broken down into chapters. I have to open a door, pull out a book, or flip through pages to explore any one of these modules. There's modularity all the way down, and it would be hard for me to get through my daily life without it.

At this point we've seen some of the most important concepts that computing has to offer. The concepts are very general, which is both a strength and a limitation. What we'll do next is focus in on the specific modules of a modern computer to see what they do. More ideas remain to be discovered.

FURTHER READING

James Essinger gives a pre-history of computing, going back to the late 1700s, in *Jacquard's Web: How a Hand-Loom Led to the Birth of the Information Age* (Oxford University Press, 2003). The Institute of Electrical and Electronics Engineers (IEEE) publishes a quarterly journal, *IEEE Annals of the History of Computing*, on the topic.

Chapter 3

Computer Architecture: The Nuts and Bolts

Computers are capable of genuinely remarkable things, and yet we also know that they're just machines. How do they do what they do?

Speed is part of the answer: computers are enormously fast. Capacity is another: computers can store almost incredible amounts of information. The earliest electronic computers of the 1940s could carry out a few thousand operations per second and could store about as much information as you'd find on a printed page in a book. The mobile phone in my pocket, a miniature computer in its own right, has half a million times the processing speed of those old computers and can hold about 50 million times as much information.

Imagine if your own brain's processing and storage received this kind of boost. You'd go into work on New Year's Day (in the afternoon, of course) and finish an entire year's worth of work in less than 15 seconds. You'd be able to recall not only the names of your 100 or so closest friends but the names of all 6 billion people living on the planet today. With your new brain, there's probably a lot you'd do that your current brain can't even imagine.

But this just begs the question. Modern computers have more speed and capacity than their forebears, but this doesn't explain *how* they do what they do. A complete explanation is complicated, and we'll have to approach it step by step—in fact, the explanation will fill this entire book. We'll start with the subject of computer architecture.

A computer's architecture, in general, is the organization of its functional components.[1] The von Neumann architecture gives a good high-level description of a computer, but it's very abstract.[2] Today, computer scientists have a much more detailed understanding of computer architecture, and they're constantly looking for architectural refinements that improve performance.

To explore ideas in computer architecture, we could follow the historical development of modern computers, but the technical details and even the vocabulary would be overwhelming. Instead, we'll look at computer architecture in a different way, using an analogy based on an imaginary company, PaniCorp.

What makes this analogy relevant? If you've ever played a team sport, or attended a meeting of a homeowners association, or worked for a large business, you have some understanding of organizations. People have different responsibilities; communication and coordination are important; formal policies and informal rules add structure to what people do; the organization as a whole has some mission or set of goals.

We can understand the architecture of a computer in the same way. We'll look at how responsibilities are distributed within PaniCorp for creating and managing documents, for storing documents, and for communicating with external clients of the company. These responsibilities correspond to architectural components for processing, storage, and input and output in a computer. We'll see that the ways people work and interact (without using modern technology) are a good match for the way computer components work and interact. Finally, we'll find that our intuitions about how to improve efficiency in a human organization apply to computers as well.

CENTRAL PROCESSING

Connie and Alun share a cubicle office at PaniCorp. They work closely together on a long-running project, managing and processing paper documents for PaniCorp clients. Connie and Alun don't pay any attention to the contents of the documents they work with; all of their tasks are so routine that they just follow the instructions they're given. Buster, the project gofer, runs errands. Connie is the decision maker on the project, and a white board across from her office rules her working life. It shows a numbered list of tasks she's to accomplish for the day.

*(PaniCorp management is not overly concerned with worker privacy.)
Here's part of a typical day:*

    Buster has just delivered a document at Connie's request, dropping it in a basket labeled R1 on her desk. Connie makes a note in her registry book to keep track of it and glances at the clock. Right on schedule. Connie's working her way down the task list; she's reached Task 4.

    Deciphering the acronym for the task, she figures out that a standard addendum needs to be attached to the document. She calls out, "Okay, Alun, here's what we need to do." Once Alun has made the change to the document, Connie updates its registry entry with a checkmark. She looks at the white board again. Task 4: done.

    Task 5 tells Connie to send a copy of the new document to the company's storage facilities. She addresses it and hands it off to Buster. On to Task 6.

What boring paper pushers Connie and Alun are! Of course, they won't mind being called that—they're just metaphors, after all.

You'll recognize Connie and Alun as the controller and the arithmetic/logic unit (ALU) from Chapter 2; as a team, they represent the central processing unit (CPU). Connie's task board corresponds to the area of memory from which the CPU retrieves instructions, one at a time. The documents being passed around the office are actually small, fixed amounts of information, encoded as individual numbers. In the CPU, such information is stored temporarily in *registers*: R1, R2, and so forth. Registers are a kind of specialized storage within the CPU.

Buster is a new character. He stands for what's called the *system bus*, which transfers information (that is, information encoded as numbers) between the CPU and memory as well as other components in the computer. (The name "bus" comes from "omnibus bar," an electrical systems term, but computer people generally think of a bus as delivering information to each of its stops.)

The system bus carries three different kinds of information: where information is stored in memory (Connie needs to tell Buster where to get the documents she wants), the actual information exchanged between the CPU and memory (the documents Buster carries), and the instructions that come from memory to the CPU (in our story this isn't up to Buster; Connie just looks up at the white board for her next task).

Here's how our example, starting from Task 4, translates into more technical terms. The CPU works by repeating an *instruction cycle*: fetch an instruction from memory, via the bus; decode it; execute it. (If the CPU were a human being, these three stages would be getting an instruction, understanding it, and then doing it.) The CPU might fetch an instruction that the controller decodes to mean, "Add 1 to the value in register R1." The controller hands the job over to the ALU. When the addition is finished, the result is put back in R1, overwriting the old value. The CPU fetches another instruction, which is decoded to mean "move the value in R1 to some memory location"; the controller puts the data on the bus to be delivered to that location (Fig. 3.1).

These instructions are part of the CPU's *instruction set*, a language of operations the CPU is capable of. Each instruction is a number that encodes a specific CPU behavior. (That's why the controller needs to decode instructions—to find out what needs to be done.)

Different CPUs have different instruction sets, but the instructions generally fall into von Neumann's four categories. We see examples of two of the categories here, telling the ALU to do a bit of arithmetic and moving data from one place to another. For examples of the other two categories, imagine a continuation of the PaniCorp daily drudgery:

Task 6 tells Connie to check if the document has an even number of pages. (Some PaniCorp clients impose arbitrary standards on document preparation.) If so, she's to skip to Task 9. This turns out to be the case. Connie scans down the white board to Task 9 and finds that she's to send the document off to the client. Connie addresses it and calls out for Buster. Once Buster takes the document off her hands, Connie moves to Task 10.

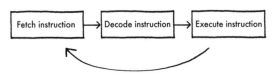

Figure 3.1. The CPU repeats the instruction cycle.

Here, by analogy, we see the CPU doing something interesting. It carries out a test on the data it has stored locally, and the result of that test can change what the CPU does next. One of the registers in the CPU, the *program counter*, points to the place in memory where the next instruction should be fetched.[3] This makes it easy for the CPU to walk through instructions in order; the program counter updates automatically after each instruction, just as Connie automatically goes from Task 4 to Task 5 or from Task 5 to Task 6. Some specialized instructions, "jumps" and "branches," change the program counter, telling the CPU to start reading instructions from somewhere entirely different in memory.

This makes two things possible. First, the CPU can make a decision (not in any deep sense, of course—it's just doing what it's told) to follow one set of instructions rather than another. Second, if the CPU returns to an instruction it has executed earlier, it can repeat some behavior. These kinds of instructions form the third category, which deals with *flow of control*. Finally, the fourth category of instructions involves communicating with system components outside the CPU and memory, such as a keyboard or a display.

Our PaniCorp analogy roughly parallels the more technical description, even if it's not a perfect match. The analogy should be helpful, though: we understand human organizations and procedures, and we can apply our intuitions to better understand the design of computers.

Here's how we'll do it. Put yourself in the mindset of an efficiency expert and ask, "What could be done to speed up Connie and Alun's work?" If you take a minute or so to think of the possibilities, I suspect that you'll come up with a good number of the possibilities I describe below. Ready?

- *Could we ask Connie and Alun to simply work faster?* Yes—or, rather, we can replace them with a new, faster team. (This is one of the more traditional benefits of modularity.) In a computer, the CPU works at a rate governed by a clock. This clock doesn't measure time, like the one on Connie's wall; it's for synchronization, to keep the CPU's internal processing in step. Different CPUs have different clock speeds, so one straightforward way to improve performance is simply to swap out the CPU for another (one that handles the same instruction set) with a faster clock. We do need to make sure that the other components in the computer, such as the bus and memory, can keep up, but these issues are manageable.

Just how fast are these clocks? We'll sometimes talk about how long a clock cycle takes—the time between ticks—but more often, we measure speed in units of frequency called hertz (abbreviated Hz). A clock with a speed of 1 Hz completes one cycle every second; a 100,000-Hz clock completes that many cycles (a hundred thousand) every second. Rather than writing out these long numbers, we generally use Greek prefixes: a thousand hertz is 1 kilohertz (KHz); a million hertz is 1 megahertz (MHz); a billion hertz is 1 gigahertz (GHz). The computer I'm typing on now, for example, has a 2.53-GHz CPU. Clock speed doesn't tell us how many instructions a given CPU can execute per second, because of differences between instruction sets and because some instructions take longer to execute than others, but it's a good general measure of performance. With a faster clock, instructions can be executed more quickly.

- *Could we give Connie a more capable assistant than Alun, or perhaps several assistants?* Yes, and this is also possible in the CPU. For example, specialized mathematical and geometrical operations are important for some kinds of computing, such as games and computer animation. Imagine watching a rotating object, like a computer-generated statue, on a computer screen or in a movie theater. You're seeing the object from different angles, and it's the job of the CPU to generate the images of that object from those different angles. A specialized graphics processing unit, or GPU, can do the job much faster than an ordinary ALU. In general, if we know that a CPU is going to be carrying out a lot of specialized tasks, sometimes we can add a new subsystem to do these tasks more quickly.
- *Could we hire more Connie–Alun teams?* Yes. In computing, this strategy is called *multiprocessing* (variations include *parallel*

and *distributed computing*). Instead of having all the work done by a single CPU in a computer, we might have two or more CPUs that split the work between them. In the real world, if we have a big problem to solve, asking more people to contribute generally helps things along. For example, imagine that PaniCorp receives a very large paper document that needs a change on every page. If there were ten Connie–Alun teams, each taking a different set of document pages, the job might be done much faster than by one team (Fig. 3.2).

But there are pitfalls we need to be aware of. Most jobs don't come naturally broken up into pieces that can be done independently; someone needs to decide how to break a job up, and someone needs to combine the results. This extra work, or overhead, wouldn't be needed if all the work were done by a single person or machine. Imagine that the PaniCorp job involves numbering the pages of the document in sequence. Unfortunately, only one of the teams (the one receiving the first pages of the document) would know where to start their numbering. If each team has to wait until some other team is finished, the job will get done no faster than if done by one team alone. Worse, it will actually be *slower*, because of the overhead of splitting up the document and then combining

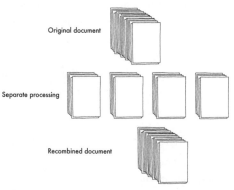

Original document

Separate processing

Recombined document

Figure 3.2. With multiprocessing, a task is broken down into smaller tasks that can be carried out in parallel.

the pieces. We could have all the teams start out by counting their pages and passing the information to all the other teams before doing the actual numbering, but this adds yet more overhead. In general, multiprocessing offers great advantages, but how much it helps can depend in subtle ways on the tasks that are being carried out and how clever we are in dividing up those tasks.

- *Connie and Alun sometimes seem to be waiting for each other to finish their respective jobs; could their cooperation be somehow streamlined, so that they can be working at the same time?* Yes. The key is to arrange for the information that Connie and Alun need, new tasks as well as documents, to be available the instant they've finished what they're currently working on. In a CPU, this is called *pipelining*. An assembly line is probably a better metaphor, though. Think about a factory with a conveyor belt that passes by several stations. At each station a worker adds a new piece or makes some adjustment, and at the end a completed widget pops out. The important thing is that the assembly line can handle many widgets at once, each at a different stage of construction. In a pipelined architecture, the CPU works in a similar way. Different CPU circuitry handles different stages of the instruction cycle, just as different stations perform different tasks on an assembly line. That is, while one part of the CPU circuitry is handling one instruction, other parts can handle other instructions. The effect is that at any point in time the CPU is processing a number of instructions, each at a different stage in execution. This can speed up processing, as long as the pipeline is kept filled. (Here we can see why the synchronization that the CPU clock provides is important: the CPU doesn't need to check whether each stage is finished for each instruction; the entire system is designed so that these activities happen right on time.)

As with multiprocessing, there are subtle factors that affect how fast a pipelined architecture can run. If one instruction to the CPU is generating information that the next instruction needs, for example, then the second instruction might have to wait, which hurts performance. Further, pipelining means looking ahead at instructions that are yet to be executed. One of these instructions might tell the CPU to jump to a different place in memory for further instructions, which means that the pending instructions in the pipeline must be flushed out. Unless we've been smart about ordering the instructions, performance slows until the pipeline fills up again.

- *Connie and Alun don't seem to do very much; could they do more?* For example, they might be given a single task that involves changing the document and sending it off to be stored, rather than the activity being broken up into two tasks. In human terms, this generally works. With computers, though, it's a bit more complicated.

Up until the 1970s, CPU instruction sets were gradually becoming more complex, enabling CPUs to do more work with a single instruction. This means that CPUs needed to be more complex as well. The question was whether the additional complexity was worthwhile. In an influential study in 1970, Donald Knuth analyzed several hundred programs to answer this question. (His collection began with what he found rummaging through the wastebaskets at the Stanford computing center for abandoned paper printouts.) Knuth found that almost half of the instructions in these programs involved nothing more than putting a specific item of data in a specific location in memory. That is, more complex instructions were generally left unused.[4]

Further, some techniques for improving performance, such as pipelining, are hard to apply when instructions vary widely in what they do and how long they take—imagine an assembly line that has to work on a Volkswagen at one point, followed by a Rolls Royce, then an electric toaster oven...

Eventually, so-called reduced instruction set computers (RISC) won out over increased complexity. Slow, complex single instructions were replaced by sequences of simpler, faster instructions that could run on simpler, faster CPUs.

The strategy was to concentrate on the instructions that were executed most often, and to make these as fast as possible.

There's a potential tradeoff here: executing even a slow complex instruction might be faster than executing a sequence of simpler instructions. But as long as this happens infrequently enough, performance will be improved. We'll call the idea of focusing performance improvements on the most common cases the *fast common case* strategy.

Let's stop for a breather. We now have a reasonable idea about how information processing works in the CPU. We've even come up with ideas for improving performance that turn out to work in practice: faster clock speeds, specialized co-processors, multiprocessing, pipelining, and sets of uniformly fast instructions. The take-home message is that improving performance is largely a matter of understanding tradeoffs. Even obvious ideas, such as speeding up a given component, need to be considered in context.

Interestingly enough, some of these strategies for improving CPU performance also apply in everyday life. Take pipelining. "Just in time" manufacturing depends on a supply chain rather than warehouses for parts, and it has had significant success in making some businesses more efficient. This has the flavor of pipelining in a CPU. On a more personal level, one of the reasons that visits to the car mechanic or doctor's office can be frustrating is that the pipelining of appointments often breaks down. You arrive for your appointment at 10 a.m., but you wait until 11:15 to be seen. It may be that diagnosing and treating automobile or medical conditions isn't predictable and uniform enough to be scheduled in a reliably efficient pipeline.

For the fast common case strategy, we can think of electronic tollbooths on modern highways. If a car has a transponder installed, then the driver can pass through a toll plaza without stopping to pay at a traditional tollbooth. (Of course, payment does occur, but that's handled independently.) When new electronic tollbooths are installed on a highway, a good proportion of the drivers who adopt the system to get through faster are those who travel the route daily. To take a more personal example, many people will try out different routes on their daily drive to work, to find the one that takes the least time. In both of these examples we see efforts to make the most common case the fastest case.

STORAGE

Let's return to PaniCorp to visit Mr. Lager, who works in a different part of the building from Connie and Alun. Lager manages paper documents for their project. He sees his job as making available all the documents that the project needs, as fast as possible.

> *Lager's desk sits before a set of doors, one leading to a storeroom lined with shelves full of documents, the other downstairs to the basement, where hundreds of filing cabinets hold a great many more documents. Lager has a simple system for organizing his documents. Every document goes into a different numbered folder, with the numbers starting at zero and going upward.*
>
> *When Buster comes to his desk requesting a document, he tells Lager the number of the folder it's in. Lager walks back to his storeroom, makes a copy of the requested document, and hands it out.*
>
> *Sometimes Buster will arrive with a document to be stored in a specific folder, which Lager does. If there is already a document in that folder, Lager simply tosses it in the trash. The rule is one document per folder. Occasionally, Buster will tell Lager that the project will need documents from the basement; Lager has entire filing cabinets of documents moved up onto the shelves in his local storeroom, swapping out the documents that are already there. To keep things simple, Lager never gives Buster any documents directly from the basement, but only after they've been put in place in his storeroom.*

Mr. Lager seems to have arranged for his job to be as straightforward as possible, at the expense of everyone else. But even though his method of organizing documents means that all of his coworkers need to keep track of where their documents are, it makes their work easier in a couple of ways. First, it's simple and predictable. For example, if Connie has a stack of ten related documents, she can ask for them all to be stored next to each other, in order, and she can retrieve them in that same order (Fig. 3.3). This is easier than keeping track of ten separate document names or locations. (Though it's not explicit in this analogy, the numbering system also makes it easy for Connie to retrieve tasks from her

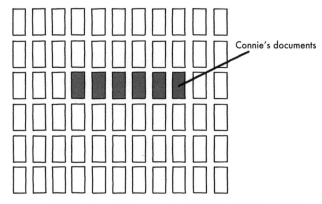

Figure 3.3. Related items of information can be stored side by side.

white board in order—Lager's storeroom holds Connie's task list as well as the documents she needs.)

Second, Lager's method is uniform. Lager might have complicated ways of arranging the folders on different shelving units, but that complexity is hidden. He can even change out or expand his storage facilities without anyone's noticing; storage is modular.

Let's switch back to a computing perspective. Mr. Lager's storeroom stands for *memory* in a computer architecture. Memory is often called *RAM*, which stands for Random Access Memory; "random access" just means that it takes the same amount of time to access any piece of information stored. The folders on Lager's shelves are *locations* in memory, and the numbers on those folders are the *addresses* of those locations. Just as with Lager's organizing system, only one piece of information can be stored in a memory location.

While it may seem drastic to simply throw old information away when we want to store new information in the same place, that's the nature of computer storage. Another feature of computer storage is that, unlike paper documents, if you have some information that you need to send elsewhere, you still retain that information. By analogy, when you tell someone something, you don't immediately forget it yourself.

Mr. Lager's basement stands for *secondary storage*, sometimes called mass storage or disk storage (after the technology that's most commonly used today). In contrast to memory, secondary storage takes longer to retrieve information from, but it can usually hold a great deal more information.

We find a pattern in the ways that documents are stored and retrieved within PaniCorp. When Connie needs a document, it might be on her desk, or in Lager's storeroom, or in the basement; that is, it could be quickly accessed, or it might take a bit of time, or it might take a lot of time. The same holds for computer storage, from registers to memory to secondary storage, in a fast-to-slow pattern that's called the *storage hierarchy*.

There's more to this than just access time. It turns out to be possible to build very fast computer storage, but that speed comes at great expense. Physical limitations mean that, all else being equal, faster storage must be smaller. The registers in the CPU are at the very top of the storage hierarchy: very fast, very expensive, tiny capacity. Memory fits in the middle of the hierarchy: relatively fast, less expensive, greater capacity. Access to data in memory may be hundreds of times slower than access to registers (Fig. 3.4).

At the level below memory we find secondary storage: slow, inexpensive, much greater capacity. Access to secondary storage may be tens of thousands of times slower than access to memory. Another general feature of the storage hierarchy is that the higher levels are volatile, meaning that they need continuous power to hold information. Secondary storage, in contrast, is permanent. We can't do without secondary storage if we want to turn off our computers once in a while without losing all of our information.

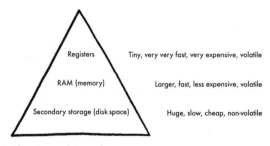

Figure 3.4. The storage hierarchy.

At this point, we're faced with a puzzle: If the CPU executes instructions fetched from memory, but memory is volatile, what happens when you press the power switch to turn on a computer and there's nothing *in* memory? In this special case, instructions come from what's called read-only memory, which is nonvolatile. These instructions initialize the system and eventually make it possible for programs to be read and executed in the way we've seen. This start-up procedure is called "booting," a reference to pulling yourself up by your bootstraps.

How much storage are we talking about? The most common unit of measure for information storage is the *byte*. A byte is enough to encode one letter on a printed page; we could store the average novel of 100,000 words, at five letters per word plus a space, in 600,000 bytes, with one byte for each letter or space.

As with CPU speed, the numbers get big fast, and so we again use Greek prefixes. A thousand bytes (though for technical reasons it's only approximately a thousand) is a kilobyte (KB); a million bytes is a megabyte (MB); a billion bytes is a gigabyte (GB); a trillion bytes is a terabyte (TB). Typical CPUs hold at most a few kilobytes (and usually much less) in register storage. The computer I'm typing on now has 8 GB of memory, more than a million-fold difference in capacity. My secondary storage is a 500-GB disk. For convenience, I can plug in various cards and drives to give my computer even more secondary storage, or to transfer information between my other electronic gadgets, such as my camera, or to keep copies of my information safe on a separate backup storage device.

All these numbers are just meant to give a sense of scale; the specifics aren't important. The basic idea is that we would like to give the CPU huge amounts of very fast storage, but for reasons of cost, physics, and technology, it's not possible. This poses a serious challenge for computer architecture. As in our discussion of the CPU, we'll try to gain some insight into what can be done to make information storage, in support of CPU processing, more efficient. Let's put on our efficiency-expert hats, and we'll test our intuitions about how to improve Mr. Lager's document storage facilities.

- *Could we move Mr. Lager's office closer to Connie and Alun's, so that Buster wouldn't have as far to go in walking documents back and forth?* PaniCorp is constrained by the laws of physics: only so much information can be stored in a given amount of space. The same general rule holds in computing. The more information there is, the more space is needed, and traversing this space takes time.

- *Could Mr. Lager work faster, just as Connie and Alun might work faster?* Unfortunately, Lager is working just about as fast as he can. Buster is, too. With computers, while memory capacity has grown very rapidly, keeping pace with the speed increase in CPUs, access to information stored in memory has remained relatively slow. Most of the other suggestions we had for improving CPU performance don't apply to memory. That is, we might imagine having more than one memory component in a system, the ability to ask for more than one piece of information at a time, and so forth, but all these ideas involve making memory responsible for processing as well as storage. We're essentially adding new, specialized processors to a computer system. This can lead to some benefits in special cases, but we face a complexity tradeoff: making a system more complex doesn't always improve its performance, and in practice most of the tradeoffs don't turn out to be worthwhile. We'll have better luck if we concentrate on the structure and organization of storage rather than the raw speed of access.

- *Could Connie and Alun keep some of the documents they've worked on, in case they're needed again in the near future?* Lager has sometimes asked about this possibility. "There's not enough room," he's told. But he has developed a strategy. He has arranged for one of his helpers, Ms. Cash, to work directly with Connie. Her space is immediately outside Connie and Alun's office, and she acts as an intermediary between Connie and Buster. Ms. Cash keeps copies of the documents that Connie has asked for most recently. Whenever Connie asks for a document, she checks her own filing cabinet to see whether she has it. If she does, it saves a lot of time. If not, it's up to Buster to get the document.

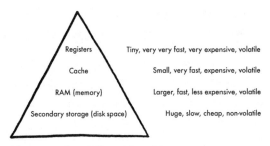

Figure 3.5. The storage hierarchy, with caching.

In computing, this strategy is called *caching*. A cache is a small, fast memory placed between the CPU and (main) memory to keep short-term information (Fig. 3.5). In the storage hierarchy, cache occupies a level between memory and registers with respect to speed, cost, and capacity. Because cache memory is smaller than main memory, it can't hold all the information that the CPU might need; there are hits and misses. But if there are enough hits, then the effect is a much more responsive memory system on average. As new information comes into the cache, older unused information is generally discarded.

What makes this all work is the *locality principle*. Studies of the behavior of computer programs have shown that when the CPU retrieves data from a given memory location, it's likely to make that same retrieval again in the near future.[5] (The CPU simply doesn't have a lot of storage space in its registers to keep old data around.) This is *temporal locality*, locality in time. Further, the CPU is also likely to retrieve data from nearby memory locations. This is *spatial locality*. A cache takes advantage of these patterns. When the CPU retrieves data from a given address, the cache copies and stores a larger "block" of memory surrounding that address. This means that later accesses to that data, as well as to data stored nearby, will be much faster.

Let's stop to recap. While increasing the speed of processing is important, it's not the only route to performance improvements.

Carefully structuring a system to make up for known limitations can also help. Sometimes even just understanding where the bottlenecks are in a system can lead to ideas about how to work around them.

Some of the storage concepts I've described should seem familiar. Take the storage hierarchy. We tend to organize our lives so that the information we need most often is ready to hand. Suppose someone asks me for a phone number. Phone numbers that I use regularly, such as for my home and office, I have memorized, and I can reel them off. Other numbers that I can't remember offhand are programmed into my cell phone. Yet others that I rarely need are available in directories. This is a real-world storage hierarchy, very similar to the one we see in computers.

My own memory is fast but it's effectively limited in size, since I'm not willing to put a lot of effort into memorizing phone numbers. My cell phone can hold thousands of numbers, but it takes more time for me to get access to them; phone books and computerized directories can in principle hold any number I'd ever need, but it takes even more time to get at the information. If I'm aware of real-life storage hierarchies, I might be able to make better decisions about which information I should store where.

A related idea is caching of information. When a middling student crams the night before a final exam, he's caching that information for short-term use—it will be gone a few days afterwards. This is a variation called *predictive caching*, in which a judgment is made in advance about whether some piece of information will be needed. Caching can be physical as well. Most cars carry a spare tire and a jack, for situations that would be expensive and more time-consuming to handle without the cached equipment. On a cloudy day, I sometimes bring an umbrella with me, even if it's not yet raining, just in case. I also lose umbrellas by doing this, just the way information is discarded from a cache if it remains unused.

Finally, we see examples of the locality principle all around us. When I get tired wandering through the side streets of a strange city and I see a taxi on a cross street, I head in that direction, because other taxis are more likely to be in the same area. That's spatial locality. When my aging car breaks down and needs to go to the shop, I should be on the lookout for other problems. That's temporal locality. Sometimes these patterns can fool us (bad things don't really come in threes), but when they're real, we can take advantage of them.

INPUT AND OUTPUT

We'll make one final visit to PaniCorp:

> *Buster arrives breathless at Connie's office: Important clients are in the building. These sorts of interruptions come rarely, but they're high priority. As they tour the building, the clients chat with Connie, which results in a few new items being added to her task list.*
>
> *In Mr. Lager's area, Connie walks the clients into the document storeroom. One of the clients stands back from the rows of shelves and says, "I can see patterns in the colors of the document bindings. Is that intentional?" Connie squints and looks. He's right—the blocks of dark and light gray seem to form a picture of a face (Fig. 3.6).[6] "That's an interesting possibility," she says.*

So far, we've treated the way that the CPU interacts with memory as if it all happens in isolation. Often, though, we humans want to *use* a computer. We move a mouse and type on a keyboard, or perhaps press buttons on a game controller, the *input devices* for the computer; we expect to see

Figure 3.6. Differently shaded squares combine to create an image.

responses via an *output device*, such as a printer or a display. These two kinds of devices are often referred to generally as *I/O devices*. One way that the CPU can communicate with an I/O device is through a specialized I/O bus. This bus works a bit differently from the way we've seen so far, in that what happens isn't always driven by the CPU.

An input device can send an *interrupt* to the CPU, which causes the CPU to jump to a new set of instructions to handle the interrupt, returning to its previous execution when finished. Why this arrangement? The main reason is speed. Imagine the CPU being responsible for handling keyboard input, regularly checking to see if a key has been pressed. The CPU can execute millions of instructions per second, however, while the fastest typists can manage only a few keystrokes per second. It's more efficient for new information from an input device to be treated as an occasional special event by the CPU. (To return to the earlier topic of storage, transfer of data between secondary storage and memory is also generally treated in the same way, because it happens so much slower than the CPU's processing, and the transfer doesn't require close monitoring by the CPU.)

Some kinds of output devices, such as computer displays, can be handled in a different way. A special area of memory, video memory, can be dedicated to display output. As in the PaniCorp example, the idea is straightforward. When we look at a computer display, we're seeing row upon row of tiny colored dots, called *pixels* (originally, *picture elements*). Each of the numbers stored in video memory (in order, just as with standard memory) encodes a specific color, and graphics hardware in the computer performs the appropriate decoding to produce an image on the display. This makes it straightforward for the CPU to generate visual output simply by sending appropriately encoded information to video memory.

Imagine what we'd see if we could stretch a fishnet stocking over a toy dinosaur. This imaginary fishnet stocking is special: each of its threads can stretch to any length, but the threads remain completely straight; the flexibility is in where the threads join together. The stocking completely covers the surface of the dinosaur. On the flatter parts (its sides and back), we'd see large diamonds formed by the threads, but on other parts (the forearms, teeth, and so forth) the diamonds would be much smaller, because they need to follow tighter angles and curves.

We've created a geometrical model of the surfaces of the dinosaur, what's some-times called a wireframe model (the more evocative term "fishnet stocking model" is never used). It's straightforward to store this information in a computer, though we generally use triangles rather than diamond shapes. If the spaces between the threads could be turned into surfaces, we'd have an angular figure that looks a lot like the dinosaur. If we see too many flat parts or angles where we expect to see curves, we redo our model with smaller shapes that fit the surface more closely.

This is one approach to *modeling*, in the area of *computer graphics*. Another important concept is *rendering*. How do we make our model look like the physical toy? Or even a living dinosaur?

When you look at a toy dinosaur (live ones are not easy to find) your eyes see light reflected from its surfaces. Rendering is essentially about reproducing the informa-tion carried by those reflected light rays well enough to create the illusion of looking at a physical object. Rendering does a few obvious things—show the front but not the back of a nontransparent object—as well as more subtle things. The light from a fluorescent lamp, for example, is different from sunlight, and the way light reflects from a surface depends on the surface's color, its texture, your viewing angle, shading, and other factors. (Human skin is difficult to reproduce in graphics, partly because it's very slightly translucent.) Rendering takes all these factors into account to create images as realistic as we'd like.

And if we wanted our rendered dinosaur model to move? That's *animation*. We need to know how the shapes and regions of the model influence each other as they move, as well as the implications for how they should be rendered. We might have to build detailed models of the internal structure of the dinosaur, down to its bones and muscles and perhaps even further. Good results in graphics depend on processing power, data, and ever-more-sophisticated programs.

How a computer handles input and output may seem esoteric, but we can find familiar analogies in real life. Think about the job of a hotel concierge, a receptionist, or others who meet with the public in the ser-vice industries. In many cases, they have regular duties that keep them busy all day, but when a customer arrives with a specific request, they put their other work aside. They're interrupt-driven. Interrupts give peo-ple (and computers) a way to handle tasks that arrive in ways that aren't entirely predictable, allowing for work to be done in the meantime.

As for video output, you've probably seen something called a card stunt if you watch sports on television. Spectators in a large stadium are given colored cards to hold in the air at a given signal, and from a distance the colors on the cards can be seen as an image: "Go team!" The image produced by a stunt is usually a bit pixelated meaning that you see the individual cards, but the effect can be impressive. Shrink it all down and speed it all up, and we have animated graphics on our computer displays.

FITTING THE PIECES TOGETHER

These are the nuts and bolts of computing. To be clear, I've just scratched the surface of topics in computer architecture, and I've simplified away a good number of practical and theoretical issues for the sake of breadth.

I hope that a useful picture has emerged, one that you'll recognize the next time you shop for a new computer. Computer advertising is heavily laden with jargon, but the ads all tend to include the same information: a CPU running at some clock speed (or perhaps a multi-core processor, which includes more than one CPU in the same hardware package, opening up the possibility of multiprocessing); memory (so many gigabytes of RAM); a video card (with its own graphics processor and memory to offload work from the CPU); secondary storage (a hard disk or a solid-state drive, with even larger capacity); and ports that allow you to plug in external devices for input, output, and yet more storage. If we're thinking about how a modern cell phone is like the computer sitting on someone's desk, or when we're making sense of a news article about CPU speeds having doubled yet again over the past two years, we need the architectural viewpoint.

What does the future hold for computer architecture? David Patterson, a pioneer in reduced instruction set computing, identifies three challenges: developing new architectures to match the needs of modern environments for developing software, ensuring that such software can take advantage of multiprocessing on multicore processors, and addressing new concerns for computer privacy and security.[7]

You'll notice a strong emphasis on programming and software. In the next two chapters, we'll look into this aspect of computing.

FURTHER READING

Most of the technical material in this chapter is based on *Computer Architecture and Organization: An Integrated Approach*, by Miles J. Murdocca and Vincent P. Heuring (John Wiley & Sons, 2007). Another popular textbook is John L. Hennessy and David A. Patterson's *Computer Architecture: A Quantitative Approach* (Morgan Kaufmann, 4th ed., 2006).

Chapter 4

Algorithms and Structured Data: Solving Problems

The architecture level gives us a very detailed view of what happens on a computer. But trying to understand everything a computer does at this level would be like watching an experimental movie shot entirely in close-ups. If all we can see is fine detail, it can be hard to grasp what's happening on a larger scale.

Here's a different perspective: computers solve problems. Solving problems, in contrast to executing instructions, means not having to worry about all the details all at once. Instead, we can think in more abstract terms. How should we represent a problem? Can we break a problem down into smaller pieces so that it's easier to solve? What would a solution procedure look like, in the abstract?

Answering these questions is a matter of *representation*. We've already encountered the idea of representation, in the encoding of data and instructions in a form that's convenient for a computer. Now we need to think more generally about how to represent problems and their solutions.

Two concepts are central to this perspective. The first is an *algorithm*, a step-by-step description of actions for solving a problem.[1] Some algorithms describe actions as detailed as those carried out by a specific CPU, but most work at a more abstract level. For example, *Multiply this list of numbers together*, whether each multiplication takes one CPU instruction or five. If you've ever followed a clearly written recipe in the kitchen, you've carried out an algorithm for preparing a meal.

A good description strikes the right level of detail. For example, it's unlikely that your recipe told you to find a small saucepan in the right-most upper cabinet and put it on the rear left burner; instead, it just told you to use a saucepan to melt some amount of butter. Detailed descriptions of some actions can be left out, because we know that they're possible and that minor differences in their execution won't affect the result. Algorithms are models of procedures at an abstract level we decide is appropriate.[2]

We also have abstract models of collections of information, in the form of *abstract data types*. Think of the term "abstract data type" as the computing equivalent of the biological term "species;" it's a way of classifying a collection by its type.[3] An abstract data type describes what can be done with a collection of information, without going down to the level of computer storage. For example, *Each item in this collection is assigned a number by which it can be retrieved*, but we won't worry about exactly where each item is stored in memory. In our cooking example, imagine adding spices in some order specified by your recipe. You may have the spices lined up on the counter, or you might instead pull them out of your cabinet one at a time. The ordering of the spices is important, but the physical arrangement of containers is not.

Algorithms and abstract data types are abstract building blocks for problem solving. If we're faced with a particular problem, we choose (or invent) an algorithm to solve it, and we choose (or invent) a way to organize the information to match the algorithm's capabilities. In general, the information representing the problem is the *input* to an algorithm, and the solution is its *output*. (I'm using "input" and "output" in a general sense here, rather than referring to input or output devices.)

It would be impractical to count all the specialized data types that have been developed in computing over the years, but many are based on a few simple abstractions: sequences, trees, and graphs.[4] In this chapter we'll see how these are used to organize information and how that information is processed by different algorithms.

ORGANIZING INFORMATION

Say I'm talking to you on the phone, and I ask you to write down some information. I tell you, "I have eight names. Here they are, in order: Smith, Johnson, Williams, Jones, Brown, Davis, Miller, and Wilson." What do you end up with on paper? You've probably written the names in a list, one after the other (Fig. 4.1).

This collection is an example of a *sequence*. Think of a sequence as a list of some given length that can hold items of information, in a way that lets us say, "Give me the first (or fourth, or hundredth) item." We call the items in the sequence its *elements*, and we call the number of an item (first, second, third, etc.) an *index* into the sequence.

If I'm running an experiment in which I record the temperature at each hour of the day, I create a sequence that can hold 24 elements, and I put temperature values into the sequence in the order I record them. We see sequences of information all around us in everyday life: a subway timetable; quarterly earnings in an annual financial report; a table of voting tallies per county for a state election reported in the newspaper; even the items on a shopping list.

Back to our phone conversation: Suppose that instead of giving you a list of names, I say, "Here's Eric's family tree. Eric has two children,

Figure 4.1. Items of information organized in a sequence.

Emily and Meredith; Emily has two children, Kylie and Kevin…" A sequence, with one item after another, doesn't preserve the family relationships between the names. Instead, you might draw something like the diagram in Figure 4.2.

This collection is organized as a *tree*. Trees give us a way to represent hierarchical relationships. In addition to genealogies, we can represent corporations and military organizations as trees (though not perfectly, because some people have more than one boss). Evolutionary biologists use trees to show ancestor–descendant relationships between species. You can even think of your circulatory system, with arteries branching out from the heart, as a tree. We find trees of information, like sequences, wherever we look.

We generally build a tree one item at a time, as with the family tree I described. We call the items of information in a tree its *nodes* or *vertices* (the circles), and we call the connections between the items *links* or *edges* (the lines with arrows). A vertex with edges pointing to other vertices is the *parent* of its *children*; the vertex at the top of the tree is its *root*, and vertices without children are *leaves*.[5] By following edges through some set of vertices, we trace a *path* through the tree. (Computing, as a discipline, doesn't object to mixed metaphors—in this case a blend of geometry, family relationships, walking trails, and woody plants—we even call trees bushy or sparse, depending on how dense they are. We

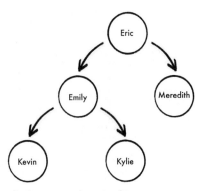

Figure 4.2. Items of information organized in a tree.

also draw trees upside down, with the root at the top, so that we can add new items without running out of space.)

One last revision of our phone conversation: Now I tell you, "James is friends with Michael and David. Michael and David are both friends with Chris, who is also friends with James..." (I'm assuming that friendship is a one-way relationship, which sometimes happens in real life.) If you start writing this down as a tree, you'll find that sometimes you end up with vertices that have more than one arrow pointing to them, and sometimes paths return to meet themselves. I might have even told you that David is his own best friend. This collection is no longer a tree; it's a *graph* (Fig. 4.3).

We talk about graphs as we do trees—they have vertices and edges, and we can trace paths through them—because a graph is a generalization of a tree, with more flexibility. Social relationships are graphs: your friends have other friends who have yet other friends and so forth, in a network of relationships that expands over the entire globe. Epidemiologists can track the spread of disease from one person to the next in graphs. Highway systems, airline flight paths, telephone systems, even spider webs can all be thought of as graphs. Whenever we have objects, people, or simply different items of information that are related to each other, we can use graphs to capture the bigger picture that they create.

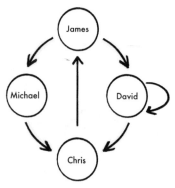

Figure 4.3. Items of information organized in a graph.

SEQUENCES: SEARCHING AND SORTING

One of the first questions we ask about a collection is how we can *traverse* it—that is, how we can access each item, one at a time. With a sequence, this is straightforward. We start at the first index and simply count upward, looking at each element, until we decide to stop or we reach the end. We can imagine other ways to traverse a sequence, systematically jumping to different elements, but going forward is the most obvious and common way. The process of finding a particular item among a set of items is called *search*, and traversing a sequence from the beginning is the easiest way to search it.

The list of names I gave earlier, in our first phone conversation, happens to be surnames ordered by popularity in the United States. Suppose that instead of reading a few to you, I'd sent you a sequence of the top 100 names. It would be easy for you to find the tenth or seventy-third most popular name—you just look at the entry for that index.

But suppose you were looking for your own name in the list. How could you do this? You'd probably check the element in the first index to see if it matched your own name, then the second, and so forth. This algorithm is called *sequential* or *linear* search. This is what it looks like as a diagram, with a smaller sequence laid out horizontally (Fig. 4.4). I've shaded the elements you've ruled out after each step; the unshaded area shows how much of the sequence is left to search.

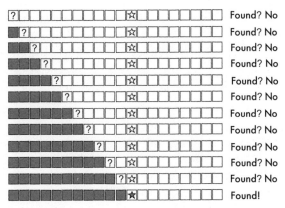

Figure 4.4. Sequential search rules out one possibility at each step.

If the names in the sequence were in a different order, alphabetized, there's a way for you to find your name with less work. Look at the element in the 50th index. If it's not your name, is yours higher or lower in the alphabet? If it's lower, then look at the 25th element. Is that your name? If not, is yours higher or lower? You continue until you've either found your name (which might happen at any step), or until you've narrowed down to a single element that's not your name, so you can conclude that your name is nowhere in the sequence. This algorithm is called *binary* search. Each decision you make divides the remaining possibilities evenly (or almost evenly) into two parts, letting you discard one of the parts. You'll notice that what's left to be searched after each step is much smaller than in sequential search (Fig. 4.5).

This may seem a small thing. After all, how long would it take you to scan through an alphabetized list of even 100 names in order? Let's take a different example. Say you're looking up the word *jabberwocky* in a thick dictionary, a thousand pages long. How much work is it to find the right page? You could start at the beginning and turn one page at a time until you reach the Js. This is a sequential search, and you'll be done after 500 pages or so. What you probably do instead is open the book in the middle, find yourself in the Ls, jump backward a bit too far to the Hs, and then move back and forth in smaller jumps until you find the right page. *Jabberwocky*: meaningless language.

The pages in the dictionary are essentially a sorted sequence, and with binary search, or something close to it, you're done in ten steps or fewer. (How do we know it's at most ten steps? Each time you take a step with binary search, you're eliminating half of the possible choices. Dividing 1,000 repeatedly by 2 gives you 500, 250, and so forth, with ten divisions until you get to 1.[6] Because you're looking at a specific page at each step, though, you might be able to stop sooner.)

Figure 4.5. Binary search rules out half of the possibilities at each step.

There's a more general way to think about sequential search and binary search, or rather the difference between the two. The first algorithm is an example of a *brute force* strategy. To solve a problem using brute force, an algorithm follows a plan for looking at possible solutions, one at a time, and it doesn't take advantage of structure in the information it's dealing with, or clues it might come across along the way. Fortunately, we can often do better than brute force.

Binary search is an example of different strategy, *divide-and-conquer*. Divide-and-conquer has the flavor of military conquest: when faced with a big problem, break it down into smaller problems that can be handled more easily. That's what binary search does to find a target item in an ordered sequence. The "divide" part involves choosing an element in the middle, to divide the sequence into two parts. The "conquer" part happens when you eliminate half of the possibilities.

Unfortunately, we can't always count on getting information that's organized appropriately. *Sorting* is the process of putting a set of items in order. To see how this works, we'll watch Evie, who runs a kitten delivery service. She's checking the latest batch of seven kittens, each with its own collar tag, each in its own carrier with a customer label—oh no! Stephen, the temp, has mixed everything up. The kittens are all in the wrong carriers. Customer 3's kitten is in the first carrier, Customer 1's kitten is in the seventh carrier, and so forth (Fig. 4.6). It's too much trouble to relabel the carriers, and Evie can't let the kittens out—they're all wide awake and full of energy—but she does have two hands. She finds Kitten 1 and scoops it up to put it in the first carrier, moving Kitten 3 to the now-empty seventh carrier (Fig. 4.7). She then finds Kitten 2 and swaps it with the kitten in the second carrier. She keeps going until she ends up with Kitten 7 in the seventh carrier. Done!

An algorithm called *selection sort* puts a sequence of numbers in order by following a very similar procedure. The main difference is that

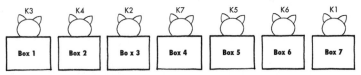

Figure 4.6. A sequence of items in no special order.

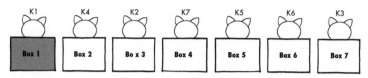

Figure 4.7. A sequence of items after one pass made by selection sort.

selection sort doesn't match each number in the sequence to one of the sequence's indexes, the way Evie matches kitten numbers to customer numbers; the algorithm is more general, putting the lowest number (even if it's not 1) in the first location of the sequence, the second-lowest in the second location, and so forth.

Here's how it works. It scans through the sequence, from the first index to the last. At each point, selection sort does a comparison. "Is this the lowest number I've seen so far? No? I'll move on. Yes? Okay, *that's* the new lowest number." When the scan is complete, the algorithm has the index of the lowest element, and it simply swaps that element with whatever element is stored in the first index. It then repeats the scan, starting from the second index and looking for the lowest of the remaining numbers. This way the second-lowest number gets put into place. In the end, selection sort will be left with the highest number in the highest index, having found and moved all the lower numbers into their correct locations.

Conceptually, selection sort has the nice property that it takes a single step, puts one item in its proper place, and then faces an almost-identical version of the original problem, except smaller by one. This approach is similar enough to divide-and-conquer that it's sometimes called *decrease-and-conquer*. If computer scientists were poets, they might describe this strategy as *A journey of a thousand miles begins with a single step*. (For better or worse, most computer scientists are not poets.)

Still, selection sort is brute force. That is, it treats sorting as the problem of putting the lowest element in place, then the second-lowest, and so forth, without paying attention to any other information that might speed up the process. Is there a better way to do this, perhaps using divide-and-conquer?

There is, with a sorting algorithm called *Quicksort*, invented by C. A. R. Hoare in 1961.[7] Imagine you're a clerk in the main census office (a bank

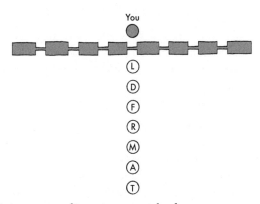

Figure 4.8. A sequence of items in no special order.

building that's been repurposed) of a small country. You're stationed behind a long row of teller windows, somewhere near the middle, and you're the only one who has come to work. All the people who have been ordered to report today are lined up in front of your window (Fig. 4.8). You beckon to the first person. "Name!" you growl. "Leutzinger," the woman says. "Wait here," you say. "Next!" "My name is Dierker," says the next man in line. "Form a new line over there," you say, gesturing toward a distant window on the left. You direct each person with a name before "Leutzinger" to the left, otherwise to the right.

When you've finished, you have one person in the middle and two shorter lines at windows on either side (Fig. 4.9). This arrangement isn't arbitrary; everyone in the left line has a name before the middle person, even if the line isn't sorted, and everyone to the right has a name after the middle person. You can probably guess what happens next: you walk to the right until you reach the window with the line in front of it (saving

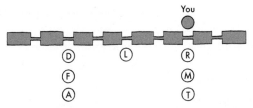

Figure 4.9. A sequence of items after one pass made by Quicksort.

the left side for later) and do it all again. "Name?" and so forth. You tell the first person to wait and you create two even shorter lines to the left and right, with names before or after *that* person's name. As long as you have enough windows for people to spread out between, eventually the entire group will be sorted.

A computer doesn't do this in quite the same way, but the idea is the same. Quicksort picks one element in the sequence, called a pivot, and by cleverly swapping data around, puts all the lower elements to its left and all the higher elements to its right. (The position of the pivot in the sequence may change as this happens.) Once this is done, the pivot is in its correct location, and there are two smaller sorting problems to be dealt with on either side. Quicksort solves these in the same way, one partial sequence at a time. Eventually, the parts of the problem get so small that no more division is possible, and all the elements are in order.

Quicksort works much faster than selection sort. To see why, imagine that we're sorting a sequence of 100 elements, and we've just finished the first stage. With selection sort, the lowest element is now in the first index of the sequence; with Quicksort, a pivot element is where it belongs in the middle of the sequence, say with 50 lower elements on one side and 49 on the other. One down, 99 left to go. Now, how much work will we have to do to put the next element in its proper place?

Selection sort walks through the 99 remaining elements to find the lowest one. Quicksort finds the next element to put in place (that is, another pivot) by looking through just 49 or 50 elements. Divide-and-conquer gives Quicksort the same advantage we saw in using binary search on a dictionary—breaking down a problem into two nearly equal parts is more effective than handling one element at a time.

I've gone into some detail about searching (sequential search and binary search) and sorting (selection sort and Quicksort) because so much information is recorded in the form of sequences, and it's much easier to find information if we can organize it properly. When I play poker or other card games, I put the cards in my hand in order. When I visit the department of motor vehicles, I expect that the clerk should be able to find my name or license plate number without difficulty, even among the millions of people who live in my state.

On a computer, think about all the applications that depend on information being sorted and easy to search: your calendar, sorted by date; the documents in your folders, sorted alphabetically; your music, searchable by title or artist; and so forth. In computing, we have dozens of different algorithms for sorting and search, appropriate for different situations, because having a lot of information is not very useful without these abilities.

TREES: BRANCHING OUT

Some kinds of information, or relationships between items of information, aren't a natural match for sequences. Let's consider trees. A good real-world example of a tree is a telephone tree. Some organizations, like community groups and the families of military personnel, use telephone trees to pass information quickly between their members. Here's how it works, in a simple example.

Archie has just taken charge of a small organization. Alison, his predecessor, has set up a telephone tree in which each person is responsible for calling at most two other people when a message needs to be passed on. (This makes the telephone tree a binary tree—no vertex has more than two children.) Alison, at the root of the tree, starts by calling Betty and Catherine; Betty then calls David and Evan; David calls Frank and Greg, and so forth. Catherine, Evan, and others who have no calling responsibilities are at the leaves (Fig. 4.10).

Archie doesn't know anything about algorithms and data types, but he does know that he's dissatisfied with Alison's telephone tree. It seems to take longer than it should for messages to reach some members of the group. He traces his finger on a path down the tree, keeping to the left as much as possible, counting as he goes. One call to reach B, two to reach D, three to reach F, and four to reach H. I is at the same level. He backs up to D (two calls away from A) and follows the right-hand edge, but going to the left again whenever he can. Six calls to reach N. He continues, for the sake of completeness (Archie is a bookkeeper at heart), and he ends up visiting the vertices of the tree in the order shown in Figure 4.11.

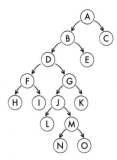

Figure 4.10. Alison's telephone tree.

Archie has just shown us an algorithm called *depth-first traversal*. The "depth-first" part means that whenever Archie reaches a vertex, he moves downward to one of its children if he hasn't visited it before. If he's looked at all the children of a vertex, he moves back up the tree to take care of vertices with other children that he missed on the way down.

It may seem that Archie is ignoring the structure of the tree when he backtracks, but he's not really: he's just being efficient. He marks off the vertices along the path he's visited (that is, he caches them), so that he can pop back upward to take a different branch from the ones he's already explored, instead of restarting from the root each time.

In computing terms, Archie is also figuring out the *depth* of each vertex—the number of edges between it and the root. Whenever he moves from a parent vertex to one of its children, the depth increases by 1. Archie thinks for a bit and reorganizes the telephone tree to look like Figure 4.12.

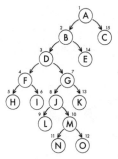

Figure 4.11. Alison's telephone tree, traversed depth first.

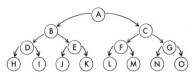

Figure 4.12. Archie's balanced telephone tree.

Archie has balanced the tree.[8] He could do a depth-first traversal to find out the depth of every vertex, but it's clear from the drawing that no one is more than three calls away. (We're ignoring the practicality that one person usually doesn't make two phone calls at once; for figuring depth it doesn't matter.) Archie's tree doesn't have anyone doing more work on average—there are seven people making calls, and eight people who don't have to call anyone else, just as in Alison's original tree. Remarkably, the entire job gets done much faster in the new tree, because responsibilities have been divided more evenly, and because the steps are carried out in parallel. If you're reminded of divide-and-conquer as well as multiprocessing, that's entirely appropriate. A balanced tree makes this work more efficiently.

Depth-first traversal is one natural way to traverse a tree, but it's not the only way. Let's imagine Archie in an uncomfortable situation: he has misplaced both the master list of all the group members *and* the telephone tree he has just put together. All he remembers is that when he needs to get a message out, he calls Betty and Catherine. He knows that someone in his group holds an important document, the original charter for the group, but he doesn't remember who. Can he find out by making calls, and at the same time rebuild his records?

Archie gets to work. He writes down Betty's and Catherine's names in a list on a piece of paper. He calls Betty. Does she have the charter? No. Betty says she's responsible for calling David and Evan, so Archie writes this down beside Betty's name and adds David and Evan at the end of the list (Fig. 4.13).

Next is a call to Catherine. She doesn't have the charter either; her calls are to Frank and Greg. Archie updates Catherine's entry, writes down the new names, and continues to David. Eventually he discovers that Jack has the charter. He continues calling, though, until finally he has reached everyone and has reconstructed his telephone tree.

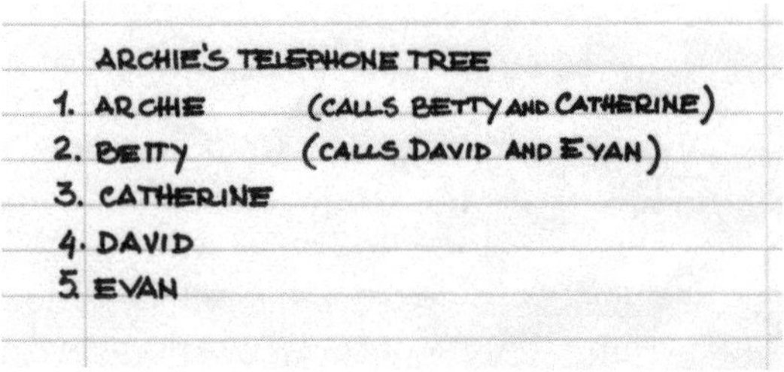

Figure 4.13. Archie reconstructs his telephone tree.

Archie has just carried out a *breadth-first traversal* of his tree, with three results: he has found his information, he has listed all the group members, and he has reconstructed his telephone tree. Not bad, given how little information he started with. The "breadth-first" part means that in visiting vertices, Archie moved across the width, or breadth, of the tree at each level before moving down to the next: all the vertices at depth 1, then at depth 2, and so forth. If we number the vertices in the order they were visited, it looks like Figure 4.14.

What if Archie had stopped on reaching Jack, who has the charter he was looking for? In that case we'd say that Archie had performed a search. Just as trees can be traversed either breadth-first or depth-first, they can be searched using either algorithm, starting at the root of the tree.

Breadth-first and depth-first searches (and traversals) are brute force, but they're still two of the most important conceptual tools for dealing with trees. They work in a different way from sequence traversal, because trees represent a different kind of relationship: not one data item following another in single file, but the kind of relationship that produces hierarchies. For example, the folders and documents on your computer form a tree. If you direct your system to search for a specific document, one way it can do this is with breadth-first search.

Breadth-first and depth-first search are also different from each other. For example, imagine that you've traced your matrilineal ancestry all the way back to Anais, your great-to-the-nth grandmother, who had two children, Beth and Chiara. You've drawn all the information in a gigantic family tree. If you were to traverse this tree breadth-first,

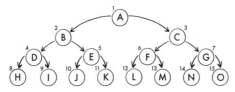

Figure 4.14. Archie's telephone tree, traversed breadth first.

you'd visit all of Anais's children before any grandchild, and all of her grandchildren before any great-grandchild. (You probably had to traverse the tree in this way when you drew it, to make sure the names in each generation were even with each other.) In a depth-first traversal you'd visit the names in a different order. You'd follow Beth's descendants all the way to your cousins of today (perhaps even yourself) before you came back to visit Chiara on her branch of the tree. Do you go wide or do you go deep? Breadth-first search gives you one, depth-first the other.

It's possible that you've carried out a search on a tree without realizing it. For example, imagine being lost in a maze inside a cave, with passages that branch but never loop back on each other.[9] A dead end stops you for just a moment; you backtrack and try another nearby route. Depth-first search. If you're at home, on the other hand, and you've misplaced the remote control to your television, you search the living room before going into adjoining rooms, and then rooms farther away. Even if you find the remote in the garage, tucked in the pocket behind the front passenger seat of your car, breadth-first search was a good choice. We can choose between depth-first search and breadth-first search depending on where we think the vertex we're searching for is more likely to be found.

Sometimes complete traversals are needed. If you're tracing the spread of a genetic condition through your family tree, a depth-first traversal would be appropriate, starting perhaps from a grandparent; it's easier to keep track of the information you learn on a path from an ancestor to a descendant. If you're writing a family history, though, your older relatives might find it appropriate if you first ask them about family stories before asking their children, nieces, and nephews. A breadth-first traversal gives the right ordering.

GRAPHS: MAKING CONNECTIONS

Let's see what we can do with graphs. Suppose you're the manager of a state park. It's a beautiful wilderness area, with many points of interest: scenic views, rock formations, a waterfall, some picnic areas, and a visitors' center. Over the past twenty years, erosion and foot traffic have taken their toll on the trails that wind between these points. You're writing a funding proposal for their restoration. You can't expect to restore all of them, and some will be more expensive than others, depending on their length, surface type, and other factors.

How do you choose a set of trails to restore that keeps all of the points of interest accessible and at the same time keeps the restoration cost as low as possible? You start with a map that shows the points of interest and the trails between them (Fig. 4.15).

Here's what you do. Beside each trail, you write down its restoration cost. Next, you copy all the names of the trails into a list, ordered from lowest to highest cost. (A sorted sequence will do.) You pick one point of interest on your map and mark it off. (You'll be marking off all the points, one at a time.) Now you scan down your list of trails until you find a trail that connects a new point of interest with one you've just marked off. You pick that trail, run a highlighter along its length, and mark off its endpoint. You return to the top of the list and scan for a trail that connects to either of your marked-off points. You repeat this process. As you go, your two marked-off points become three, then four, and so on, and they're always connected by the lowest-cost trail that

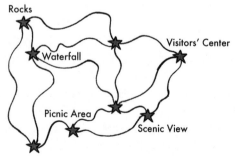

Figure 4.15. A graph of locations and the trails between them.

you find. When you've marked off trails that connect all the points of interest, you're finished. The highlighting shows the trails you've chosen (Fig. 4.16).

Your original map of trails is a graph, with vertices being the points of interest and the trails being edges. This graph has a twist we haven't seen before: the edges have *costs*. (Also, the edges are *undirected*, which means you can move along them in either direction.) Your algorithm for choosing trails is Prim's algorithm, and it generates what's called a *minimum spanning tree* for a graph. The "spanning" part means that all the vertices in the graph are included in the tree, even if not all the edges are kept. The "minimum" part means that of all the different sets of edges you could have chosen (trails between two locations, in our example), you've ended up with a set that has the lowest overall cost.

Prim's algorithm gives us two new ways to think about algorithms. First, because we've brought cost into the picture, we can imagine algorithms that find solutions that have different total costs. Prim's algorithm finds an *optimal* solution. There are many spanning trees on our graph, but Prim's finds one with the lowest cost. It's possible to prove that the algorithm is guaranteed to find an optimal solution, for any graph it's given. As you might expect, finding an optimal solution is often harder than finding just any solution.

Second, instead of looking at the quality of the result of Prim's algorithm we can think about how it makes decisions. At each step, the algorithm commits to the lowest-cost edge that connects a new vertex to the tree it's building. This commitment to a short-term gain, without ever

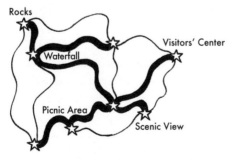

Figure 4.16. A minimum spanning tree showing selected trails.

looking back, means that Prim's algorithm is *greedy*. ("Shortsighted" or "eager" might be better descriptions, but "greedy" is the technical term.) Greediness doesn't rise to the level of being a strategy, but it's a useful way of describing how some algorithms work. Greed is good if, after having solved a problem, you can say, "Looking back, I wouldn't change any of the choices I made." Greed works for Prim's algorithm, but of course a short-term gain doesn't always lead to a good solution in the long term—think of playing the stock market.

Let's consider another graph example. It turns out that because graphs are a generalization of trees, some of the same algorithms can be applied. Imagine yourself in this situation (it won't be hard): You say to a friend, "The other day I bumped into Jane Doe. You don't know her…" Your friend says, "But I do know her. We went to school together."

"That's funny," you say. "It's a small world."

How small is it? In the 1960s, Jeffrey Travers and Stanley Milgram decided to find out with an experiment.[10] They sent letters to 296 volunteers, giving them the name and a brief life history of a stockbroker in Boston. Travers and Milgram didn't make the stockbroker's name public in writing about their research; for convenience let's call him K.B.

The instructions for the experiment ran along the following lines: "Do you know K.B. personally? If you do, send the enclosed packet to him. If you don't, think of a personal friend or acquaintance of yours who is more likely to know K.B.; send the packet to that person." Volunteers also filled out some paperwork so that the process could be tracked over time. K.B. eventually received 64 letters. By analyzing this information, Travers and Milgram found what we'd now call the degrees of separation between K.B. and a sampling of other people in the country: 5.2, on average.

We could replicate this experiment today in an online social network, such as Facebook, using email instead of letters going through the U.S. post office. Or, if we had direct access to the information in the social network, we could try a more direct approach. A social network is a graph, with vertices representing people and edges representing friendships. If friendships go in both directions (that is, I can be your friend only if you're my friend as well), then we can carry out a breadth-first search on the graph to get the same kind of information.

We start at the vertex representing you, and we move outward to all of your friends, one edge away. We then visit vertices two edges away, then three, and so forth. We skip any vertices that we've encountered already. We'll probably find what Travers and Milgram did—a small number of hops between you and most other people in the social graph.

Social networks are *small-world networks* (here "network" and "graph" mean the same thing). Pick two vertices at random in a small-world network, and the path between them is usually short, even if the network is very large.

Not all graphs are small-world networks. For example, if we think of a highway system as a graph, with intersections being vertices and the stretches of road between intersections being edges, two non-adjacent intersections chosen at random usually won't have a very short path between them. Interstate 90, which runs from Boston to Seattle, is just such a graph, but (unfortunately for long-distance drivers) the average distance between intersections is about 1,000 miles.

It turns out, though, that graphs of many kinds of relationships in the real world do have the small-world property.[11] It's surprising for social networks, because we tend to think of groups of people as form- ing social clusters, and it's not obvious that tracing relationships within and between these clusters would give us short chains. The World Wide Web is also a small-world network, with pages related by links between them. A graph of actors who have appeared in the same movies is a small-world network; this is the basis for the trivia game "Six Degrees of Kevin Bacon."

In fact, there's even evidence that the small-world property applies to how we store information inside our heads. In *Alice in Wonderland*, Lewis Carroll posed a now-famous riddle: "Why is a raven like a writing desk?" Carroll was aiming for a riddle that had no answer, but fans of *Alice* have come up with dozens of possibilities.

It's actually hard to think of two things that aren't related to each other in *some* short chain of associations. In the 1970s, psychologists developed a model of concepts in human memory called a *semantic net- work*, represented as a graph.[12] In simple form, each concept is a vertex, and vertices have edges between them if there's an association between their concepts. Chains of associations are produced by *spreading activation*. For example, the vertex for the color "red" has edges to vertices representing other color concepts, some fruit concepts, and so forth. When the "red" vertex is activated, its activation spreads to those other vertices, and the activation continues to spread outward (Fig. 4.17).

As a model of our brain, spreading activation would happen in parallel, with all the neighbors of one vertex being activated at once, but we can create a similar effect by doing breadth-first search. From any vertex, we visit all of its neighbors, then all of their neighbors (that haven't already been visited), and so forth.

Spreading activation works in more than one direction as well. If I ask you, "What's the connection between fire engines and flowers?" you might say that some flowers, like roses, are red, and so are fire engines. This corresponds to one breadth-first search starting at fire engines and another starting at flowers; they stop when both searches come across the same vertex, the concept red. You might have thought of a different path between fire engines and flowers, perhaps through the concept of

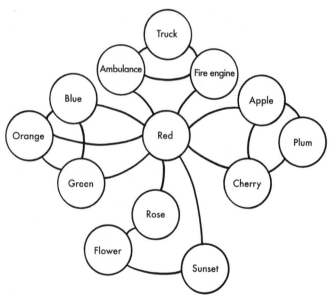

Figure 4.17. A semantic network.

parades, but there isn't enough room in an entire book to draw *all* of the concepts even a single person has.

Think about what makes it possible for us to find short chains of associations between distant concepts, given what we know about graphs. It could be that everything is directly related to almost everything else, in a graph that is very dense with edges. But there's another plausible explanation: relationships between concepts could form a small-world network.[13] That is, every concept doesn't *have* to be directly related to almost every other concept, and yet we can find short paths between them. Who would have expected similarities between social networks, the World Wide Web, and the knowledge in our heads? Now you have a new short path linking all three concepts.

ABSTRACT DATA TYPES AS BUILDING BLOCKS

Abstract data types and algorithms are building blocks for organizing and processing information. We combine them as needed, and if we encounter new problems, we invent new abstractions. We're looking for the right tool for the job—one that gives us as much power as we need.

For example, if I'm running shopping errands in town, I might have a collection of stores in mind, and for each store a separate collection of items to buy. I can organize the collection of stores as a sequence, then sort that sequence to minimize my driving time, and do the same for the items in each store to minimize my browsing time. I'm combining algorithms and abstract data types to capture complex behavior or structure.

This kind of combination suggests an interesting possibility: we can create new abstract data types, new ways of describing how collections of information can be organized. Here are a few examples. Suppose you have a list of tasks to be done, and some tasks are higher priority than others. New tasks of different priorities arrive regularly (you have a tough job), but when you pull the next task from your list, it should always be the highest-priority task remaining. A *priority queue* is a good match for this problem. A priority queue is a collection of information that automatically keeps itself sorted as new items are added and, when you remove an item, it's always the highest-priority item in the collection.

If data items added earlier have higher priorities than items added later, then we get a first-in, first-out *queue*, similar to people standing in line at a grocery store. ("First-in, first-out" is usually shortened to "FIFO" and pronounced as in the "Jack and the Beanstalk" fairy tale.) People join the line at the end and are checked out only when they reach the front. If items are kept sorted in the reverse order, with newer items having higher priority, we have an organization closer to a stack of papers or books, where we can add to or remove only from the top. This is a last-in, first-out (LIFO) queue, or a *stack*.

Sometimes we find it convenient to define entirely new abstract data types. For example, suppose you have a collection of information about the cars you've owned in your lifetime: make, model, color, year, and so forth. We could represent each car as a sequence, with the first element being the make, the second the model, and so forth, but we're forcing an ordering onto the information that really isn't there. Instead, we could use a *tuple* abstract data type.[14] ("Tuple" comes from the words "quintuple," "sextuple," and so forth.) A tuple is a collection that lets us ask for its items by name rather than by a numerical index. We could define a "car" tuple, for example, so that we could ask, "What value of 'make' does this car have?" instead of "What's the first element of the sequence containing information about this car?" Tuples give as much power as we need, but no more.

Priority queues, FIFO queues, tuples… These can be built from trees and sequences, but I won't go into the details of exactly how. Aren't those details important? Not necessarily. There's a riddle that runs along these lines: You're an army officer with a sergeant and a platoon of soldiers under your command. There's a 25-foot flagpole to be put up, and you have 200 feet of rope. How do you raise the flagpole? The answer is this: You say, "Sergeant, get that flagpole up."

We can treat algorithms and abstract data types in the same way. It's important to know the basics about how information can be organized (as sequences, trees, or graphs) and what can be done with the information (it can be searched, sorted, and so forth). But we don't always have to think about the details. For example, it's enough to know that you can add items to a priority queue and get them back one at a time, in highest-priority order, without worrying about how the information is managed or processed internally.

We can treat an algorithm as a unit of computation itself, and we can similarly think of a collection of information as a unit. We say that these abstractions *encapsulate* their internals; that is, as long as we know something about what they do or what they're for, we don't have to look inside. Encapsulation is a form of modularity that lets us think about the bigger picture of computing.[15]

Imagine creating a table on paper, with columns labeled make, model, year, and so forth, and filling up the rows of the table with a tuple for each car you've owned. You've just built a **relational database**. (The term "relational" comes from the logical foundation of databases, as developed by English computer scientist E. F. Codd.) You can find information about specific cars in your database by scanning across the column labels and then down through the rows, or tuples. In database terms, you're carrying out a **query**.

For example, I keep a contacts database of friends and colleagues on my computer. Each tuple contains a first and last name, an email address, a phone number, and sometimes other personal information, such as a birthday. I could find out whose birthday is today by running a query to select tuples with a birthday value of today. If I were ambitious, I might chain the results to a query in another database of information about what my friends' interests are, and those results to third query in an online shopping database to give me ideas for possible birthday gifts. (My friends know I'm not *that* ambitious.)

Databases are part of the broader area of information management in computing; they're important in part because they encapsulate information on a grand scale. When you use a search engine on the Web, for example, you're executing a query—or perhaps several queries, chained together behind the scenes—on a very large set of databases. Today's companies and government agencies would quickly break down without the ability to handle large amounts of data, organized to make it easy to retrieve. Work on databases, relational or otherwise, constantly improves our ability to get relevant information as fast as possible.

RECURSION: A SPECIAL KIND OF BUILDING BLOCK

At this point, we're ready to take a deep dive into abstract thinking. We'll start with the structure of a tree. Imagine that the genealogy bug has bitten someone in your family, and you've been sent an enormous drawing of your family tree: parents, grandparents, aunts and uncles, cousins and so forth, going back several generations. Here are the top three levels of the tree (Fig. 4.18). I've elided Mary's and John's children and further descendants (including yourself); Joseph and Abigail had no children.

Joseph and Abigail have family trees consisting of only themselves. Emma's family tree contains her two children and all of their descendants. Jane's family tree is Jane plus the family trees of her three children. Notice that a family tree can contain other family trees, and that the links between them are parent–child relationships.

That is, if we think of abstract data types as building blocks, some can be building blocks for *themselves*, which is a remarkable thing. We can define trees, for example, in this way. A tree is...

(a)   A single vertex, or

(b)   A vertex that is the parent of one or more trees.

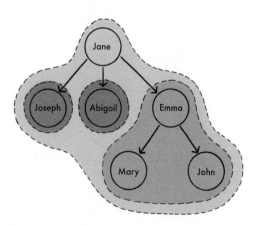

Figure 4.18. Trees contain other trees.

This is a *recursive* definition, one that refers to itself. The second part of the definition says that trees are built out of other trees. The first part ensures that the definition isn't circular—at the very bottom of a tree we'll find single-vertex trees, without children.

Recursion is a fundamental concept in computing. Recursion has elegance in the eyes of a computer scientist: it lets us describe large ideas concisely, in simple terms. The number of possible trees is infinite, and yet our definition captures them all in just two rules. It explains how trees can be broken down into smaller trees (there's a root vertex, and below it there are subtrees) and it also explains how small trees can be combined into a larger tree (you can make them all the children of a new root vertex).

Algorithms can be defined recursively as well. Remember *A journey of a thousand miles begins with a single step*? A very literal-minded person might say, "But after a single step, you're still . . . well, if a step is about a yard and there are 1,760 yards in a mile . . . you're still 1,759,999 steps away!"

A more natural interpretation is that after one step, you face nearly the same problem, so you solve it in the same way. A computer scientist would express the idea like this:

To take a journey of so many steps,
> *Check whether you have zero steps to take. If it's zero, you've arrived. Otherwise, subtract one from the number of steps.*
> *Now take a journey of that many steps.*

This is a recursive solution for the problem—a solution that refers to itself. Recursive algorithms don't treat an entire problem as a whole, but rather break it down into smaller parts. If a part is small enough, it's solved directly; if it's not, the algorithm creates a copy of itself to repeat the process on that remaining part.

Here's a different example of the same idea. You're standing in a long line of people, and you're handed a strip of paper containing a list of numbers. Your job is to add up all the numbers. You'd rather not do all the work yourself, so you tear off the top number, hand the list to the person behind you in line, and ask that person to add up all the numbers on the now-shorter list. When you get the total back, you'll add your own number to it and be done. *Everyone* in line does the same thing. Eventually, because each time the strip of paper gets passed down the line it contains one number fewer, it will reach someone who sees a single number. That person simply passes the number forward again. An increasing total is passed forward up the line, getting larger as each person's number is added to it. Eventually you receive the total and add your number to it, and you're done.

This idea becomes powerful when we think about decrease- or divide-and-conquer. Let's assume that a sorting algorithm stops if it's given a sequence that contains just one element. Then we could define the selection sort algorithm recursively in this way:

> *To apply selection sort to a sequence,*
> > *Check whether the sequence has more than one element. If not, stop. Otherwise, find the lowest element and swap it with the element in the lowest index.*
> > *Now apply selection sort to the rest of the sequence, leaving out the lowest index.*

A recursive algorithm can even create multiple copies of itself if the problem needs to be broken down into several parts. Hoare originally presented Quicksort in a recursive style:

> *To Quicksort a sequence,*
> > *Check whether the sequence has just one element. If it does, stop. Choose a pivot element and rearrange the sequence to put lower-valued elements on one side of the pivot, higher-valued elements on the other side.*
> > *Quicksort the lower elements.*
> > *Quicksort the higher elements.*

These recursive definitions of the algorithms work in the same way as our examples of taking a journey and adding up numbers. We're describing how some potentially enormous amount of work should be done, and yet our description has just a few simple steps.

Recursive algorithms also turn out to be effective when we combine them with information that has a recursive structure. How could you find an item in a tree using depth-first search, starting at the root? *Check to see whether the root holds your item. If not, perform a depth-first search on each of its child vertices.* Or how would you tell whether you're a direct descendant of Charles Babbage by looking through your family tree? Put your finger on the vertex representing you. *To find Charles Babbage... Check whether the vertex under your finger is Charles Babbage. If not, and if the birth date is later than 1791, move your finger to the father vertex. Now find Charles Babbage.* These are brute force algorithms, as we saw earlier; simply because we've described the algorithm in recursive terms doesn't make it a divide-and-conquer algorithm. But in some situations, where the information in a tree has the right structure, we *can* deal with it using divide-and-conquer.

Imagine that you play Twenty Questions at the championship level. How would you convey your expertise to a protégé? One way is to write out what you know as a binary tree. Say that you've been told the answer is an animal. At the root you ask, "Does it have four legs?" The "Yes" child vertex asks, "Does it have claws?" while the "No" child vertex asks, "Does it live in the water?" At each level, the tree contains more and more specific questions, until the leaves are reached, where specific animals are guessed.

The recursive algorithm for playing Twenty Questions, based on this tree, is straightforward: *Ask the question at the root vertex. Depending on the answer, go to the "Yes" or "No" vertex. Now play Nineteen Questions from that vertex.* This is the equivalent of binary search, but on a tree rather than a sequence. It's divide-and-conquer—it eliminates half of the possibilities at each step.

THE BOTTOM LINE

We've seen different kinds of structure in information, which can be captured by abstract data types. Sequences, trees, and graphs are all around us, whether we're running a finger down a shopping list, trying to remember how we're related to someone at a family reunion, or planning a road trip across the country.

We've also seen algorithms for processing information structured in different ways: traversal, searching, sorting, finding paths, and more specialized procedures. More importantly, we've learned how to think about solving problems by following general strategies, such as brute force or divide-and-conquer strategies, and different abstract ways that we can describe algorithms that rely on these strategies—this one might give optimal solutions, this other one is greedy. New algorithms based on these ideas are developed every day—after all, we never run out of problems to solve. That's part of what makes the theoretical side of computing important and rewarding.

But it's all still theoretical. I've left a gap between abstract strategies for solving problems and how these strategies can be put into action on a real computer. In the next chapter we'll see how this gap can be bridged, with programs.

FURTHER READING

Some of the material in this chapter related to abstract data types is based on *Data Structures in Java*, by Simon Gray (Pearson Addison-Wesley, 2007). The most popular and complete textbook on algorithms today is *Introduction to Algorithms*, by Thomas H. Cormen, Charles E. Leiserson, Ronald L. Rivest, and Clifford Stein (MIT Press, 3rd ed., 2009). It's nicknamed "CLRS," after the last names of the authors. John MacCormick gives an accessible account of modern algorithms in *Nine Algorithms That Changed the Future: The Ingenious Ideas That Drive Today's Computers* (Princeton University Press, 2012).

## Chapter 5

Programming: Putting Plans into Action

Algorithms and collections of information, organized by abstract data types, need to be translated into a form that a computer can process. This is what programs are for: they translate between the abstract and the concrete.

Programming means expressing abstractions in a language that a computer can deal with.[1] Given what we know about computer architecture—the CPU marching through a set of instructions, data being shuffled between different storage components, all carefully synchronized—I suspect programming may sound a bit daunting. And it can be, working with the low-level language of machine instructions. Remember how little a computer can accomplish with the execution of a single instruction: move a number from memory into a register, or the reverse; carry out a single arithmetic operation; execute this instruction instead of that one. Now imagine writing down one of the algorithms in the previous chapter using only these instructions. Developing, analyzing, and removing errors from machine language programs of even just a few dozen lines can be amazingly tedious.

This was a major challenge for the field of computing in the 1950s: how could programs of any size or complexity be written in a reasonable amount of time? To put this challenge in perspective, an organization interested in scientific computing at that time could easily spend over $1 million per year (in today's dollars) leasing a single computer, and personnel costs for programmers would be about the same. Writing a program might take months or years, with each programmer contributing a dozen or so instructions per day.

In 1954, John Backus took on this problem, as leader of the Programming Research Department at IBM.[2] (Backus found his calling only after leaving medical school and, earlier, the chemistry program at the University of Virginia. About his high school experience, he said, "I flunked out every year. I never studied. I hated studying. I was just goofing around."[3] He's remembered today as an accomplished computer scientist and mathematician.) Backus and his team revolutionized the theory and practice of programming with the creation of Fortran (FORmula TRANslation), a *high-level programming language*. Instead of instructions, a Fortran program contains *statements*. A single statement stands for some common, useful sequence of machine instructions.

Here's an analogy for what a high-level language brings to programming. Suppose you're writing a program to keep inventory of your collection of exotic jams. You have just two kinds, mango and kiwi (you're just starting out). At some point your program needs to add up the number of Kiwi jars and Mango jars to get the total number of jam jars. This is how you might naturally express this operation, in a Fortran statement:

```
Jams = Kiwi + Mango.
```

In contrast, if you were writing your program in machine language, you'd have to write instructions that look more like this (as translated into English):[4]

Copy the data from some specific memory location into Register R1.
Copy the data from a different memory location into Register R2.
Add the values in Registers R1 and R2 and put the result in Register R3.
Copy the data in Register R3 to yet another memory location.

The Fortran statement is much more concise than the equivalent machine instructions, but there's more to a high-level program than just being shorter. Notice that the single statement has meaningful names for the information we're dealing with. "Jams," "Kiwi," and "Mango" stand for specific memory locations in the machine instructions, and we can use those names instead of numerical memory addresses. Further, it's reasonable to expect that addition operations will be common enough that we *should* have a shorthand for them, rather than writing out very similar sequences of machine instructions again and again. Fortran turned out to be much more powerful than machine language in terms of programmer productivity; writing and debugging Fortran programs could be done four times as fast.

High-level languages represent two key insights in computing. We've talked about a computer as having an abstract functional organization—the CPU, memory, and so forth—above the level of its wires and electronic components. Another level of abstraction can be added on top of this. Backus described this level as the language of a "synthetic machine" for programmers to work with, instead of the "hardware language" of the actual computer. By defining new abstractions in such a language, programmers can build their own conceptual tools to do whatever is needed. For example, our Fortran statement is about jam inventory, rather than strictly about arithmetic, and if we were to extend our work to an entire program, we'd see further abstractions, perhaps related to physical storage space and ordering forms.

Of course, it isn't enough simply to say, "Now you don't have to worry about machine language." A program in a high-level language (we generally call such a program *source code*) needs to be turned into machine instructions that an actual computer can run. This translation can be automated, which leads to the second insight: Programs can be treated as data.[5] That is, a specialized kind of program, called a *compiler*, takes a source code program as input, and it generates machine instructions as output.[6]

If this seems unintuitive, think about assembling a piece of furniture you've just bought from a Swedish manufacturer. The instruction booklet is written in English, but that's probably not its original language. The manufacturer sent out its Swedish-language booklet to a translation service that produced a new version in English, and of course that service didn't start building furniture by following the instructions. It translated those instructions into a different language.

Roughly speaking, a compiler does what the translation service does, though we'd have to imagine the new instruction booklet being enormously larger than the original—one benefit of working in a high-level language is that individual statements can stand for dozens or more machine instructions. There are various strategies aside from compilation for making a high-level language program executable, but I won't go into the details; I'll use the general term *translator* to encompass them all.[7]

With the release of Fortran, other high-level languages quickly followed, notably Lisp, for work in mathematics and artificial intelligence, and Algol, whose influence can be seen in most popular languages today, including C and its descendants, Java, and Python. Today it's possible to write exceedingly complex programs in a very short time, taking advantage of the flexibility and abstraction that high-level languages offer.

In this chapter, we'll walk through the process of writing a simple program to see what programming is about, on both the technical side and the creative side.

That there's a creative side to programming may surprise you. How could writing "code" be anything but drudgery? It does take work to learn a programming language and to write programs to solve problems, but for many programmers, the payoff is in the act of creative expression.[8]

Conceptually, you begin by sketching an idea, or perhaps several conflicting ideas, on a blank canvas. You set to work expanding and refining your thoughts. At one point, you throw out your canvas and bring in a new one; at another point, you stop to invent a new, more expressive tool for your work. Eventually a design emerges that gives you confidence you're on the right track, and you fill in the details. The result is a program that solves a problem and gives you a good deal of personal satisfaction.

If I've made programming sound as much like an art or craft as a technical topic, that's intentional. Many programmers see elegance and beauty in the best programs they write. It's a specialized aesthetic sense (by analogy, I'd guess that most art appreciation classes don't begin with Jackson Pollock), but it's widespread—there are even books about programming aesthetics.

We take it for granted that artists must understand their materials, and we'd say the same about structural engineers, fashion designers, and race car mechanics; metaphorically speaking, it's true as well for military commanders and movie directors. Alan Kay, a computer scientist (and former professional jazz guitarist) whose work has influenced the design of most popular programming languages today, writes, "It is software that gives form and purpose to a programmable machine, much as a sculptor shapes clay."[9] Programs are the materials of computing.

PROGRAMMING A ROBOT

Programming is the most practical skill in computing, and to understand the process, it will help to concentrate on a concrete task. In this chapter, we'll move away from information processing toward interaction with the physical world: programming a robot. We'll see how algorithms and abstract data types translate into a high-level language, based on general concepts that apply equally well to information processing and robot movement. We might not find beauty or elegance in the program we eventually write, but we'll be able to see a few important elements: simplicity, clarity, and some generality.[10]

Imagine that we've been hired by Martha, a dance choreographer and noted robotics enthusiast. She hands us a kit for a robot, the Lego Mindstorms NXT, and says, "I'd like you to write a program that makes the robot move along the outline of a square and reports the distance it's moved. Can you do this by next week?"

We're relieved. Martha hasn't asked us, "Could you program a six-foot-tall robot to waltz with a human partner?" It's not clear whether that's even possible with current software and hardware, and trying to do it would involve more research than programming. Having a manageable problem like moving in a square is a good start for a program.

The NXT robot is used in college courses and in real robotics research, but it's also simple enough for schoolchildren to assemble and program (Fig. 5.1). The core of the robot is a plastic "brick," a self-contained computer with a CPU, memory, a keypad for input, and a

Figure 5.1. The Lego Mindstorms NXT robot.

tiny LCD display for output. The brick can be connected to other input and output devices that let it interact with the physical world. In robotics, we call the input devices for a robot its *sensors*, and the output devices its *actuators*. Sensors typically include cameras for visual information and microphones for auditory information. Actuators include motors for independent control of the wheels of the robot.

We'll be using a simple version of the robot, configured like a backwards tricycle, with no sensors. Each front wheel can be driven independently by loading a number into a specific memory location, a positive number for forward, negative for reverse.

We'll write the program together. Programming isn't necessarily a solitary activity, where you retreat alone to a cubicle or basement room for hours or days, emerging only for basic bodily needs. The first professional programmers in the history of computing (Kathleen McNulty Mauchly Antonelli, Jean Jennings Bartik, Frances Snyder Holberton, Marlyn Wescoff Meltzer, Frances Bilas Spence, and Ruth Lichterman Teitelbaum) worked together in teams to write programs for the ENIAC, one of the earliest electronic computers.[11] Today, a common technique in so-called agile development is pair programming, in which one person types on a keyboard while another observes and comments; the two switch places regularly. We'll give it a try here, though I'll remain in the driver's seat throughout.

The first step is to make sure we understand the problem (Fig. 5.2).[12]

You: "Does the robot have some built-in way to follow a path around a square?"
Me: "Not that I know of. We can send power to the two wheels, though, so that it can move forward and backward. And if we have the two wheels turn in the opposite direction from each other, the robot can do turns."
You: "Then a square is easy. Just move forward, turn right or left, move forward the same amount, turn the same direction, and so forth, four times. At the end report the distance. Does the robot need to end up facing the same way it started?"
Me: "That sounds like a good idea. If we had it do another square, it would roll along the same path."
You: "What does it mean to 'report' something?"
Me: "We'll keep things simple. Our program can produce the distance as its output."
You: "I have a few more questions…"

Even though we haven't yet committed a word to paper (or rather a statement to a program), we've made progress. We've realized that if we clarify some assumptions, this will make the problem easier to solve. Writing a very general program to handle any contingency would be nice, but we have limited time.

We return to Martha and ask for clarification. Are squares of different sizes needed? Should the robot end up facing its original direction? Should the robot be able to turn either right or left around the square? Does the speed of movement make a difference? Martha tells us yes, yes, yes, and no.

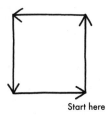

Start here

Figure 5.2. Moving along a square path.

Good. Now we have a clearer target for our work, and we're less likely to end up with a program that performs exactly as we expect, but solves the wrong problem. We've also developed a vocabulary to describe the robot's behavior—terms that aren't included in the problem statement: moving forward and turning at right angles. We're following the same approach I outlined at the beginning of Chapter 4. We identify abstractions that let us concentrate on the important parts of the problem, and ignore the details, such as how exactly the robot performs these actions.

Our choice of language here may seem natural, even too obvious to mention, but it's a critical step. This is a very general aspect of problem solving, which cognitive scientists call *problem decomposition* or *goal decomposition* and software engineers call *top-down design*. (The difference is whether we're thinking about the problem or its solution, but in the early stages of programming we often shift back and forth.) The abstractions we choose will guide our further thinking, so we'll take some care establishing them. Moving forward and turning left or right are reasonable choices, given what we know so far.

We've now covered enough ground to start sketching out our approach in a very simple algorithm for what we'll call a "following a square path." In this stage, we'll use *pseudocode*, which is just structured English, for our description. I'll number the lines to make the algorithm easier to talk about.

```
Version 1: Move, turn, move, turn, etc.

To follow a square path:               1
   Move eight inches forward.          2
   Turn left.                          3
   Move eight inches forward.          4
   Turn left.                          5
   Move eight inches forward.          6
   Turn left.                          7
   Move eight inches forward.          8
   Turn left.                          9
   Output the number 32 as the result. 10
```

Our algorithm breaks down the problem of following a square path into smaller problems: moving in straight lines and turning. The comment at the top, without a number, is for the benefit of human readers rather than part of the procedure. Each of the remaining steps is a statement. Line 1 gives the algorithm a name, and the rest, lines 2 through 10, form a *block:* a list of steps to be carried out in order.

This algorithm steers the robot around a square eight inches on a side, which isn't very general, but it sometimes helps to start by solving a more specialized problem than we're given, so that we can see how our ideas play out.

I have to be honest with you, though: Version 1 is terrible. The pseudocode is easy to read, and it does what it's supposed to do, within limits, but that's not enough.

Consider how much work you'd have to do to see whether it's correct or not. First, you'd need to count the number of turns to make sure there are four; then see that the distances are all the same; and finally, recognize that eight inches times 4 is 32 inches. (And if I'd made a mistake in my multiplication, accidentally writing 64 instead of 32, the last line would be hard to make sense of.) Let's see how we can fix these problems.

We start by noticing that the block of statements, lines 2 through 10, contains an obvious pattern. Two of the statements, which I've emphasized below, are repeated four times.

```
Version 1, as above

To follow a square path:              1
  Move eight inches forward.          2
  Turn left.                          3
  Move eight inches forward.          4
  Turn left.                          5
  Move eight inches forward.          6
  Turn left.                          7
  Move eight inches forward.          8
  Turn left.                          9
  Output the number 32 as the result. 10
```

In Chapter 3 I described a class of machine instructions that tell the CPU to fetch an instruction from a new memory address, rather than marching through instructions in order. We could do something similar here, changing the algorithm's *flow of control*: "Move forward, turn left, then go to Step 2 and repeat." But this leads to problems. Reading through a long algorithm with so-called "go to" statements is like being in a scavenger hunt, where each location you visit tells you where to go next. (And there are no treasures anywhere to be found.)[13] Instead, it's typical to handle repetition in a more structured way. We can say in advance how many repetitions are needed, and then we give the statements that are to be repeated. This is called a *loop*, or an *iteration*.

```
Version 2: Repeat move/turn four times
To follow a square path:                    1
  Do the following four times in a row:     2
    Move eight inches forward.              3
    Turn left.                             4
    Output the number 32 as the result.     5
```

This is slightly better. We've turned the repeated moving and turning statements into a smaller block (in lines 3 and 4). This block is inside a *compound statement* (in line 2) that specifies how many times the inner block is to be repeated. Our algorithm now has a better conceptual connection to a square: four sides of the same length, four repetitions of the same block. The algorithm is also more concise. Version 1 had a block of nine statements at the top level; now we have a top-level block of just two statements: the loop and the output statement. Let's take care of that output statement, by having the system do the additions for us.

In Version 3 we've used a *variable*, named "total distance." A variable gives a name to an item of information we're keeping track of, in this case the distance traveled by the robot. Each time the algorithm goes through its loop, the total distance is updated by eight inches. Whenever an algorithm can do work for us, we'll let it; among other things, this gives us fewer opportunities to make mistakes.

```
Version 3: Repeat move/turn four times.
Total distance is updated each time and
produced as output.
To follow a square path:                    1
  Set the total distance to zero.           2
  Do the following four times in a row:     3
    Move eight inches forward.               4
    Turn left.                               5
    Add eight to the total distance.         6
  Output total distance.                     7
```

The algorithm still has obvious weaknesses. First, not all squares are eight inches on a side, and we'd prefer not to write different algorithms just to handle different squares. Second, the algorithm always tells the robot to turn left, as if it's in a NASCAR race. We'll fix these problems with two changes.

One will involve considering different possible inputs to the algorithm: the distance to move forward, and the direction for the robot to turn, either clockwise or counterclockwise. The other change is a further refinement to the algorithm's flow of control. It should pay attention to direction inside the repeated block. For a clockwise square the robot should turn right each time, and for a counterclockwise square the robot should turn left.

We could rewrite the algorithm to ask two separate questions, "Is the direction clockwise?" and "Is the direction counterclockwise?," but because there are only two possibilities, we can do this more concisely. We'll simply have the algorithm check whether the direction is clockwise. If it's not, we'll assume that the direction is counterclockwise. To do this check, we'll add an *if-then* statement, or a *conditional*, to our algorithm. An if-then statement runs a test (in our case, "Is the direction clockwise?") and carries out either one block (if the test is true, "Turn right") or another (if false, "Turn left").

Here's the latest version of the improved algorithm. We'll call the length of the side of the square its "side length," and we'll use "clockwise or not" to specify which direction the robot should turn.[14]

```
Version 4: Repeat move/turn four times.
Total distance is updated each time.
Side length and total distance are
in inches.
Clockwise is true or false.

To follow a square path                    1
  (of a given side length, clockwise or not):
  Set the total distance to zero.          2
  Do the following four times in a row:    3
    Move forward by the given side length. 4
    If clockwise,                          5
        Then turn right.                   6
    Otherwise, turn left.                  7
    Add side length to total distance.     8
  Output total distance.                   9
```

We now have a reasonable, preliminary solution. I've gone into some depth to illustrate a few important concepts in programming.

Our main refinements to the algorithm were to improve its flow of control. We've seen flow of control at the machine level, but here we're taking a more abstract, structured view of the concept. We have three basic forms:

- A block is a sequence of statements to be executed one after the other.
- An if-then statement runs a test that can turn out to be true or false. If the test is false, one block of statements is then executed; otherwise a different block is executed. In our case, it's "Should we move in a clockwise direction?"
- A loop specifies that some block of statements should be repeated some number of times. In general, the number of times a loop repeats its inner block depends on the result of a test; in our case, it's "Have we repeated four times yet?"

Flow of control is also involved in a fourth way that's less obvious. What happens when the robot moves forward or turns? The algorithm transfers control to another procedure—either "move forward" or "turn"—which we haven't yet defined. Those procedures carry out their tasks before transferring control back to our algorithm (we say that those procedures "return" to the original algorithm when they've finished execution). By nesting different blocks or procedures inside each other, we can build up behaviors that are as complicated as we need them to be.

The later versions of our algorithm also make use of *variables*. A variable gives us a convenient way of storing information that the algorithm needs. From a computer architecture perspective, a variable is simply a location in memory that we can refer to by name. We *assign* the value zero to a variable with the name "total distance" in the beginning of the algorithm, and then we assign it a new value each time through the loop, to keep track of how far the robot has moved. Version 4 adds the variables "side length" and "clockwise or not." These are specialized variables, called *parameters*, which are used to give input to an algorithm.

Finally, all of the elements of our algorithm—the variables and procedures, even the algorithm itself—have meaningful names. Naming our algorithm might seem grandiose for such a small piece of work, but it lets us refer to it in a convenient way. (We do this all the time in real life; doctors have names for medical procedures, for example, and sports teams give names to their plays.) We give algorithms and programs names for modularity, more specifically for encapsulation. That is, it could happen that we'll want to include the behavior of following a square path within a different algorithm, and to do this we'd like to refer to it without having to list all of its steps.

TURNING AN ALGORITHM INTO A PROGRAM

We're now ready to turn our algorithm into a program. We'll be using a high-level language called Python; there's an active community of software developers using Python for robotics.[15]

For historical reasons, a program might be called a "program," a "procedure," a "function," a "module," or a "routine," depending on the programming language. In Python, we write "functions," like the one below. When you read it, imagine that you're reading in a foreign language: you might not understand all of the words and phrases, but it should be possible to make some sense out of it.

Version 4, as above

```
To follow a square path                       1
  (of a side length, clockwise or not):
  Set total distance to zero.                  2
  Do the following four times in a row:        3
    Move forward by side length.               4
    If clockwise,                              5
        Then turn right.                       6
    Otherwise, turn left.                      7
    Add side length to total distance.         8
  Output total distance.                       9
```

```
# Version 5: Repeat move/turn four times.
# To save space, side length is shortened
# here to side, and clockwise to cw.
# Notice that the structure of Version 5
# is identical to Version 4, with matching
# line numbers.
# Ignore punctuation when reading the code
# below, but pay attention to indentation,
# which shows how compound statements are
# related to the blocks they contain.

def follow _ a _ square _ path (side, cw):    1
  distance = 0                                 2
  for stage in range(4):                       3
    move _ forward(side)                       4
      if cw:                                   5
        turn _ right()                         6
      else: turn _ left()                      7
      distance = distance + side               8
  return distance                              9
```

And you actually *do* understand this function, if you understand the Version 4 pseudocode that I've copied here. The numbered lines match exactly. I've also included comments in the Python code (beginning with a # symbol) for explanation.

This function, as expressed in Python, will seem less familiar than the more English pseudocode we've written. Every programming language has its own vocabulary of *primitives*, the terms that have specific meanings for all programs in the language, and its own *syntax*, which specifies how the primitives can be put together. Version 5 is a Python program that respects Python syntax.

I hope that you can guess at the meaning of most of this program: for example, def is a Python primitive that means "define a function"; else means "otherwise"; the input to a function like move _ forward needs to be enclosed in parentheses; a distance is returned as the output of the function.

Two Python idioms are less obvious. Line 2 is an *assignment statement* that stores the value zero in the variable distance. In math and sometimes in ordinary English, we think of an equals sign as saying that if you were to compare two things, you'd find out that they're the same.

In Python and many other languages, an equals sign means something more active:[16] "Compute the value on the right side of the equals sign and store it in memory, in the location with the name on the left side." This should help make sense of line 8, which otherwise seems strange—how can something be equal to itself *plus* something else that might not be zero? Rather, line 8 in this program means, "Add two values together—those held by the variables side and distance—and store the result in distance." That is, line 8 updates the value of distance, overwriting its previous value, each time through the loop.

Line 3 begins the loop. In most programming languages, a loop involves a variable that counts upward from some number until it reaches a limit, executing the body of the loop each time. In Python, we do the equivalent with a variable (here called stage) that takes on the values in a range of four numbers, specified here by range(4). Using for to mean "repeat something some number of times" is not a very good choice of wording, but the usage has a long history in programming languages.

Whew.

You've just learned the basics of reading—reading a program, that is. It may no longer surprise you that programmers refer to programs as code.

There are no deliberate secrets behind the complexity, though. Programs are written in order to make the computer do things, but they still need to be understood by people, including the person who's writing the program. Good code is written to run on a computer *and* to be understandable. This means that a well-written program contains comments—explanations in plain English aimed at human beings; the different parts of the program have meaningful names; the program includes tests to ensure that all is going according to plan. For a large program, entire written documents will explain how different factors contributed to its design.

All this makes it possible for a knowledgeable reader to make sense of a program.

What does "knowledgeable" mean? It helps to know something about what's called the *domain* of the program. By working out in advance how the robot should behave, we already have a good understanding of this domain. It also helps to know how concepts are expressed in the programming language, with its primitives, syntax, and idioms.

We put knowledge to use in reading a program by looking for *beacons*. A beacon is a term or feature of a program that carries meaning.[17] Our program, for example, contains terms like `move _ forward` and clockwise, which suggests that our program deals with navigation, rather than, say, spreadsheet calculations.

When reading a program, expert programmers look for beacons that help them understand two things. One is control flow, which I've already mentioned. The other is *data flow*. Our program doesn't contain much in the way of data flow, except for giving the value of the `side` parameter to `move _ forward`. Other programs spend a great deal of time shifting information from one place to another, and being able to follow that information through different parts of the program is also an important part of our understanding.

FINISHING THE PROGRAM

So, what's left?

Remember that we've built `follow _ a _ square _ path` on top of abstractions for moving forward and turning, but we haven't yet said exactly what should happen at a lower level of programming, when our function must run those procedures.

Fortunately, Python programmers have made their robot programs public in a library of functions for controlling the robot. Software is often stored in libraries in the same way that real books are, freely available to anyone. Instead of writing our own functions from scratch, we can use existing software.

Examining the library, we discover a minor problem—or rather, an opportunity. The library software has just one function for turning, rather than separate functions for turning right or left. The library function follows a convention in geometry—a positive number of degrees means a turn to the left, negative a turn to the right.

This gives us a tradeoff to consider. We could revise our initial abstractions to follow the same geometrical convention, letting us use one turn function rather than the separate turn _ right and turn _ left functions. This would simplify follow _ a _ square _ path.

The tradeoff is that whoever reads or uses our work needs to be aware of the same convention. This seems worthwhile; it's actually a slight improvement to our abstractions, in that we treat moving forward and turning more consistently by specifying how far to move or turn.

```
# Version 6: Repeat move/turn four times.
# The if-then statement of Version 5 has
# been replaced by a call to the turn
# function.
# A positive angle means a left turn
# (counterclockwise); a negative angle
# means a right turn (clockwise).

def follow _ a _ square _ path(side, angle):   1
    distance = 0                               2
    for stage in range(4):                     3
        move _ forward(side)                   4
        turn(angle)                            5
        distance = distance + side             6
    return distance                            7
```

To take advantage of this opportunity, we write two lower-level functions—move _ forward and turn—and we revise follow _ a _ square _ path so that its second parameter is a number of degrees, which must be either 90 or –90.

We should also think about one more thing.

Remember the old joke about going to the doctor and saying, "It hurts when I move my arm like this"? The doctor says, "Then don't move your arm like that."

Suppose we hand off our program to Martha, and, by accident or out of curiosity, she gives it a negative number for side. It turns out that this works, after a fashion, but move _ forward causes the robot to move backward, and follow _ a _ square _ path returns a negative number for the distance moved. This probably isn't what Martha wants.

We've assumed that the values of side will only be positive, but we haven't done anything to test or enforce that assumption. We'll take care of this with *error checking*—not finding errors in our own code, but instead making sure that our function is used in the way we've intended. We'll add tests to our move _ forward function so that it gives a warning if the value it receives isn't a positive number. (We could also do the same to ensure that the number of degrees given to turn is always 90 or –90, but we'll get to that later.)

Let's stop, for the moment at least, to look back over the conceptual ground we've covered. A high-level language gives us a level of abstraction above machine instructions, and in that language, we can build our own abstractions. Here's what this looks like in our case.

- *At the top level:* We've defined a function for moving the robot in a square with a given side, in a given direction.
- *One level down:* We've defined more basic functions that specify how the robot should move forward and turn.
- *At the level of the programming language:* We've used the language to define variables and functions, to combine these in different control structures, and to put information where it's needed to drive the robot.
- *At the machine level:* We depend on the CPU to carry out instructions that reflect the behaviors we've described at higher levels.

This isn't a strict hierarchy, in that the higher levels rely on the primitives and syntax of the programming language. But at each level, we're able to dispense with many of the details that are important at lower levels. Furthermore, our "top level" is just where we happen to be working. Martha might later ask us to build a higher level, in which we develop abstractions for more complex patterns that include squares, and then perhaps more levels, in which our abstractions would deal with coordinated movements of many robots, and so forth. Abstraction reduces the complexity of whatever problem we're trying to solve.

Indirection also plays a role in our function. We first saw indirection in a story about Clark and his filing cabinets, in Chapter 1; here it's put to better use. Version 1 of our program includes a specific distance, eight inches, for the robot to move for each side of the square. The later versions include variable parameters, side and angle, that act as indirect references to specific values. This means that the program can handle *any* distance or angle, within practical constraints.

Indirection, using variables, breaks the connection between a program and a specific number, making the program more general. We could even have two different variables that point to the *same* item of information, just as Clark has two differently labeled folders, both pointing to the location of the same physical documents.

Indirection works for functions as well. When we chose moving forward and turning as the lower-level abstractions for our program, we simplified the problem. We could put off thinking about the details of those procedures; we could think of them in terms of what they would eventually do, rather than how they'd do it. In this way, indirection helps us write modular programs.

In Chapter 4 we learned about recursive algorithms, which do work through indirection by referring to themselves. We could write follow _ a _ square _ path in a recursive style, but the task isn't a natural match for recursion. Instead, let's revisit Archie's telephone tree. How could we write a Python program to do a depth-first traversal of his binary tree? Here's one way.

Let's assume that we've defined two new functions. The functions left _ child and right _ child return the left and right child vertices of a vertex they're given. If a child doesn't exist, each function returns False.

```
# Perform a depth-first traversal to
# print vertices in a binary tree.
# This is a recursive traversal.

def df _ print(vertex):
  print vertex
  # If left child exists, traverse it
  if left _ child(vertex):
    df _ print(left _ child(vertex))
  # If right child exists, traverse it
  if right _ child(vertex):
    df _ print(right _ child(vertex))
```

When df _ print is first called, it treats the vertex it's given as the root of a tree. It then checks whether there's a left child; if so, df _ print calls itself on that child. As df _ print calls itself, it's diving deeper and deeper into the tree, always keeping to the left. Notice, though, that on each call there's work left to be done to handle the right child (if it exists). The function does this work on the way back *up* through the binary tree, handling each right child after the left child and all its descendants have been taken care of.

Understanding recursion takes some practice, but it's worthwhile. Because they're so concise, recursive functions can often be easier to hold in your thoughts, all at once, in comparison with other ways of expressing the same procedures. For example, Quicksort was originally presented as a recursive function, and we can write the top-level function in Python with just half a dozen lines of code; it looks very much like the function above.

A PROGRAM IS NEVER FINISHED

Looking over our work, you may have a thought: "We call this function 'follow a square path', but there's no square path in the code." You make a good point. The information about the path is scattered through the function, in the side and angle parameters and the number 4.

Let's apply what we know about organizing information to create a collection of information that represents a square path. We can think of a square path as having three elements: the number of sides (always 4),

```
# Version 6, as above, with
# square path information emphasized.
# The relationships between side, angle,
# and the number 4 are not explicit.
def follow _ a _ square _ path(side, angle):    1
    distance = 0                                2
    for stage in range(4):                      3
        move _ forward(side)                    4
        turn(angle)                             5
        distance = distance + side              6
    return distance                             7
```

the direction to turn (either 90 or –90 degrees), and the length of a side (which is different for squares of different sizes). What kind of abstract data type would be appropriate? A tuple will do, as we saw in Chapter 4: a collection that lets us ask for its elements by name.[18]

Remember, though, that abstract data types are theoretical models of structure in information. That is, they don't tell us specifically *how* the information in a collection should be stored on the computer, or how programs should be written to manage and access that information. This is the role of a *data structure*.

Data structures connect abstract data types to the computer architecture level by filling in these details. While an abstract data type says, "Here's what can be done with this collection of information, in theory," a data structure adds, "...and here's how to do it on a real computer."

Most high-level programming languages have built-in data structures that correspond to different abstract data types. In fact, because an abstract data type doesn't specify the "how" of information management, we often have a choice between several different data structures for the same abstract data type.

Python offers us a data structure for tuples that's well suited to our robot-programming needs. We'll define a square _ path data structure to contain three elements. (I'll leave out the details of exactly how to do this.) We access the elements of a square _ path with the names n _ sides, for the number of its sides; side, for the length of a side; and angle, for the angle to turn.

This is how to create a specific square path.

```
square_path(n_sides = 4, angle = -90, side = 8)
```

This data structure describes moving clockwise along a square eight inches on a side. Now we can say, "*This* is a square path." Instead of having the information associated with this square path scattered through our code, it's organized in a collection that can be treated as a unit of information itself.

We'll need to rewrite follow _ a _ square _ path to handle square _ path data structures. To avoid confusion with the original function, we'll give it a different name: follow _ a _ path. Instead of parameters for the length of a side and the direction to turn, follow _ a _ path will have just one parameter to hold a square _path.

We'll need a new bit of Python syntax for this version. To access an element in a square path, we use the name of the variable holding the data structure, then a dot, and then the name of the element. For example, if we name the new parameter in our function path, we can access the angle with path.angle. Below is the last version of follow _ a _ square _ path, for comparison, and then the new function follow _ a _ path.

The control structure of the new function is identical to Version 6 of the old function. We've just replaced the original references to the parameters and the number 4 with references to information stored in the square _ path data structure.

Notice how indirection is being used. For example, in Version 6, we get the side of the square, in inches, in the parameter side. That's one level of indirection.

In the new function, we have *two* levels of indirection to get that value: we look at the path parameter, which holds a square _ path data structure, and from there, we go to an element named side within that data structure.

```
# Version 6, as above.
def follow _ a _ square _ path (side, angle):    1
  distance = 0                                   2
  for stage in range(4):                         3
    move _ forward(side)                         4
    turn(angle)                                  5
    distance = distance + side                   6
  return distance                                7
```

```
# Version 7:
# The side and angle parameters change to
# a single path parameter, which holds a
# specialized tuple data structure. That
# data structure contains elements that
# correspond to the side, the angle, and
# the number 4 (n _ sides), in a single
# collection.
def follow _ a _ path(path):                     1
  distance = 0                                   2
  for stage in range(path.n _ sides):           3
    move _ forward(path.side)                     4
    turn(path.angle)                             5
    distance = distance + path.side             6
  return distance                                7
```

What have we accomplished? We have modularity in our data, just as we have modularity in our functions. We've also gained a few interesting side benefits.

First, Versions 6 and 7 are as short as any of the earlier versions. All else being equal, a knowledgeable reader will find them easier to understand.

Second, it turns out that follow _ a _ path will work for paths around regular polygons in general, not just square paths. All we have to

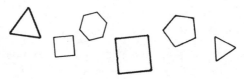

Figure 5.3. Paths around regular polygons.

do is create new paths with different angles and sides for input, and our program will steer the robot around regular triangles, regular pentagons, and so forth (Fig. 5.3). Working toward a more abstract representation of the information in the task has given us more generality in our program.

PROGRAM, MEET THE REAL WORLD

All of our effort so far has been writing a program, describing what the robot should do. Now it's time for execution.

With Martha watching, we start up the Python translator, load our program, and enter the statement,

```
follow _ a _ path(square _ path(n _ sides = 4,
angle = -90, side = 8))
```

The robot follows an eight-inch square, moving clockwise, and the program returns 32 as a result. Success!

Sadly, our success is limited. As we test our program, running it several times, we discover that the robot never moves exactly the same distance or turns at exactly the same angle. The robot's performance simply isn't very precise. We've encountered just one of the reasons that robotics programming is hard.

Although you wouldn't realize it from watching TV or movies, robots face the same challenges as people when they carry out actions in the real world. Professional golfers miss putts, and basketball players miss foul shots.

A factory robot may be able to depend on precise actuators and a tightly controlled environment, but our robot can't. When it moves, its wheels slip slightly; its movement speed isn't perfectly constant; its motors take a small amount of time to start and stop. (This is another set of problems I've glossed over; our functions for moving forward and turning should pause at the end before the next movement starts.) We've given the robot no sensors, and so it has no way to detect the errors in its movement, much less correct them, and the errors will accumulate. The robot can't even tell whether you've picked it up as it's moving.

Remember that a computer is a discrete processing system, jumping from one state to another as if riffling through a series of photo snapshots. The real world, in contrast, is continuous. When we write programs that connect to the real world, those programs miss whatever goes on *between* the snapshots, and the snapshots themselves have limited resolution. We're building models that are, at best, approximations.

This is more than just a problem with robotics; it applies throughout computing. For example, you probably know that there's a name for the ratio of a circle's diameter to its circumference, the Greek letter π, which is about 3.14. Why do you suppose we have a name for this number? Partly it's for convenience, since it pops up in so many different situations, but it's also because *we can't write down all of its digits*—the number of digits in π goes out to infinity. This means that we can't represent it perfectly in a computer.

Worse, it turns out that there are infinitely many such numbers that we can only approximate in digital form. Imagine that we're planning to build a perfectly circular beltway around a small town, ten miles across, and we need to know how long the road will be. If we use 3.14 for π, we get one result, but if we use a closer approximation, the result is different by about 85 feet. This may seem like a minor issue—we should figure out in advance how precise our numbers need to be. But that's the point. We choose specific approximations to put bounds on the errors we can expect, because in many cases we can't avoid errors.

There's an even deeper difficulty in writing programs that work well. We've naturally made assumptions about what the various numbers in the program mean. For example, we're using inches and degrees to describe the size and shape of the square (rather than, say, centimeters and radians), but this information is only in comments intended for a human being to read and interpret. Often, these assumptions aren't documented, and programs are combined or used in ways that don't make sense. But the programs will still run—computers have little in the way of common sense.

It's very difficult, sometimes impossible, to make every relevant assumption explicit in a program, so that errors of meaning can be detected automatically. Instead, programmers often depend on the common sense of other programmers who read their code.

LAST BITS

I've described a somewhat artificial evolution of our program; it wouldn't be surprising for an experienced programmer to think for a few minutes and then write the last version of our program from scratch, or perhaps a better program.[19] An experienced programmer would also rely on sophisticated computer tools (other programs) to help. These tools organize and keep track of the thousands of functions that might be part of a large program, and they help us test, modify, and run programs that we're developing. An important part of the future is discovering new ways to make programming easier. We're still following in Backus's footsteps.

I've gone through a single, simple program in detail to illustrate some important programming concepts. These concepts aren't limited to robots; in fact, they're better suited for the kind of information processing we saw in Chapter 4. We haven't seen programming examples for all of the abstract data types and algorithms we know about, but they're generally handled in the same way.

What have we accomplished? We've learned how to read a program, to follow the syntax to understand its procedural structure and how its information is organized. This is a specialized skill, but only in a way. Whenever you encounter an unfamiliar description of some situation or activity, you probably look for clues, or beacons, to tell you what it's about. You need to know what individual words mean, whether it's a program or perhaps a legal or financial document. It also helps to have background knowledge of what the description is about: a program for robots, a legal brief for a criminal case, or a mortgage statement.

Many of the concepts we've covered *are* specific to programming. Variable assignments. Control flow in terms of conditionals (if-then statements), iterations (loops), and transfer of control to other procedures. Data structures. This is the technical side of writing programs, which involves understanding how to express algorithms and abstract data types in a way that an actual computer can handle. The syntax of different programming languages can be complex, even baroque, but it's the concepts that are important.

At a more abstract level, we have standard strategies for writing programs. Programming starts well before a single line of code is typed. Much of it happens in your head as you figure out how to approach a problem:

how to break it down into smaller pieces, how those pieces should interact, and how they come together in a reasonable design. Are the components at the right level of abstraction? Does each component have a clear responsibility, cleanly separated from other components? Finally, abstraction, indirection, and modularity are critical to a well-designed system.

At an even more abstract level, we've learned something about the nature of structured activities. If you're trying to explain a complex procedure to someone—you might be diagramming a football play, or handing out responsibilities for a family reunion, or giving someone instructions at work—then computing concepts may be helpful, even if your modules are other people rather than software.

For most of this chapter, we concentrated on writing our program, and only at the end did we execute it. Program execution is somewhat more involved than I described, though. In the next chapter, on operating systems, we'll see why.

FURTHER READING

This chapter is essentially a very brief survey of concepts in problem solving that are relevant to programming. I've drawn on George Polya's mathematics book, *How to Solve It* (Princeton University Press, 2nd ed., 1957). Math and computer science are closely linked in many ways, and some of Polya's advice generalizes well. For really learning how to program, I'll mention one book that has influenced the presentation in this chapter: *Introduction to Computing and Programming in Python, A Multimedia Approach*, by Mark J. Guzdial and Barbara Ericson (Prentice Hall, 2nd ed., 2009). If you're interested in the deep relationship between programming and computer science, two books are indispensible: *Structure and Interpretation of Computer Programs*, by Harold Abelson and Gerald Jay Sussman with Julie Sussman (MIT Press, 2nd ed., 1996), and *Paradigms of Artificial Intelligence Programming: Case Studies in Common Lisp*, by Peter Norvig (Morgan Kaufmann, 1992). These books are well known by their initials: SICP and PAIP. Frederick P. Brooks, Jr.'s classic book *The Mythical Man-Month: Essays on Software Engineering* (Addison-Wesley, 20th Anniversary Edition, 1995) describes the difficulties faced by large software projects.

## Chapter 6

Operating Systems: Working Together

In Chapter 5, I described the robot as if executing that program were all it would ever have to do. That might be true for a robot, but general-purpose computers typically don't run single programs in isolation. Instead, the programs run in a computational environment called the *operating system*.

If you've ever used an Apple Macintosh or a computer running Microsoft Windows or Linux, you've encountered its operating system. You explore your documents and launch applications in the file system, which is under the control of the operating system. When you connect a new keyboard to your computer or add a new disk drive for extra storage, it's the operating system that handles the details of setting up and managing these devices. If your word processor automatically inserts today's date into a letter you're writing, it's getting that information from the operating system.

The operating system acts as an executive manager for your computer. It's responsible for managing information in storage, for managing communication between programs and I/O devices such as the keyboard and display, and for other housekeeping and maintenance tasks.

One of the typical responsibilities of the operating system is management of information on secondary storage: the *file system*. On a personal computer, we see files contained in folders, presented in graphical form as in Figure 6.1.

Figure 6.1. Files and folders in the file system.

Each of these files has a name, such as "Doc1.txt," and contents on secondary storage. They're all contained in a folder called "Documents." One of the files, "Spreadsheets," is actually another folder that contains more files not shown.

When I say that a file contains information or a folder contains files and other folders, I'm actually speaking metaphorically. Files and folders aren't physical holders like cups and boxes, but *containment* gives a useful way to think about how information is organized. The interesting thing about the relationship "one thing contains another" is that it matches the structure we can represent in trees, "one item is the parent of another." That is, the relationships between folders and files can be captured in a tree-structured file system (Fig. 6.2).

Remember Clark and his trick with his file cabinets in Chapter 1? Instead of moving a large amount of information from one place to another, he solved his problem with indirection. He put a pointer from where the information "should" be to where it actually is, which avoids moving the information at all. The file system relies on indirection in the same way. In secondary storage, files can be stored in any way that's convenient; they can even be broken up into several pieces. The file system keeps track of a file by associating its name with its secondary storage address. That association is what I mean by a pointer. The file system is essentially the collection of these pointers plus the information they point to. A file system can even include more than one pointer to a single folder or file (which makes it a graph rather than a tree—edges in a graph can revisit a vertex). In a graphical user interface, additional pointers to a

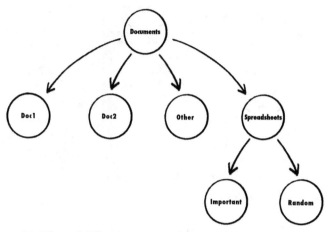

Figure 6.2. Files and folders are organized in a tree structure.

given place are typically called *aliases* or *shortcuts*, which gives a good idea about their purpose. They're edges that take you from one vertex to another in a potentially large graph, in a single step.

In this chapter, we'll look below the surface of the operating system at the *kernel*—its core component—which is responsible for coordinating the execution of programs. Say you're watching a video, and you decide to send an email message. You open up your email application and start typing. Half a dozen other applications are open at the same time, and some of them are doing work without your attention. The video is still playing, your Web browser automatically updates the news page you were reading earlier, the Sudoku game you've abandoned still shows a clock ticking forward...all these applications are apparently running at the same time. You can add new applications, and these also work seamlessly with those already on your system.

It's possible to imagine writing a program to manage all these activities, given what we know about programming concepts, but it would be exceedingly complex. Here's an analogy. Some days my life gets very busy: I have classes to teach, students to meet, papers to read, errands to run, and so forth. New tasks flood in unexpectedly. Some are important, others less important. Different tasks place different demands on my time and my mental resources. If I were to try to plan out my day in advance, down to all the details of what I should be doing at each point in time, I'd get very little work done.

Instead, I set up a rough schedule along with some general rules for managing what I do. I prioritize—I take care of the most important things first. Whenever I start working on a given task, I focus on it and try not to be distracted by other demands. For some tasks, I'll arrange not to be interrupted. I'll spend a limited amount of time on any given task, so that it doesn't take over my entire day; if I don't finish it, I'll come back to it later.

The kernel of the operating system handles programs in a comparable way. The general rules it relies on are *policies* for behavior in specific situations. *Every task has a priority, and higher-priority tasks are handled first* is an example of a policy. *Some kinds of tasks are not to be interrupted* is another. Policies give us an abstract way of thinking about how a complex system should perform as a whole—not, "How should we write this program so that it produces correct results?" but instead, "How can we arrange for dozens or perhaps even thousands of programs of different types to run without problems?" Different policies for the same situations produce different results, and understanding the tradeoffs will be the focus of this chapter. We'll be taking a "systems" view of computing.[1]

I should say at this point that when I talk about "the" operating system or "the" kernel, I'm oversimplifying. Dozens of different operating systems have been developed over the history of computing, some similar to each other and some very different; there's no such thing as a typical operating system. I'll be describing the kernel of a simple imaginary operating system, designed for a computer with a single CPU, in just enough detail to make connections with computing concepts from earlier chapters and to illustrate some new ideas.[2]

A PROGRAM THAT RUNS OTHER PROGRAMS

To start, think of the kernel as a program (which it is) that coordinates other programs. When you first turn on a computer, the kernel is copied into memory from secondary storage. The CPU fetches the first instruction and begins execution. The kernel builds the data structures it relies on, storing those in memory as well. All this happens when the operating system starts up. The kernel doesn't take up all of memory when it runs; the remainder is left free, but under its management.[3] Conceptually, the situation looks like the diagram in Figure 6.3.

Now, remember that computers are discrete systems. They work step by step, with each instruction executed by the CPU putting the system into a new state. If we stop a discrete system in a given state and then let it continue some time later from that state, the system will behave as if there had been no interruption at all.

Here's something interesting: Once we've stopped the system, we can record all of the relevant information about its current state, *then do something else with the system,* and later recreate that recorded state and let the system continue with what it was doing originally. (There's an analogy here to a creation myth sometimes called "Last Thursdayism," in which the universe was created last Thursday, but with the appearance of being much older—imagine this happening over and over and over…) Because computation is discrete, nothing is lost except time.

This is essentially how the kernel runs another program. In the simplest approach, the kernel allocates some amount of free memory for the program and its data, then loads the program into that space and directs the CPU to the first instruction of the program. The program takes over the CPU and the rest of the computer until it finishes. The kernel takes back control, reclaims the memory of the now-finished program, and picks up where it left off, possibly to run another program (Fig. 6.4).

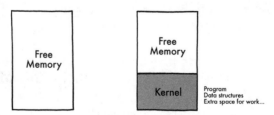

Figure 6.3. Memory, before and after the kernel is loaded.

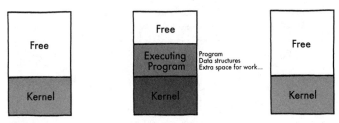

Figure 6.4. Memory, before, during, and after a program runs.

This idea of pausing one program (the kernel) to run another seems quite powerful. Could we apply it to any program? We can. The kernel can load several programs into different regions of memory and choose one to begin execution. After some fixed period of time (a *time quantum*), that program is interrupted and another can begin executing.[4] To show how this works, I'll need to revise a diagram from Chapter 3 describing the instruction cycle, to add one more stage at the end (Fig. 6.5).

In this cycle, the CPU fetches an instruction from the location indicated by the program counter, which is automatically updated to point to the next instruction. The CPU decodes the instruction it has fetched and then executes it. Before it goes on to the next instruction, though, the CPU checks for an interrupt. If an interrupt has been signaled, the CPU ignores the program counter and instead fetches its next instruction from elsewhere in memory, an area holding instructions that tell the CPU how to deal with the interrupt—for example, to give back control to the kernel once the time quantum of the currently running program has expired. (The shortcut arrow from the execute stage directly back to the fetch stage is needed because in some specialized situations, interrupts can be turned off.)

In this way, the kernel switches back and forth between the programs, giving each its turn with the CPU. This is *multitasking*.

Multitasking requires careful management. Imagine a program that has loaded the number 2 into one CPU register and the number 3 into another, and it's just about to add those two numbers together—when it's interrupted by the kernel. To resume this program at some later time, the kernel needs to store away information about its state at the point it was interrupted, including the contents of the registers and the addition

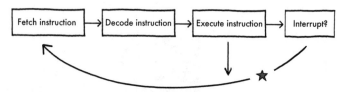

Figure 6.5. The CPU's instruction cycle, with interrupts.

instruction just about to be executed by the CPU. (This doesn't mean predicting the future; the address of that next instruction is held by the program counter.)

The kernel keeps a table of the executing programs that it's managing, and it records such information whenever a program is interrupted. This information is used again when the program resumes executing. The changeover from one executing program to another is called a *context switch*. Context switches take time, but it's necessary overhead for a multitasking operating system. A context switch also turns out to be the best thing for the CPU to do in some situations. For example, imagine that an executing program needs data from secondary storage before it can execute its next instruction. Copying the data into memory will take a long time, relative to the speed of the CPU. Instead of simply waiting, the kernel can perform a context switch, giving the CPU to some other program that's ready to run.

Multitasking is an appealing concept, inside and outside of computing. It's sometimes used to describe people doing more than one thing at a time. You're multitasking when you're in the kitchen making dinner, cutting up vegetables, stirring a pot, keeping track of what needs to happen next, and holding a conversation. Some students in the classes I teach are multitasking (I suspect) when they surf the Web on their laptops during the brief moments when my lecture is boring.

If the human mind is at all like a computer's operating system, then we'd expect multitasking to be less efficient than completing each task and then moving to the next. This is the case, even though the human mind is much more complex than an operating system. For many kinds of activities, it's only an illusion that you're doing more than one thing at once; you're really following a strategy, probably unconsciously, of switching between different tasks. For example, imagine driving your car and talking on your cell phone, or sending text messages as you drive.[5] (You probably don't drive and text, but just imagine.) It might seem as though you should be able to share attention between driving and holding a conversation—after all, you can walk and talk at the same time. But brain imaging studies show that even listening to someone speak degrades the spatial processing abilities you rely on when driving—for example, to keep your car on the road. In simpler computing terms, we'd say that driving and texting at the same time involves context switches and thus overhead, and that performance on both tasks will be worse than we might otherwise expect.

PROCESSES AND RESOURCES

Managing activities on a computer can grow complex, even at this level of description. Fortunately, we have two abstract concepts to help us make sense of it.

The first concept is a *resource*, which in general is something that a program needs in order to run. Resources in an operating system aren't very much different from resources we think about in everyday life. For example, you'll sometimes hear, *Time is money*, or *Take care of the minutes, for the hours will take care of themselves.* Time is a resource. There's also *A place for everything, and everything in its place.* It's possible that *For want of a backup system, information was lost* would make a good modern proverb. Space is a resource. And *You can't always have what you want* . . . Sometimes we even think of being able to get or do something as a resource. In an operating system, resources for a program include memory (space), being able to run on the CPU (time), and devices such as printers that the program might need to reserve for its use.

The second concept is a *process*, a program-in-execution. I've used the phrase "an executing program" in my description of what the kernel does, and you may wonder how that's different from simply saying "a program." Here's an analogy. Suppose I've written down a description of my daily schedule at work, down to the minute: I teach a class for so long, then I return to my office to work on a paper, and so forth.

While I'm in my office, the fire alarm goes off. I gather my thoughts for a second or two, put a bookmark in one of the journals I'm looking through, and type a line on my computer to remind me of what I plan to write next, all before I leave the building. When I get back to my office (it was a false alarm), I look at my schedule, the equivalent of a program. But this isn't enough for me to get back to what I was doing when I was interrupted. I also need the same arrangement of books and journals on my desk, the bookmark I've left, the line I've typed, and so forth. Additionally, I need the mental snapshot I've taken of my thoughts, so that I can move on to the very next thought I would have had without the interruption.

A process keeps a record of analogous information, all the resources a program makes use of in its execution. The contents of the program counter and related CPU registers correspond to my mental snapshot; this information is what we call the *thread of execution* of the process. It's the information needed for the process to continue with the instruction it was about to execute when it was interrupted.

The operating system is a resource manager for processes. It manages time by deciding which process should have the CPU at any point and how long it should be allowed to run. The operating system manages space, from CPU registers down to secondary storage. It decides how memory should be divided up and which parts should be assigned to different processes. Its file system manages secondary storage; it keeps track of how storage should be allocated to new files, where all the files are stored, and how they're organized. The operating system also manages hardware devices as resources, providing ways for processes to control or get information from the display, keyboard, printer, and so forth.

The concepts of processes and resources give us a new way to think about what happens on a computer at an organizational level. In our program of Chapter 5, we broke down a single activity into smaller parts and carefully designed modular functions for each. We arranged for these functions to work together from start to finish. The operating system must deal with many of these activities at the same time, and they may change dynamically and unpredictably. There's no practical way for the operating system to keep track of why a particular function or operation is being executed; the operation could be part of a game, or a spreadsheet application, or a photo editing tool. The operating system manages this complexity at an abstract level. Instead of asking, "What does this program do?" it concentrates on other questions:

- What resources does the process (the program in execution) need, and when?
- How long will the process run?
- How important is it?

The operating system doesn't need to be concerned with the specific purpose of any given program. It relies on general policies for handling processes and resources, to ensure that the computer performs well as a whole.

SELF-PROTECTION

Managing a computer poses subtle challenges. We'll approach these by way of a story that continues through the rest of the chapter.

Eunice is at her family reunion. Her rich Uncle William has rented an entire small hotel with dozens of rooms for the event, enough space for the entire family—grandparents, parents, aunts, uncles, and a dozen or so children. Unfortunately, it's raining. The children have divided themselves up into three adjoining playrooms for the afternoon, and Eunice is acting as chaperone for all of them until the weather clears up.

Eunice moves between the three rooms, talking with the Toddlers, the Preschoolers, and the Teenagers. (She has named the groups of children in her head.) Being an organized person, Eunice decides that she'll rotate between the rooms, spending time with each group in turn.

In the hallway between the rooms, on a white board, one of the parents has written down all of the children's names, to help Eunice keep track of them. While talking with the Preschoolers, Eunice realizes she has forgotten one of the children's names. She goes out into the hallway to check her white board, and there she finds Jimmy, whose name she does remember. Jimmy has sneaked out of the Preschooler room while her attention was elsewhere, erased all the names on the white board, and drawn a portrait of Eunice in their place. "Thanks, Jimmy. It's a good likeness," says Eunice, but she'd rather still have the list.

Eunice represents the kernel of the operating system.[6] She's giving her attention to the activities of three groups of children, who represent processes. The activities take place in different playrooms, memory allocated for those processes. This isn't an exact analogy, in that whenever Eunice leaves a room, we'll have to imagine the children in that room freezing in place, returning to life only when Eunice comes back (as if they're playing a game of Red Light, Green Light). But the story will help frame a few important concepts.

Protection is critical in an operating system: protecting information (and even hardware) from being inadvertently or maliciously damaged by running processes. When the operating system schedules a process to run, eventually it will need to take charge of the system again.

But what if the process has used the memory that the operating system reserves for itself, perhaps even changing the memory locations that hold the kernel program? The multitasking scheme I described earlier allows this to happen, and it could cause havoc. A single misbehaving process could destroy enough data to bring down the computer. A malicious process could keep control over the computer for its own ends.

A basic solution is a policy that divides processing into two categories, or modes. The operating system itself runs in *privileged mode*, while ordinary processes run in *user mode*. Privileged mode gives unrestricted access to the hardware and all parts of the software system. In user mode, processes are limited in what they can do. Some areas of memory are off limits to user processes. A user process is given its own area of memory, separate from that of the operating system and other processes. Some kinds of CPU instructions can't be executed directly by user processes. For example, a user process can't draw directly on a computer display— some other process might be using that part of the screen. Other instructions, such as those that change some CPU registers or alter the time that processes are allowed to run, are reserved for use by the kernel.

But processes do need to carry out some of these tasks, such as displaying information to users; how do they get this done? Processes go through the operating system, issuing *system calls*. System calls can be used for managing files, controlling I/O devices, communications, and other functions. The operating system can check whether a given system call is appropriate and, if so, carry it out on behalf of the process. (In our story, some of the children might have to ask Eunice to do things for them, such as cutting up sandwiches with a sharp knife.)

Two important principles are at work here. One is already familiar. With system calls and other services, the operating system provides a layer of abstraction for programs. Common problems can be solved just once (by programs written and tested by experts) and used by any process running on the system. This makes some programs much easier to write—the programmer doesn't need to consider as many low-level details. For example, programmers can build interactive applications to use system calls so that they have a common look and feel. Opening and saving files, choosing from menus, and so forth are consistent across most applications, because these tasks are handled by the operating system through the same system calls.

The second principle is *least privilege*.[7] The kernel has the highest level of privilege, but ideally processes are given only enough leeway to accomplish the tasks for which they're designed. This limits the possibility of errors (or mischief) that can bring the entire system down. We see the least privilege principle in action when the operating system asks for a password to allow new software to be installed, or when it prevents some file under its control from being moved or deleted.

Least privilege is also common outside of computing. At airports, on military bases, in courthouses, and on construction sites, it's not unusual to see signs reading, "No unauthorized personnel beyond this point." Security clearances are part of a least privilege approach to managing sensitive information in government and industry. We can think of least privilege as a way to make a computer system or even a human organization more robust and secure.

COMPETING FOR TIME

When we think about time as a resource, we ask whether we're using it wisely. Dividing up time into blocks isn't enough. Some people carefully schedule their days, hour by hour, and still don't seem to get very much done—this happens with me sometimes. For an operating system, the question is how blocks of time should be allocated to different processes so that work can be done efficiently.[8] Let's return to our story:

> *Eunice makes her rounds, rotating between the rooms in order and spending about ten minutes in each. Just as her conversation with the Teenagers ends, she hears a Toddler wailing. When Eunice appears in the doorway to the Toddler room, Henry runs up to her, tears on his face. Eunice picks him up and says a few soothing things, then looks around. She sees a plush rabbit, with brown and white spots, a bit threadbare but otherwise in fine shape. She gives it to Henry, and he's happy again.*
>
> *Raised voices are coming from the Preschooler room. Eunice goes in to find Harriet arguing with Oscar. Eunice quickly resolves the dispute. "No, I don't think that if a million people jumped up and down at one time, it would cause an earthquake. But you can try it if you like." Eunice moves back and forth between the Toddlers and the Preschoolers, until she realizes she has left the Teenagers alone for some time. Oh, well. They're not starving for her company.*

Eunice is scheduling her time between the rooms. Ordinarily we think of scheduling as setting up specific times for specific events (a meeting with the boss from 10 a.m. to 11 a.m.), but for processes we think in terms of *scheduling policies* to handle any mix of processes. Eunice's first policy, moving from one room to another after spending a fixed amount of time, is a *round-robin* policy. Round robin is used in some sports tournaments, in which every player or team plays every other. Its advantage is fairness—everyone is given a chance.

In the operating system, processes can be organized in a collection that works like a grocery store line, or queue. New processes are added to the tail of the queue. The process at the head of the queue runs for a fixed amount of time, the time quantum, and if it doesn't finish, it's returned to the tail of the queue to wait its turn to run again. If it does finish, so much the better (Fig. 6.6).

If the time quantum is long enough for any process to finish in the time it's given, round robin turns into a *first-come, first-served* policy.[9] If

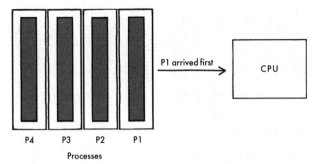

Figure 6.6. With a round-robin policy, processes are handled in the order they arrive.

the quantum is too short, on the other hand, the operating system could spend more time context switching than allowing processes to run.

When Eunice dashes to the Toddler room, she has changed her scheduling policy: it's a *priority-based* policy. She makes a judgment about which room to visit next, depending on what's most important at the time. In the operating system, processes can be given different priorities. For example, user input, such as a key press or a mouse click, is usually important. Imagine playing a video game or typing a letter and having to wait half a second or so for the system to respond; it wouldn't be very interactive. Processes for handling user input are high priority. Checking for new email and updating the time on the clock in the corner of your display, in contrast, are lower priority. The higher the priority of a process, the sooner it gets to run. In Figure 6.7, darker processes have higher priority.

Priority-based scheduling can be used for another useful policy: a *shortest-remaining-time* policy. We could imagine Eunice setting up a different board game for the children in each room to play. A shortest-remaining-time policy would have her start with the Teenagers, because they'll take much less time to get going than the younger children. Following this policy, the operating system gives the CPU to the process that can be expected to finish earliest. The intuition is that if shorter-running processes are taken out of the mix as quickly as possible, the operating system will need to do less context switching in the longer run. In Figure 6.8, the shaded level within each process shows how much time it has left to run.

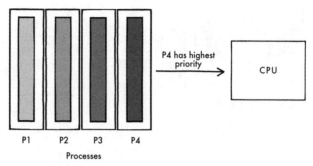

Figure 6.7. With a priority-based policy, higher-priority processes are handled before lower-priority processes.

It might seem that any of these policies will do (and there are other possibilities I haven't mentioned), as long as the CPU is kept busy. But this isn't the only way to judge a policy. Here's a different example that shows why.

Years ago, I was stranded at the Heathrow airport, waiting in line at a public telephone. The person at the front of the line was making a dozen calls in a row, apparently trying to find a hotel; the rest of us in line were getting restless. The phone was in almost constant use, which was good. By other measures, though, the arrangement was terrible: everyone else in line had to wait a long time to reach the phone, and someone who had to make a call by a certain time might have been out of luck.

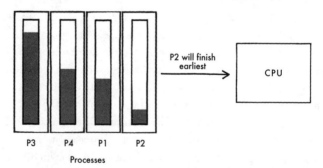

Figure 6.8. With a shortest-remaining-time policy, the process with the least time remaining to run goes first.

Similarly, there's more than one way to judge how good a scheduling policy is. *CPU utilization* measures how much work the CPU does. If a process makes a request to an I/O device and needs to wait for it, then the operating system can switch to a different process, increasing utilization. The number of processes that use the CPU over some period of time is *throughput*, the average amount of time that processes have to wait before running is *latency*, and *fairness* tells us whether every process gets a chance to use the CPU (processes that don't are said to starve).

No single policy is best on all these measures, and depending on the mix of processes in a system and what can be known about them, different policies may be appropriate. For example, round robin is fair, but if there are a lot of processes to handle, each might end up waiting a long time to run. Shortest remaining time gives the highest throughput, but if new, short-running processes are constantly being created, longer-running processes may starve. Also, it's not always possible to predict how long processes will take to finish. Priority-based scheduling is a reasonable compromise if we can decide on a good way to set priorities. For example, we can say that the priority of a process starts with some estimate of how important it is and it increases over the time that it hasn't used the CPU. This way, even low-priority processes will eventually have a high enough priority to run.

Scheduling policies may seem esoteric, but sometimes we can find them hiding under everyday activities. For example, airports typically follow a first-come, first-served policy when several planes are ready for takeoff.[10] This may produce high efficiency for airplane runways, but if several small planes are in line before a large one, this efficiency doesn't extend to the average passenger. We can even see scheduling policies in much simpler situations, such as a police officer directing traffic around an accident at an intersection. The officer is likely to be following a round-robin policy—first letting the cars in one direction go, then the cars in the opposite direction, and repeating the alternation. If the officer sees an ambulance or a police car coming, he'll change to a priority-based policy to let it through first. And if you're in the sole car in line watching a stream of traffic go by in the opposite direction, you'll hope that the officer will change to a shortest-remaining-time policy, but that's probably just wishful thinking; the context switch is too expensive.

COMPETING FOR SPACE

Space must be managed just as carefully as time in an operating system, but the strategies are different. In contrast to time, space can be reused. On with our story:

> When Eunice next visits the Teenagers, she finds them in a group, star-ing at the wall. The wall is decorated with a row of framed manuscript pages at eye height, in haphazard order (Fig. 6.9).
>
> "'First Witch: Give me the eye,'" reads Karsten, peering at the page in front of him. "It looks like a play. It says 'Perseus and the Witches' across the top."[11]
>
> "Let's act it out," says Suzy. "Is that how it starts?"
>
> "No, this is page 72. Where's page 1?"
>
> They walk along the walls until Eunice spies page 1. Karsten begins to read the first role. The other Teenagers join in for the other parts. By the time they've reached the end of the first page, Eunice has found the second page. She eventually leads them around the room, from page to page, until they've finished Act I, Scene 1.

We can think of the pages of the manuscript that Eunice and the Teenagers are looking at in two different ways. There's the actual order-ing on the wall, with page 72 followed by page 17, then page 56, and so forth, and there's the conventional ordering of pages, starting from 1. We call the first the *physical* ordering and the second the *logical* order-ing. What Eunice is doing as she leads the Teenagers around the room is translating between the two orderings. The Teenagers don't have to worry about the physical ordering; Eunice ensures that they read the pages following the logical ordering.

Figure 6.9. Pages, in their physical order.

This story would be unusual in real life, but it illustrates a way for the operating system to solve a tricky problem. I've described the kernel as allocating a single region of memory for each new process. Among other things, this makes it straightforward to walk through memory in the execution of a program: "Fetch the next instruction" means "Find that instruction in the next location in memory."

When a process finishes running, its region in memory is reclaimed for later use by other processes. But there's a problem: *memory fragmentation*. Processes need different amounts of memory, and as memory is allocated and reclaimed, the entire space gradually gets broken up with free regions scattered irregularly throughout (Fig. 6.10).[12]

By analogy, think about room reservations at a hotel (one like Eunice's, after the reunion is over). Different groups might reserve blocks of neighboring rooms at different times, and when each group leaves their rooms can be rebooked. If it's busy, though, there's no guarantee that a new group will get rooms next to each other; even if the hotel has enough space, the rooms might be scattered across different floors. The hotel might ask existing customers to change rooms to consolidate blocks of free rooms, but this would take a good deal of time and it would irritate a number of people.

For an operating system, the situation is similar. Consolidating free space by copying regions of memory around would take too much time. Instead, the operating system resolves the problem with indirection. With the assistance of hardware, memory is broken up into numbered blocks of fixed size. These are called *frames*, and they correspond to the physical organization of memory. To manage memory, the kernel keeps a list of unused frames and allocates them to new processes as needed.

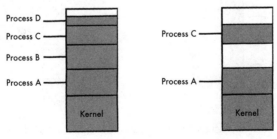

Figure 6.10. As processes execute and finish, memory becomes fragmented.

But there's a twist. A kernel might allocate frames 43, 61, and 88 to a new process, but there's a layer of indirection between the process and these scattered regions of memory. From the process's point of view, it has been allocated a single block of three adjacent regions, numbered 1, 2, and 3. Each of these regions is called a *page*; a page is a frame that has been renumbered to produce a logical organization of memory. When the process accesses memory on one of its pages, it uses a logical memory address, and the operating system translates that logical reference into a physical memory location, just as when the Teenagers are looking for the next (logical) page in the manuscript, Eunice leads them to its (physical) location. This technique for managing memory is called *paging* (Fig. 6.11).

We can push the idea of paging a bit further. What if we had a process that required an enormous amount of memory to run, more memory than is available in the system? Remember two things. First, secondary storage is typically a great deal larger than main memory. Second, the locality principle applies to memory accesses: a running program is likely to execute an instruction that's located immediately next to the previous instruction in memory, and it also tends to retrieve data from memory locations close to each other.

We can take advantage of these observations with what's called *demand paging*. When a process is created, the kernel doesn't allocate it all of the memory it might need. Instead, the kernel allocates enough memory for the process to do whatever it needs to at the time.

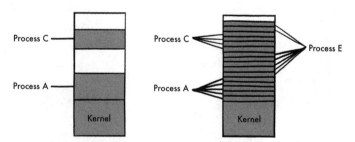

Figure 6.11. Breaking up memory into smaller regions, with indirection, lets a process see different areas of memory as a single block.

The rest is kept in secondary storage. If the process hasn't used one of its pages for some amount of time, the information on that page can be copied to secondary storage and that page reused by another process. (A workable policy is to reuse pages that haven't been touched in a while.)

The operating system brings the information on the first process's page back into memory only when it's needed next. The effect is that the operating system is reusing memory, often between processes, allocating frames to one process and then taking them back and reallocating them to another process. Individual processes can still run *as if* they have as much memory as they need, because they don't need it all at once. Alternatively, we can think of memory as being a relatively fast cache for process information on secondary storage.

Demand paging is a way to implement *virtual memory*, which lets processes act as if there's much more memory than there actually is. This is a powerful idea that extends beyond the operating system. For example, imagine wandering through a large virtual computer environment, which could be an imaginary city or an alien planet. You can look around and walk (or perhaps fly) from one place to another. But your display shows you only a small part of the scenery at any time. If the system can make the right information available at just the right time, you're given the impression that the space you're moving through is enormous. Your virtual environment can even be infinitely large, if the system can generate the necessary information on the fly.

We can also see analogies to virtual memory in the physical world. Have you ever played basketball on a half-court? You're applying the same idea. When your team controls the ball, you treat the basket as your own, until control changes over to the other team. At that point there's a conceptual shift—the physical space gets reused, with the other team now treating the basket as their own. Or in a movie, we might see actors wandering through the rooms in a large mansion. That mansion probably doesn't exist in reality, and some of the rooms might even be reused in different scenes, slightly redecorated, as if they were other rooms. The same idea is at work, in which we have a small physical space that, practically speaking, we can reuse at different times for different activities.

COMMUNICATING AND COOPERATING

In the Preschooler room, Leo approaches Eunice and hands her a note.
"Could you please give this to Anne? She's in one of the other rooms."
"Sure. I'm heading over there in a couple of minutes."

Processes, like people, don't always work independently, fighting over resources. Sometimes they cooperate and communicate with each other. One simple way for processes to communicate is through *message passing*. Suppose that one process has a message for another process, perhaps a request for information. The first process can make a system call to open a *socket*—an endpoint for a communication link with the second process. That process, waiting for such requests, opens a socket of its own to create the other endpoint. The two processes can then exchange information, with the operating system handling the details of temporary storage and management of the information.

In Chapter 4, we saw a different way for programs to communicate information. One function called another function, passing information through its parameters: "Start running now, and use this information." With message passing, each process can work at its own rate, determining when and how to deal with the messages it receives. We say that message passing *decouples* the behavior of different programs or processes, making them less dependent on each other.

Another advantage of message passing between processes is that they don't even need to be running on the same machine, managed by the same operating system. If processes can identify each other, they can pass messages over a network of computers.

This decoupling is surprisingly useful, and we see it in everyday life. If you've ever watched the interactions between the wait staff and the cooks in a diner, you might have seen your order, written on a slip of paper, placed at the end of a queue. A cook removes the order at the front of the queue, prepares the meal, and signals when it's ready to be brought out. This arrangement is much better suited to the ebb and flow of customers in the diner than if each order were handed directly to a cook.

You rely on message passing, as well, whenever you listen to messages on your telephone's answering machine or voicemail, or when you read your email. Passing messages takes more time than giving instructions or information directly, but it can make some coordination tasks much simpler.

The time delays and storage of messages count as overhead—additional cost in comparison with more direct communication. In the operating system, there's the cost of maintaining the communication link, as well as the storage needed for messages, and a context switch must happen before a process can receive a message that another has sent.

What if processes were allowed to communicate more directly with each other, for example, by sharing access to memory? In Eunice's situation, this would mean a child in one room talking directly to a child in another, or sharing information by drawing on the white board without Eunice's oversight. Perhaps we should think of our story differently: the separate rooms represent different activities to be managed, but each room alone is also a microcosm of activities.

The operating system can support this idea as well. Remember that a process has a *thread of execution*, the current state of the program being executed. We allow a process to have *multiple threads*, all sharing the resources of the process. These threads can then communicate by reading and writing information to the memory reserved for the process. This can be much faster than message passing, because the threads don't need a communication link, and the context switch between threads of a process involves much less work. The downside is that there's no longer a hard separation between the activities of threads, as there is with processes. Threads require more careful management, but the tradeoff is generally worthwhile.

MANAGING AN ECOSYSTEM

Operating systems are important in computing for a number of reasons. There's the practical perspective, which I outlined at the beginning of this chapter—it's hard to do anything interesting on a computer, either as a user or a programmer, without knowing something about the facilities of the operating system. But there's a conceptual side of operating systems that's just as important. Operating systems work at a larger scale and handle different problems than most programs. To understand the complexities, we need new concepts: processes, resources, and policies that govern their interaction.

It's possible to think of the operating system as an ecosystem for computer processes. Even the jargon of operating systems, which I've largely tried to avoid, suggests this view. For example, parent processes can spawn child processes, and processes can die or be killed by other processes; a child process with no parent is even called an orphan. Fortunately, it's a clean, bloodless environment. Also fortunately, the operating system has policies in place that make the environment quite a bit more orderly than any natural ecosystem, despite all the competition.

Where does the future of operating systems lie? One place to look is in your pocket. Today's smart phones are full-fledged computers, with as much processing power and storage as their desktop cousins of just a few years ago. New operating systems are being developed and refined to meet specialized requirements for size, mobility, and connectivity. These constraints may mean that mobile operating systems can't do everything I've described in this chapter; for example, multitasking is still limited on some mobile phones.

Looking in a different direction, we might wonder whether the concepts we've seen so far extend to the hundreds of millions of computers that exist today in the world. How do they communicate and coordinate? We'll take on this subject in the next chapter, on networking.

FURTHER READING

Most of the technical material in this chapter is based on *Operating System Concepts*, by Abraham Silberschatz, Peter Baer Galvin, and Greg Gagne (John Wiley & Sons, 8th ed., 2008). It's nicknamed "the dinosaur book," after the illustration on the cover. If you are interested in learning how to program an operating system (a daunting task), Minix is designed for this purpose. Andrew S. Tanenbaum and Albert S. Woodhull's book *Operating Systems: Design and Implementation* (Prentice Hall, 3rd ed., 2006) describes Minix, which has a core that contains only a few thousand lines of code. For contrast, an entire commercial operating system typically contains tens to hundreds of millions of lines of code.

Chapter 7

Computer Networks: Making Connections

Let's imagine an alternate universe. It's a bright fall morning in the year 1950, and you've just arrived at your office. You have a job in a new sector of the economy: you're a knowledge worker.

You settle in at your desk. (If you're a man, you've just hung your fedora on the office hat rack; if you're a woman, you've just folded your stylish cotton gloves and put them in a drawer.)

Your first task for the day is to respond to a request for information from Frank, a colleague who works for your company at a remote site. You flip a switch and a small light comes on behind one of the screens built into your desk. The screen shows a story on the front page of yesterday's newspaper, projected from microfilm underneath: the National Science Foundation (NSF), a new government agency, has been created.

Turning to another screen, you move a slider to skim through recent material from the Library of Congress. Eventually, you find a report written by Vannevar Bush, Director of the Office of Scientific Research and Development (OSRD), outlining the need for the new organization.

You tap a button to create a link between the news story and the report. You draw arrows with your stylus between the relevant passages of text (captured by dry photography), and type a few lines to document the connection. Satisfied, you press another button and a few small sheets of microfilm emerge from an opening on your desktop. You place these in a plastic capsule, mark it with Frank's address, and insert the capsule into the opening for the pneumatic tube running along the wall. With a whooshing sound, it's carried down to the mailroom in the basement. A day later and 500 miles away, Frank will read your work and make further connections on his own.

Most of the world became aware of the Internet in the early 1990s, when the World Wide Web burst onto the scene. The conceptual roots of the Web go back much earlier in history, though, to a 1945 *Atlantic* article by Vannevar Bush.[1] (Bush, as the director of OSRD, reported directly to the President; he actually did make the case for what he called a national research foundation, which became the NSF in 1950.)

In his article, Bush imagined a future device called a *memex*, an "enlarged intimate supplement" to a person's memory. The memex would contain an entire library of information, built into a desk much as I've described. Books, pictures, periodicals, reference materials, and encyclopedias would be included, all indexed for easy access. Users of the memex would blaze trails through masses of information, identifying associations, constructing narratives, and sharing their findings with others.

Does this sound familiar? Bush's precomputer vision inspired decades of research into what came to be called *hypertext*.[2] We see the results today whenever we browse the Web, an enormous repository of information distributed over hundreds of millions of computers networked together across the world.

These networked computers, including your own, form the *Internet*. The Internet is what lets us surf the Web, send email, share music and movies, play multiplayer games, and try out new network applications that appear almost daily.

The conceptual roots of the Internet are more ambiguous than those of the Web, but a good starting point is the writing of J. C. R. Licklider.[3] Licklider envisioned a universal network of computers that would form symbiotic relationships with human beings, actively helping us as individuals and in groups. "Universal" is an exaggeration, of course, but a famous memo from Licklider in 1963 was addressed to "Members and

Affiliates of the Intergalactic Computer Network." His efforts as a director in the U.S. Defense Advanced Research Projects Agency (DARPA) started a wave of research and development that led to today's Internet.

The Internet and the World Wide Web are part of the world of *networking*, an area of computing that deals with communication. The Internet is one example of a network, and the World Wide Web is an example of a network application. To understand these systems, as well as more general concepts in networking, we'll continue with my alternate-universe history. Even if the story bears no resemblance to any real system, the parallels should give some insight into the challenges of building a global (if not intergalactic) network of computers. We'll avoid the details of sending signals through wires or across the airwaves, and we'll even avoid discussion of specific algorithms. Instead, we'll take a systems perspective on networking.

A MEMEX NETWORK

The essential idea behind the memex is the association between related items of information, which may be in different places in the same document or in different documents entirely. Bush wrote, "The process of tying two items together is the important thing." His idea of *associative indexing* is the key to hypertext.

We're all familiar with an ordinary book index. We can think of an index as a tree, going from categories to terms to page numbers.[4] Bush's insight was that this type of categorical index misses some important relationships. If you read the term "Office of Scientific Research and Development" in a document, you can look it up in the index and perhaps find the line "See 'Government Agencies'." That's one kind of relationship.

Here's a different kind: The term you're reading in a two-year-old document has just been used in a news article yesterday. How can a static index hope to capture that kind of future association? The memex is designed to make it easier for its users to find new associations, by providing them with a large library of information, both public and private. It's also designed to make it easy to record those associations, so that they can be called up again later or shared with other people.

The memex does this by integrating an associative index into the body of a document. When you (the 1950s you) found a connection between a newspaper article and a report in the Library of Congress, you created a link between those two documents—you added a new relationship to the associative index.

In modern computing terms, an associative index is a graph of connections between documents, or locations within documents. When you read a memex document, you can move forward through the text in the usual way, but whenever you come across an associative link, you can follow it instead to look at related material.

The memex, as I've described it, is a network application—one that depends on communication with other, independent systems. It's easy to imagine extending its capabilities. Suppose that documents contain more than text; they also include pictures, movies, and music. Your bank sends account information to your memex and you send information back; you order real books, clothing, appliances, even cars from store catalogs designed for the memex; you exchange information with different groups of friends who have memexes of their own. Workers come into your office at night (with your permission) and copy all of the connections you've made between documents you've looked at during the day. They compile your findings with everyone else's in the organization, and the next day you can see what other people have thought is interesting.[5] Your memex eventually includes games and other dynamic ways of interacting with information. If we continue along these lines, we'll reach something that looks very much like today's World Wide Web.[6] Most of your actions involve typing and clicking on Web addresses, rather than writing on capsules to be sent through the mail, but the basic concepts are the same.

Bush described the memex as a device for managing information, but I've pushed his description in a slightly different direction. It can also be a device for communicating information, with exchanges structured in a specific way. In our example, Frank is your client, and you provide a service in responding to his requests. We call this arrangement a *client-server model*. A client-server model is an attractive way to organize a network of memexes, in that a server memex can maintain resources in one place. Frank doesn't need to have subscriptions to all the sources of information that you have; he simply sends you requests for specific information. (You, in turn, are also acting as a client for the servers for your information sources.)

This separation allows for scaling on both sides. Many other clients might use your services, delegating responsibility to you for expanding and maintaining the information you manage. And if your client base grows too large for you to handle alone, you can call in helpers; none of your clients need to know. Here we have another analogy to the World Wide Web, which also follows a client-server model, with client-browsers requesting information from Web servers, and with the separation motivated for similar reasons.

To make the organization of memexes work, we'd need to think about *infrastructure*. How do documents get from one place to another? Bush's article doesn't mention the communication and transportation technology of the time, but I've always imagined it to include the pneumatic tubes that used to run up the walls and overhead in banks and department stores, capsules handled by clerks in busy mailrooms, and packages in postal trucks crisscrossing the country.[7]

Let's consider what a memex network based on 1950s technology would look like on a grand scale.

Hedy, your new junior colleague, has arrived for her first day at work, and you're showing her the ropes. You hand her a small capsule.

"Earlier this morning I sent off a document to Frank, in our Springfield office," you say. "I put the microfilm in a capsule like this one, I filled in the address—his name and the department he works in—and then I put it in this tube receptacle."

"What happens then?"

"When the capsule gets to the mailroom, they package it up and send it through regular mail. The package should get there a day or two later. And when a capsule arrives for you..." (you pull a waiting capsule out of the receptacle) "you pop it open and slide in the microfilm here."

"Neat. So it runs like clockwork."

"Mostly. For some important documents I'll give the microfilm to Nick, our office assistant. He makes a copy before he sends it down to

the mailroom, and he checks the next day to make sure it has arrived. Usually that's not a problem, but if a package gets lost or damaged, Nick sends another copy."

These are the basics of how to use our imaginary memex network. If we were interested in what should happen to make this possible, we'd have to answer several questions:

- *How should a package be addressed?* In any communication network, we need a way to identify different locations. Fortunately, our memex network relies on the post office, so there's a scheme for addresses already in place. Also fortunately, the memex network doesn't require you personally to know every detail about an address. All you have to know to send a document to Frank is his name and department, which you write on the label of a capsule. A clerk in the mailroom boxes up the capsule in a package and adds the street address, city, and state (but not a ZIP code, which won't be created until 1963). When the package is picked up, it's brought to a processing center managed by the post office, where more labels are added to the outside. Your package moves from one processing center to another on its way across the country, until it finally reaches its destination (Fig. 7.1).[8]

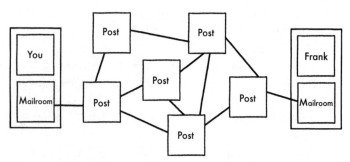

Figure 7.1. Information may pass through many locations on the way from its source to its destination.

This strategy for handling addresses involves two computing concepts we've seen before. First, what you've written on the capsule is a "logical" address. If Frank's department were moved to a new building at a different physical location, the mailroom would be informed about the move, and the address you have for him would still work. This is indirection, an abstract reference to a physical location; you'll remember that an operating system uses the same concept for managing memory. Second, once your memex document is in its capsule, no one pays attention to the information it contains; it's just a package to be delivered, with only the address being relevant. This is a nice example of modularity—it's encapsulation in a literal form. Each person adds new information to the package, but no one looks inside.[9]

- *How does a package get to its destination?* By this question, I mean which route is taken; we'll assume that packages are carried by ordinary vehicles. In the memex network, the route for a package isn't planned in detail from start to finish. Instead, when the package arrives at an intermediate location, it's directed to another, closer location. This might be the final destination, but it might instead be another intermediate location. After a few hops, the package eventually arrives. This adds uncertainty to the transportation process, but it has advantages. If a road is blocked or a postal station becomes too busy to deal with incoming packages, for example, then packages can be rerouted to avoid trouble spots.

- *Are there limitations on where a package can be sent?* For example, how can international boundaries be handled? We're in luck. The postal systems of different countries can work with each other already. As long as workers in one postal system can make sense of the addresses used by another postal system, then the packages holding memex capsules can be handed off between countries without difficulty, and no one on one side needs to know the details of what happens on the other side.

- *How fast can a package be delivered?* Once you've addressed a memex capsule and sent it off, it's out of your hands. The best you can hope for, in general, is that a package should make as few intermediate stops as possible, and that it shouldn't sit in one place for long periods of time. We should also think beyond individual packages. What would happen if you sent a large number of memex documents through the system the day before Christmas? It's possible for the postal system to become overloaded, so that packages will be delayed. You can avoid some problems if you pay attention to timing, but sometimes this may also be out of your control: some packages must be sent when they need to be sent.

- *What happens if something goes wrong?* A memex document with scratches, scuff marks, or boot prints on it wouldn't be readable, which is why you put it in a capsule. Still, perhaps due to snow or rain or gloom of night, packages can be damaged or even lost.[10] We might ask the postal system to guarantee delivery, but that's not enough. That guarantee is a cash substitute that doesn't magically recreate a lost or damaged package. If a package really needs to get from one location to another, then it needs to be re-sent. In the memex network, as in the real world, this is the responsibility of the sender (or rather, your office assistant). There are alternatives, but they're not very attractive. For example, we could require the post office to take responsibility, but this would mean that postal workers would be opening each package and copying its contents, just in case it were lost or damaged, so that a substitute could be delivered. Aside from privacy and security issues, where would the post office store all that information?

All of these are reasonable questions to ask about a communication network. The specific answers for the memex network involve some complexity, which we'd see if we watched the network in action, with flurries of human activity and packages moving in all directions. This complexity can be managed, though, with the help of two abstractions.

The first deals with how activities are organized in the network, in *layers of services*. When you fill out an address label on a capsule, for example, you add the name and department of your colleague, but you don't have to do more than that. The rest is handled by the services of the mailroom, one layer below. The mailroom depends on the services of the postal system, and these dependencies continue down through the layers to the physical transportation of packages.

Layers give us modularity, which makes it easier to maintain and improve the memex network. Changes can be isolated within a layer.[11] For example, I haven't included airmail delivery in the memex network, but it's a possibility. If airmail were introduced, it would operate at the layer responsible for physical transportation. The layers above, all the way up to the layer that includes the human sender and recipient, don't have to know about the change. Documents will simply arrive sooner.

The second concept is that of a *protocol*. Ordinarily we think of protocols as the arbitrary rules of etiquette that diplomats follow so as not to offend the leaders of other countries, but we also use the term to describe what happens in a network. A protocol is a set of rules for packaging up and exchanging information.[12] Protocols are centrally important to networking; by analogy, communication is about protocols in the same way that computation is about algorithms.

In the memex network, there's a different protocol for the services of each layer. You're following a protocol when you fill in the address fields on a capsule. If you ignore the rules by leaving out information, writing the information in the wrong order, or scribbling elsewhere on the capsule, there's no guarantee that the capsule will be delivered properly. The clerks in the mailroom follow another protocol when they add the street address to your package. The postal workers also have their own protocols, and we'd even find protocols being used by the drivers of the postal trucks carrying packages; they're following the rules of the road. Protocols make the rules clear for everyone involved, and they're designed to work well individually and in combination with each other.

The protocol you follow in the memex network has an interesting property: it's an *end-to-end* protocol. (The mailroom clerk's protocol is end to end as well.) That is, once you address your capsule to Frank and send it off, your job is done. You don't have to worry about how packages are handled by a postal processing center or which roads the postal trucks will take—which is good, because you probably don't have enough information to make the best decisions at those lower levels. It's as if Frank were right next door, with the only difference being the delay in delivery. Your protocol supports what's called "logical" communication between you and Frank, in the sense that you don't have to worry about the physical aspects of the communications.

Just as processes and resources give us a systems view of an operating system, service layers and protocols give us a systems view of a network. Rather than focusing on individual documents and how they travel between specific locations in the memex network, we think about the rules that govern these exchanges of information. Is the overall system reliable? Is it efficient? When is it most likely to break down, and what could we do to make that happen as seldom as possible? With protocols working in different layers, we gain all the benefits of modularity and abstraction that we have in designing algorithms and programs.

I recently received an email message from an old high school friend, Joe, with the subject "Help!" It began,

I am in a hurry writing this mail to you, I travelled to Wales for an urgent situation and unfortunately for me all my money was stolen at the hotel where I lodged…

Joe went on to ask that I send him £1,300, which he would refund immediately when he got home again. Of course, the message wasn't really from Joe. The writing isn't native English, and Joe's American—he would have written "traveled" instead of "travelled," and Americans don't "lodge" in hotels.

This is just one of the countless scams that fill our networked, computerized world. If I can't see Joe or hear his voice on the phone, I have to be careful that it's really him I'm communicating with. This can be tricky if I'm not aware of what it's possible to do with computers. If I visit a Web page that asks me for personal information, is it really my bank or is it someone trying to get access to my bank account? The latter is an example of *phishing*. If I open an email attachment that hijacks my computer by copying itself onto the hard disk and running a malicious program (one that might even visit my email address book and send a copy to all my friends to infect their computers), then I've fallen prey to a kind of computer *virus*.

Part of improving security is raising awareness among everyday users about all the plausible-seeming ways that their private information can be compromised. *Computer security* takes a broader perspective on the problem: people can be vulnerable, but so can systems. We've seen a specialized form of security in operating systems, in Chapter 6, with the concepts of protection and privilege. Similar considerations apply down to the behavior of modules within applications and up to communications between computers over a network. Security has close connections to operating systems and networking, and it's a constant battle between the white hats and the black hats.

A COMPUTER NETWORK

Back to the real world, though not yet to the present. Let's translate what we know about the memex network into a network of computers.

By the 1960s, computers (very large, very expensive computers) could be found at hundreds of companies, universities, and government agencies. It had become possible for people to use these computers remotely, with a keyboard and display communicating through the telephone lines. It was even possible for many people to use a single computer at once, with the computer dividing its processing time between them (this was called "time sharing," but we know it as multitasking). The world seemed ready for computer networking.

There was a challenge to be met, however. You may have noticed the oddness of my memex network relying on the post office, airmail or no. Even in the 1950s of an alternate universe, it would be reasonable to build on the technology of telephones and fax machines, which have existed since the 1800s.[13] In the real world, it's certainly possible for computers to communicate over telephone lines, and this is still common today. But the ordinary way that information is handled in telephone communications turns out not to be ideal for computer networking.

When you call a friend, a circuit is opened between your phone and your friend's phone. This circuit has a capacity for carrying information—the sounds of your voices, including pauses and background noise—and that capacity is reserved for your use over the duration of the call.

What happens if you've called on Mother's Day? There's some chance you'll hear, "All circuits are busy," because the telephone network is running close to its maximum capacity. Now imagine your computer communicating with another computer in the same way. You might be browsing a Web site, reading different pages, stopping to make a cup of coffee, and then reading more. If a circuit were reserved for the entire duration of your visit to that Web site, most of the capacity of that circuit would be going to waste, unused by you and unavailable to others.

In the early 1960s, a computer scientist named Leonard Kleinrock devised an alternative.[14] Computers can break up the information they exchange into small messages, or *packets*.[15] These messages are bursts of information to be sent only as needed. The advantage is that if we have many computers communicating over the same network, we don't need to create and maintain an open circuit for every pair of computers exchanging information. Instead, the capacity of the network can be divided more dynamically over time, in a scheme called *packet switching*.[16]

Packet switching has another advantage for sending information, in that an initial connection doesn't have to be established before information is exchanged. (A telephone call does require that initial connection, with one person dialing and another responding to the ring.) Packet switching can be *connectionless*: messages can be individually addressed and delivered without an advance signal of their arrival.

It took less than a decade to put theory into practice. A succession of directors at the Advanced Research Projects Agency, including J. C. R. Licklider, Ivan Sutherland, Robert Taylor, and Lawrence Roberts, oversaw the development of a new packet-switching network, the ARPANET. In 1969, it connected four computers, or *hosts*, from California to Utah; within the next few years, the ARPANET crossed the entire United States.[17] Specialized "gateway" computers were installed at each site to handle the flow of packets. Email and file transfers became possible. Each gateway was connected to two of the others, so that the failure of one communication link wouldn't leave a host completely isolated.

We can think of the ARPANET at this stage as being something like the memex network we've imagined. Each ARPANET host had an address—a numerical encoding of its identity—so that messages could be directed from one host to another. Gateways chose routes for the messages to be sent from one host to another. Responsibilities were separated between hosts and gateways.

Protocols handled communication: protocols on one host would package up a message for transfer, and other protocols on its gateway would communicate the packets to another gateway to be unpackaged on its destination host.

The ARPANET was a remarkable demonstration of both the theory and practice of computer networking. It grew rapidly, and by the early 1970s, other independent networks had sprung up. Then a new challenge arose: computers within a single network could communicate with each other, but communication across networks was more difficult. Dozens of different kinds of computer systems were in use at the time, running different software systems.

How could there be communication between "multiple independent networks of rather arbitrary design," as networking researchers of the time put it?[18] Two of those researchers, Robert Kahn and Vinton Cerf, developed a set of ground rules for a new approach to networking, which led to the Internet of today:

- *The Internet would have a global addressing system.* Every system on the Internet has a unique address following the same format. (This handles the "international boundaries" problem on the memex network.)
- *The Internet would have an open architecture.* The Internet doesn't place requirements on how information is communicated *inside* any specific network. Between networks, though, a common protocol is respected. (The layers in the memex network follow a similar rule.) We've seen modularity at the level of hardware components inside a computer, in programs we've written, and in the operating system—here it applies to entire networks of computers. The effect is to make it easy for networks and individual computers to connect to the Internet.
- *Complex processing would be pushed to the edges of the Internet.* Gateways in the ARPANET evolved into what are today called *routers*. A router handles network communications in a similar way, but it's not necessarily tied to a specific host. Instead, routers can be distributed throughout the network, receiving information from hosts or other routers and sending it on. (Routers are the equivalent of the postal processing centers in the memex network.) Licklider described this way of handling messages as "store-for-just-a-moment-and-forward-right-away." Routers should be as simple as possible, for fast delivery of information.

Routers can't be *too* simple, however. They're responsible for the choice of where to send the messages they receive, as you'd guess from their name. Fortunately, routers don't need to store huge amounts of information about the structure of the Internet to do this. They simply keep track of which other routers in their neighborhood they can communicate with.[19] Addresses on individual messages can be analyzed, similar to the way that modern ZIP codes can be analyzed (codes starting with 9 are on the West Coast, while those starting with 2 cover much of the Eastern Seaboard). Routers can take advantage of the information encoded in an address to choose where to send a message next.

- *The Internet would have no global controller.* Computers and networks on the Internet are only loosely coupled, with systems communicating as "peers" rather than one giving commands to another. Aside from avoiding the complexity of building a single global system to control millions of others, this also makes the Internet more robust. Imagine a connection to a hypothetical global controller becoming unusable, or even the controller breaking down: delivery of information would be brought to a halt. By distributing responsibility for communication over many different systems, this kind of fragility can be avoided.

- *The Internet would deliver information on a "best effort" basis.* This last design principle may surprise you. At a basic level, the Internet is an unreliable system. For example, routers need to store messages long enough to forward them, but new messages may arrive too fast to keep up. In this case a router will simply discard any messages it can't handle. Messages can be garbled, in the same way that your words might be drowned out by static on a telephone line. A lack of reliability may seem like a tremendous flaw in a communication network, but as we saw in the memex network it can be resolved, at some cost.

Kahn and Cerf's work led to two protocols that are considered the core of the Internet. The first is the Internet Protocol, which is supported by every system on the Internet. IP defines the format of addresses for systems on the Internet. (Addresses are encoded as four numbers separated by dots. If you ever see something like 127.0.0.1 in a computing context, you're probably looking at an IP address.) IP also defines the format of message headers, all of the bookkeeping information needed to get messages from a source to a destination.

IP is designed to be simple and general. It's connectionless, which means that it can simply send messages from one host to another (through some sequence of routers) without setting up a connection in advance. It's a "best effort" protocol, which means that it's unreliable. If a message is riddled with transmission errors or even lost completely, or if a series of messages is delivered out of order or with duplicates included, IP does nothing to repair the problems. These design decisions make it possible for IP to be fast, given the lower-level constraints on communication technology.

The second protocol is the Transmission Control Protocol, which adds services not provided by IP. TCP supports logical communication between hosts. To send information from one host to another, TCP first sets up a communication session for the exchange.

TCP is reliable. For a series of messages to be delivered in order, TCP ensures that they actually arrive in order (rearranging them if necessary), without errors, losses, or duplication. It does this by keeping track of the "state" of a communication session, tracking messages by their number, and handling problems by retransmitting messages. TCP even manages congestion to avoid overloading the network. TCP does all this by relying on the services of IP; the messages sent at the TCP level are encapsulated in a form appropriate for handling at the IP level.

IP and TCP are often referred to together as TCP/IP. They're actually just two of the protocols (though the most important two) in the *Internet Protocol Suite* (Fig. 7.2)[20]:

- The *link layer*, lowest in the suite, includes all the various protocols for handling the physical transmission of information between hosts and routers.
- Above this layer is the *network* or *Internet layer*, where we find IP and thus the basic ability for systems on the Internet to communicate with each other.
- Next is the *transport layer*, which includes TCP. It turns out that the services TCP provides, such as reliability, aren't always

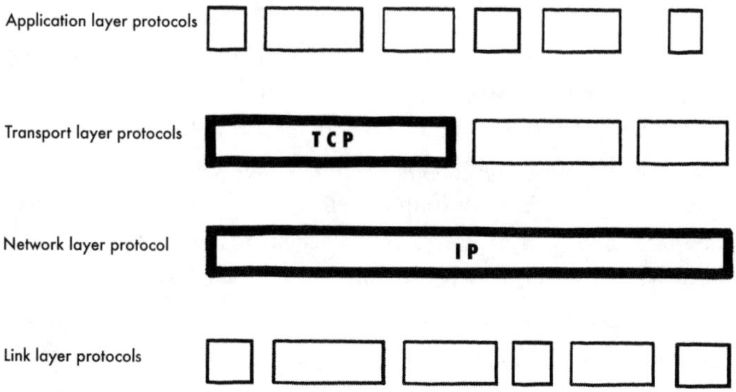

Figure 7.2. The Internet Protocol Suite.

needed, and so there are other, simpler protocols as well in the transport layer.

- The top layer is the *application layer*. We find a variety of protocols in this layer as well, specialized for different network applications such as Web browsers, email applications, Internet telephony, and so forth. Application layer protocols vary because of different requirements for handling information to be communicated: a voice message, for example, is different in many ways from the text of a Web page.

ORGANIZING COMMUNICATION

We haven't gone deeply into networking topics, but we have gained an overview of basic concepts in the area. Our interaction with the Internet is through network applications, such as Web browsers, email applications, and so forth. Many of these network applications have two parts—a client side and a server side.

A client-server architecture for a network application makes it easier to maintain and expand common resources, because they're in one place, and it means less complexity on the client side. The client-server model isn't limited to computer networks, of course: we find the same model at work in the practices of lawyers and doctors, in the businesses of electricians and general contractors, in libraries, and in service organizations.

For almost any situation where many people need access to specialized information or services, a client-server model provides a reasonable organization.

But those services require infrastructure. The specialized breakdown of the Internet into layers doesn't perfectly match any real-world activities, but we can see some aspects of its design elsewhere (aside from postal delivery systems). For example, consider a national organization for youth development or sports. The organization makes it as easy as possible for local groups to join; that's an open architecture. The local groups all have identifying names; that's global addressing. The national organization sets up guidelines and policies but in general leaves local groups in charge of planning their own activities; there's no global control. And what makes one organization more attractive to join than another? In part, it's the activities that it supports, which we can think of as being analogous to specific services.

Finally, we have protocols. Protocols are everywhere, not just in computer networks. If you send me an email to make an appointment to talk to me in my office, you're following a standard academic or business protocol. When you arrive, I invite you in and ask you to sit down; that's also protocol. Even during our conversation, we follow protocols, sometimes unconsciously. For example, we'll take turns speaking in our conversation, and when I finish saying something I'll make eye contact, a nonverbal cue that tells you it's your turn to talk. (You can experiment with this if you like; it's possible to hold the floor a very long time if you never make eye contact at all—but of course the point of protocols is for communication to flow more smoothly, not to violate them for your own benefit.)

Protocols can also be found in legal proceedings, wedding ceremonies, and legislative sessions. In these cases, protocols are used for formal communication in a situation of some importance. How does the defendant plead? Do you take this person to be your lawfully wedded spouse? How does the senator vote? Protocols ensure clarity, so that afterwards there's no question about the information that has been communicated.

This chapter and the previous two, on programming and operating systems, are part of a systems perspective on computing. In the next chapter we'll shift attention to the theoretical side of computing. We've seen that computers have an enormous range of capabilities; you've probably seen these capabilities yourself, in your everyday experience. Are there any limits? Let's find out.

FURTHER READING

Most of the technical material in this chapter is taken from *Computer Networking: A Top-Down Approach*, by James F. Kurose and Keith W. Ross (Addison-Wesley, 2010). It's a comprehensive, readable introduction to computer networking. The historical analogy in the beginning of the chapter is based on Vannevar Bush's article "As We May Think," *Atlantic Magazine* (July 1945).

## Chapter 8

Theoretical Computer Science: Pushing Boundaries

In a 1967 monograph titled *Calculating Space*, German computing pioneer Konrad Zuse wrote, "The possibilities arising from the ideas of calculating space are in themselves so interesting that it is worthwhile to reconsider those concepts of traditional physics which are called into question and to examine their validity from new points of view."[1] Mathematicians and scientists still debate this issue today. Could life, the universe, and everything be a kind of computation?

This is too grand a question for this chapter, but it raises another that we *will* look into: Just what is computation? Clearly Zuse and his colleagues are not imagining a gigantic CPU that controls all of existence. Computation is something more abstract, and it's the focus of the *theory of computing*.

Theoretical computer scientists study what can be computed and how efficiently it can be computed. The theory of computing is founded on abstract mathematical models that give us insight into what a real computer—*any* real computer—is capable of.

Here's an analogy. Part of the long-lasting appeal of the television show "Doctor Who" is the TARDIS. The TARDIS is a combination of a spaceship and a time machine, disguised as a 1960s British police box, and it's bigger on the inside than on the outside. That last part seems impossible—but how do we know?

One way is to build police boxes and measure their dimensions, inside and out. We'd be doing a lot of sawing and hammering, and we'd never be entirely sure that all the possibilities had been covered. Or we could just apply what we know about geometry and physics.

In computing, we do something similar. We develop theoretical models of computation and see what they're capable of. If a model is a close enough match for a real computer, then the conclusions we draw about the model also apply to the computer. We can even stack the deck by developing a model more powerful than any real computer—a model that could in theory carry out computations for centuries, using more memory than can exist in the universe. Surprisingly, we'll discover that even with all that power, some things can't be computed.

We also look at problems that we know *can* be solved, to ask how easy or hard they are. How long does an algorithm take to solve a particular kind of problem? A wide range of techniques have been developed for analyzing problems and algorithms over the past several decades. Again, surprisingly, we'll find that for some interesting and important problems, we can only guess how hard they are.

The theory of computing builds on the past hundred years of research in logic and mathematics, and it's typically thought of as one of the most difficult areas of computing to work in. On the other hand, it's also one of the most important areas. Theoretical results are foundational—they can guide us in choosing the best way to solve problems on a computer, and they can sometimes tell us that what we might like to do is impossible or impractical.

A SIMPLE MACHINE

If you ask a computer scientist to draw a diagram of a switch for a light or an appliance, you'll probably see something like Figure 8.1.

This is a *finite state machine*.[2] You flip the switch up to turn the light on, down to turn it off (or the opposite, in the UK). "Off" and "On" are *states* that the switch can be in—it can be in only one state at any point—and "Up" and "Down" are symbols that cause *transitions* between the states. We think of a state machine as processing a series of symbols by moving from one state to another, or possibly staying in the same state. In the Off state, an Up action causes a transition to the On state; in the

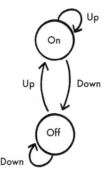

Figure 8.1. A finite state machine for a light switch.

On state, Down goes to Off. Pushing up on a switch that's already on doesn't change the state, and neither does pushing down if it's off. The "finite" part of a finite state machine means that it can include any number of states, as long as it's not an infinite number of them.

We draw a state machine as a graph, but there's more to it than that. State machines are models of computation, one of the simplest models that we have. Of course, being a model, our state machine leaves out some aspects of real switches. For example, the state machine doesn't represent the short time it takes to flip the switch from one position to the other, or what will happen to the light if you are able to balance the switch between its two positions, or how the switch is affected by wiring problems in your house. These limitations may sound familiar—in fact, all the terms I'm using should sound familiar. I described computers in the same way, though in less detail, in Chapter 2.

You might be wondering how such a simple abstraction can be a model of computation. Let's take a different example. Imagine you're a marine biologist, and you're on a dive counting fish of some species. You carry a clicker with two buttons: one for male fish ("M"), the other for female fish ("F"). The clicker has an LED that glows green whenever you've clicked as many Ms as Fs. (The clicker also displays the total count, but we'll ignore that part.)

Here's how we can model the clicker with a state machine. It keeps track of the number of Ms and Fs you've clicked at any point, and it follows a transition to a specific state if the number of Ms matches the number of Fs. If you click several Ms in a row, for example, the machine will need to see the same number of Fs before it turns the LED green (Fig. 8.2).

Our clicker state machine can do some very simple kinds of computation: it can add and subtract by one. It can also handle simple logical decisions, for example to follow one path rather than another if it sees an M rather than an F. It even includes a kind of loop, flipping back and forth between two states if it sees alternating Ms and Fs. In general, state machines can handle some kinds of problems without difficulty.

But it's obviously cumbersome. The clicker machine needs to distinguish between different numbers (one more M than F, or three more Fs than Ms), and the only way it can do this is with a different state for every such number. Worse, the machine can count only so high before it loses track. I've drawn the machine to count up to four (four more Ms than Fs, or the reverse), but what happens if you come across five female fish before a single male fish? I haven't included transitions for when this happens, but the most plausible approach would be for the machine go back to an earlier state, such as "M = F."

Unfortunately, this is less than ideal. When the LED turns green, it could mean that "M = F," or it could mean that there have been 56 more Ms than Fs or 128 more Fs than Ms; any difference that's a multiple of four will bring the machine back to the "M = F" state. You face a similar problem if you've ever thought about buying a car with, say, 27 miles on the odometer. From this information alone you can't tell whether it's

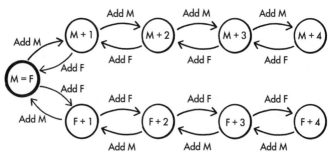

Figure 8.2. A finite state machine for counting male and female fish.

a new car, an old car, or perhaps a *very* old car. And unlike cars, state machines don't show wear and tear.

What do state machines tell us about the nature of computing? Not very much, because as a general model of computation, they're too weak.[3] I've given a few examples of what state machines can do, and they're actually quite useful in some ways, but there's much more that they can't do. For example, given an arbitrarily long string of As and Bs, here are some simple questions that no state machine can reliably answer:

- Does it have the same number of As as Bs, in any order?
- The same number if all the As come before all the Bs?
- Are there more As than Bs?
- Is the string a palindrome, reading the same forward and backward?

We know that state machines can't answer these questions because of what's called the *pigeonhole principle*. If you have some number of pigeons and they're all sitting in a smaller number of pigeonholes, then some hole *must* contain more than one pigeon. By the same principle, if you have 367 people in a large room, then at least two of them *must* share the same birthday (even if it's on February 29th during a leap year). If a state machine is given a series of symbols that's longer than the number of states it has, then it will revisit some state as it makes its transitions. When that happens, the state machine can't tell whether it's entering that state for the first time or the tenth time or the millionth time.

The most that a state machine can tell us about computation in general is that some kinds of problems can be solved easily, but if a given system is trying to solve a problem and it runs out of space, it will fail. Even if this is true in principle about computers in the real world, it's not a very interesting insight. (And we can always add more storage to a real computer. What would the state machine model of computation tell us about our upgraded computer? Only that if it runs out of space, it will fail again, which we already knew.)

Let's try a different approach.[4]

ANOTHER SIMPLE MACHINE

This different approach is a model of computation developed by English mathematician Alan Turing in 1936. Turing developed this model at age 24, while a fellow at King's College, Cambridge. Within the next fifteen years he would help the British government break the Enigma cipher used by the German military in World War II, design one of the earliest electronic computers (the Automatic Computing Engine), and lay the foundations for a new area of computing, artificial intelligence. Turing is the single most important figure in the history of computing.[5] The annual Turing Award, named in his honor, is the equivalent of the Nobel Prize.

Turing's model looks like this. Imagine a paper tape that stretches out to infinity in both directions. (You can imagine it lying on an infinitely long table, if that helps.[6]) The tape is divided into squares, each square blank or inscribed with a symbol. A machine trundles back and forth over the tape, moving one square at a time. On each square, the machine can read the symbol on the tape, and it can decide to erase the symbol, overwrite it with a different symbol, or leave it untouched. The machine can then move one square to the left or right. The machine has a controller making these decisions, an internal state machine. Turing called this an automatic machine, or *a*-machine, but today we call it a *Turing machine* (Fig. 8.3).

Let's see how a Turing machine can handle one of the tasks we looked at for state machines. Suppose we have some number of As on a tape, followed by some number of Bs, with blanks surrounding the list on either side (Fig. 8.4). Can a Turing machine tell whether there are more As than Bs?

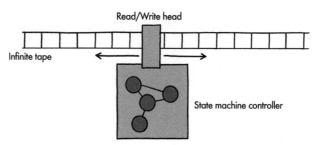

Figure 8.3. A Turing machine.

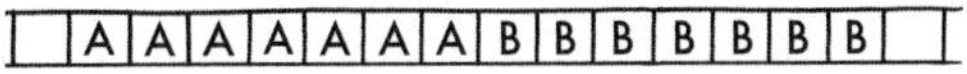

Figure 8.4. A tape containing a sequence of As followed by an equal number of Bs.

Here's one way a human being might answer this question. It's even possible to do it without counting. Start at the beginning of the As, on the far left. Erase the A (leaving that square blank), then move to the far right, to the end of the Bs, and erase the B there. Now move back to the beginning of the As and repeat. You're gradually reducing the number of symbols on the tape, one A paired with one B. When you run out of pairs, check to see what's left. If you have any As, answer Yes, otherwise No.

A Turing machine can do essentially the same thing. It starts at the first A on the tape (the next square to the left will be blank). To keep things simple, we'll ignore the case where the list is empty, with no As and no Bs. The Turing machine scans back and forth between either end of the list, matching up As and Bs and erasing them, one match at a time, just as you would. If it's scanning for a B to match an A and doesn't find one, then there are more As than Bs. In this case, the machine should stop and output some encoding of "Yes," such as writing a Y on the tape; otherwise it's N for "No." (The state machine controller for this Turing machine can be built with about a dozen states, but I'll spare you the details.)

Writing Turing machine programs is even more tedious than building state machines, but in the end, we don't run into the same problem of limited space. We don't run into any obvious problems at all. We can build Turing machines to do arithmetic and other kinds of numerical processing; they can manage and process information in all the ways I described in Chapter 4. We can encode the input and output in different forms, and Turing machines can operate on that information to handle any problem we expect a real computer to solve. That's remarkable, given how simple a Turing machine is.

There's something even more remarkable about Turing machines. David Harel puts it this way:[7]

Turing machines are capable of solving any effectively solvable algorithmic problem.

This is the *Church-Turing thesis*, one of the central ideas in theoretical computer science. There are subtleties in what it means to be "effectively solvable," but the upshot is that when we talk about algorithms, we're talking about what Turing machines do.

This isn't as restrictive as it might sound. Alonzo Church, working slightly earlier than Turing, developed a way of describing computation in terms of mathematical logic, but his approach turned out to be equivalent to Turing's. In fact, all the different theoretical models that mathematicians and computer scientists have developed to describe algorithmic computation are equivalent to each other: each can compute exactly the same things as the others—no more and no less. In the end, what we say about Turing machines applies to all algorithms, which makes the Turing machine an excellent model for what real computers—*all* real computers—are capable of doing.[8]

Turing's most famous result was this: Some things can't be computed. We'll spend the rest of this section following his reasoning.

Remember one of the early historical insights about programming: programs can be treated as data. The translation of a program in a high-level language into machine language depends on this idea, and there are many other practical ways that this idea can be put to use. For example, if you've started a program on your computer and had to wait a very long time for it to finish, you might have wondered, "Is it possible that this program will never finish?" It would be very useful for programmers to be able to find this out about their programs, especially if that behavior isn't intended.

Suppose I've written a program that allows you to type in some number, and it prints out all the numbers from yours down to 1. For convenience, I've written this program in Python, but imagine that it's a program that could be run on a Turing machine. Turing machines can handle numbers just as easily as the abstract symbols A and B I've used above; it's just a matter of encoding. A program in any language you might think of can be translated into a Turing machine program, which will become important later.

In this program the `while` loop repeats the statements in its body until the number that's being tested reaches zero. Will it halt

```
# A buggy program
# This program counts downward to
# zero... but where does it start?

def print _ downward (number):
  while (number is not 0):
    print number
    number = number − 1
```

on all inputs? No, because it's not a very good program. I've left out the possibility of the input being a negative number. If you give it −2, the program just keeps counting downward forever (in principle, at least). An experienced programmer will see the bug in this program immediately. Could we write another program, to find such bugs automatically?

This is harder than it sounds. If instead of simply subtracting 1, the program carried out a very complex function, written by a genius and understandable only to other geniuses, it might be harder to tell whether the program would ever halt. We can imagine writing more and more complicated code to figure out more and more complicated patterns that cause a program not to halt. Could we ever claim with certainty that we've written a completely general program that could take any other program and determine whether it halted or not?[9] Or, in computer jargon, can we solve the *halting problem*?

Unfortunately, no.

Turing proved that it's impossible to write an algorithm general enough to solve the halting problem for all possible programs. This may sound like a straightforward problem, but there are many ways that a program might run forever. If we were talking about Turing machines, we can imagine a Turing machine that repeatedly writes a symbol in a specific place on its tape and never stops; it might move along the tape in one direction and never stop; it might go back and forth over its tape, reversing over larger and larger distances, but never stop. Comparable behaviors are possible in all programming languages. We can catch some of these problems, by writing a program to analyze other programs, but we'll never catch them all.

To see how Turing established this, we'll need to understand the style of logical argument he used. I'll use a story to illustrate, in which you're getting your hair cut by Sally in her shop.

> *"I've been taking an evening class on logic," Sally says, "and I noticed something. I'm the only hairdresser in town, and I get all the business."*
>
> *"This sounds familiar," you say.*
>
> *"Right. I'd like to say that all the women in town either always do their hair themselves or always have it done by me."*
>
> *"That would be good advertising for your shop. But…"*
>
> *"But it can't be true. What about me? If I'm in the group of women who don't do their hair, then as the only hairdresser in town I have to do it—but that doesn't work. And if I'm in the group that does their hair themselves, then I don't do my own hair—but I've just said that I do!"*

This is a variation on a famous paradox in logic usually attributed to Bertrand Russell. The strategy is to make an assumption (here, Sally's universal rule) and reason with it to reach a contradiction. This tells us that the assumption is false.

The other relevant part of this example is its use of self-reference. (We saw a related form of self-reference in Chapter 4, with recursive algorithms that could create copies of themselves.) Sally has identified a relationship between herself and another set of people: she does their hair if they don't do it themselves. Then she asks, "Am I one of those people?" That's the self-referential part, and it leads to the contradiction.

Let's see how this strategy plays out in the halting problem. I come to you with an ambitious claim. "I've written a program that solves the halting problem. I call the program `Halter`. It takes two inputs. The first is a program and the second is an input to that program. My program `Halter` is guaranteed to tell you whether that program halts or not on that input."

We run Halter on several examples, different programs with different inputs. Halter chugs along, and for each example it correctly returns either Yes or No. For one example, Halter runs for quite a long time. "Don't worry," I say. "It'll eventually tell us." And it does.

"How does it work?" you ask.

"It's complicated," I say. "At the top level, here's the pseudocode for the actual Turing machine program…"

```
# Yes if the input program halts

def Halter (program, input):
  if (something very complicated):
    return Yes
  else: return No
```

That's not very helpful. But then, remembering the idea of self-reference, you hit upon a clever idea.

"Give me your program," you say. You write another program, called Clever. The pseudocode looks like this:

```
# Clever inversion of Halter

def Clever (program, input):
  result = Halter(program, input)
  if result is No:
    return Yes.
  else: loop-forever()[10]
```

Clever does something tricky. It calls Halter and then inverts its result in a particular way. For a given program and input, Clever does one of two things. If Halter returns No, saying that the program *does not* halt on the input, then Clever *does* halt and returns Yes. If instead Halter returns Yes, saying that the program *does* halt on the input, then Clever goes into an infinite loop and never halts.

Now for the big question: What does Clever do when given itself? (Clever has two parameters, another program and some input for that program, but let's say that the input can be anything.) There are two possible results, based on what Halter does. Suppose that Halter says, "Yes, the program Clever halts." In that case, Clever will loop forever—that's what the function shows us above. Suppose instead that Halter says, "No, the program Clever does not halt." In that case, Clever *will* halt and return Yes. In other words, we've reached a contradiction.

Whatever we say that Clever does, we find that it actually does the opposite when we reason it through. And because Halter is the only part of Clever that's at all questionable (the rest of the Clever program is very ordinary), Halter is where the problem lies. My guarantee is incorrect—there can be no completely general program that tells us whether another program will halt on a given input. We say that the halting problem is *undecidable.*

There's worse news. The halting problem is just one example of an infinite number of undecidable problems.[11] Could we work around this? For example, we might say that programs aren't allowed to call each other the way that Halter and Clever do. Unfortunately, this would disallow so much that computers wouldn't be able to do much in the way of computing. And how could we detect whether any given program was breaking the rules on a modern computer? That's also an undecidable problem.

Here's why we've done this in the context of Turing machines: it's not a peculiarity of a specific programming language that produces this result, or of a particular computer. It's a result that applies to algorithms in general, as we understand them, and due to the Church-Turing thesis we can say that it applies to *all* algorithms, running as programs on all the different kinds of computers we now know of. Unless someone comes up with a fundamentally different explanation of what computation is, there are some things that computers simply can't do.[12]

You may be familiar with Gödel's Incompleteness Theorem, which roughly says that if you develop a formal system of logic that's powerful enough to represent basic arithmetic, your system will include true statements that, using your system, you can't actually prove are true.[13] And in quantum physics there's Heisenberg's Uncertainty Principle, which says (again roughly speaking) that if you're measuring the position and momentum of an elementary particle, you can't indefinitely increase the precision of both measures simultaneously; you'll reach a point at which the more you know about one property, the less you know about the other. Turing's finding is closely related to Gödel's and not at all to Heisenberg's, but the three have something in common: they're about the limits of our knowledge and abilities. At the very beginning of this book I wrote, "Sometimes it seems as if computers can do almost anything we can imagine." Now you'll understand the "seems" and "almost." What computers can do is limited not only by our imaginations—they're also limited by the nature of computation itself.

A BIT OF MATH

Let's shift gears. In the next section we'll move to another area of theoretical computer science, to consider problems that we know we can solve, but to start we'll need a few intuitions about the math that's involved. Imagine that a business is moving into a historic office building, and you've been hired to oversee the renovation.

> In the morning you talk to Lynne, who plans to install railings in an old stairwell. "You'll need two railings, one six feet long and the other 20 feet long," she says. "The sections of railing come by the foot, and the unit cost is $50 per foot, so that's $300 for the short railing and $1,000 for the long."
>
> "Okay," you say.
>
> Around lunchtime you talk to Audra, who is putting in carpeting. "You have two rooms, one six feet on a side, the other 20 feet on a side. So one is 36 square feet, the other 400 square feet, and it's $10 per square foot... $360 for the small room, $4,000 for the large one."
>
> "That sounds reasonable," you say.
>
> In the afternoon, you bump into the business owner who's moving out of the building, and you fall into conversation. "I've owned XPT— that's the name of my business—for 20 years," she says. "The first year my accountant told me the business was worth exactly $2. The next year it had doubled in value, to $4. The value kept doubling every year. We hit $64 at six years. It's been 20 years now, and I decided to sell."

"Are you retiring?"

"Maybe. With over a million dollars, I can take my time to decide."

You think, "Too much information," but you say out loud, "That's nice."

I've told this story to illustrate three different mathematical functions, each of which has a name. Lynne uses a *linear* function to calculate her railing costs. She thinks, "My unit cost is $20, and if I have *n* units, the total cost is $20 × *n*." In shorter form, this is 20*n*. Linear functions are all around us. If you're driving at 60 miles per hour, then *n* hours will take you 60*n* miles. If you buy *n* candles at $3 apiece, the total will be 3*n*.

Audra uses a *quadratic* function for her carpeting costs ("quadratic" is derived from the Latin for "square," a shape with four sides). We write Audra's calculation, $10 × *n* × *n*, or, using power notation, $10n^2$. Quadratic functions also make an appearance in our everyday lives, whether we're figuring the square footage of a house, the amount of fabric needed for sewing a pattern, or how many square inches of brownies are in an 8 × 8-inch pan.

Linear and quadratic functions are part of the more general class of *polynomial* functions. If you're not familiar with the idea of polynomials, here's a simple way to think about them. Variables (such as *n*) and constants (such as 10 or ½) are polynomials, and if you add, subtract, or multiply two polynomials, the result is also a polynomial.

That's it—recursive definitions are very concise. For example, Lynne's 20 × *n* and Audra's 10 × *n* × *n* are both polynomials, and so is the total cost of their work, 10 × *n* × *n* + 20 × *n*. For convenience, we write polynomials in power notation, such as $10n^2 + 20n$, and for polynomials with just one variable, the highest power tells us what kind of polynomial it is; $10n^2 + 20n$ is quadratic.

The owner of XPT uses a different kind of function, an *exponential* function. Think about a barrel-style combination lock for bicycles. If you have three digits to work with, you can choose any number between 000 and 999, giving 1,000 possibilities. This is 10 × 10 × 10, which we

Table 8.1 A LINEAR, A QUADRATIC, AND AN EXPONENTIAL
FUNCTION.

N	Linear	Quadratic	Exponential
1	50	10	2
2	100	40	4
3	150	90	8
4	200	160	16
5	250	250	32
6	300	360	64
7	350	490	128
8	400	640	256
9	450	810	512
10	500	1,000	1,024
11	550	1,210	2,048
12	600	1,440	4,096
13	650	1,690	8,192
14	700	1,960	16,384
15	750	2,250	32,768
16	800	2,560	65,536
17	850	2,890	131,072
18	900	3,240	262,144
19	950	3,610	524,288
20	1,000	4,000	1,048,576

write 10^3. If you were looking for a more secure lock, you'd get one with more digits, because each new digit gives you ten times as many combinations: four digits give you 10,000 combinations, or 10^4; six digits give 1,000,000 combinations, or 10^6. These are numbers raised to some power, as in a polynomial, but in an exponential function, that power is a variable. A lock with n digits, each with 10 settings, has 10^n combinations. In XPT's exponential function, each year multiplies the value of the business by 2, and so for n years we have $2 \times 2 \times 2 \ldots \times 2$, or 2^n.

We're not so much interested in the exact values that linear, quadratic, or exponential functions produce when given some specific n, but rather their *rates of growth*. Table 8.1 shows what the functions in my example look like for n from 1 to 20.

The rates of growth are easier to see if we translate these numbers into a graphical plot. On the left we see the three functions, linear ($20n$), quadratic ($10n^2$), and exponential (2^n). For very small numbers, the linear function has the highest value, but it's quickly overtaken by the quadratic function. If we were to look at more examples of linear and quadratic functions, we'd find that quadratic functions always grow faster than linear functions. If Audra's unit cost were only $1 and Lynne's were $1,000, it would take just 32 units before n^2 is more than $1,000n$.

Both the linear and quadratic functions are eventually overtaken by the exponential; in fact, the exponential grows so quickly that I've shown its values only up to $n = 12$. If we zoom out to see the entire range, the linear and quadratic functions are so small in comparison that they can't even be distinguished from each other. We'd find the same in a comparison between any polynomial and any exponential function: in the long run, the exponential will have much, much higher values (Figs. 8.5 and 8.6).

The differences between these functions may be surprising, because we don't often compare them in real life. Here's a slightly different perspective to help with our intuitions. I've described these functions in terms of dollar cost—the cost of railings, the cost of carpeting, the cost of buying a business. But they're just mathematical functions. They can be used to describe other measures of cost as well.

What about time?

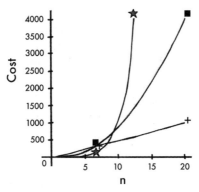

Figure 8.5. A linear, a quadratic, and an exponential function, for a small number of units.

Imagine that you're a competitive walker. You're quite tall, so that every step you take is a meter long, and you take one step every second. You perform very predictably: in a 100-meter race you finish in 100 seconds; in the 10-kilometer race (10,000 meters) you finish in 10,000 seconds, about 2 hours and 45 minutes. One day your walking partner, a mathematician, says, "These linear races are getting boring." He tells you about a more challenging kind of race, both physically and mathematically, in which the distance to the finish line is described by a

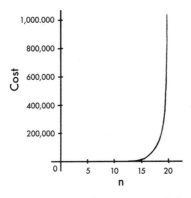

Figure 8.6. A linear, a quadratic, and an exponential function, for a larger number of units.

nonlinear function. You enter your first quadratic race, where the function is n^2 and n is 100. You finish in 10,000 seconds. "Do you want to try an exponential race?" asks your friend. "It's a 2^n race, with n equal to 100." You start figuring. Eventually you find out that 2^{100} meters is about five times the size of the observable universe. It would take you more than a trillion times the current age of the universe to go that distance at your one-meter-per-second pace. "No thanks," you say.

Polynomial time, such as linear and quadratic, is reasonable, but exponential time is almost unimaginably long.

THE ANALYSIS OF ALGORITHMS

We now have enough background to start thinking about the analysis of algorithms.

Suppose we have a sorting algorithm, and we'd like to know how long it takes to run. Working with algorithms is like asking someone to do a job for you; you're naturally interested in how long it will take. (How much memory an algorithm needs is another good question, but we'll leave that aside.) We could write a program for the algorithm, give it a sequence of 1,000 elements as input, and time how long it takes to run on a computer—32 milliseconds, perhaps.

But this approach doesn't tell us very much. We could have gotten different results with a different programming language, or if we'd used a slower or faster computer, or if we'd used a sequence of 100 or 10,000 elements.

Here's what we do instead:

- We analyze an algorithm by picking a specific kind of step that it takes and asking how many times that step is repeated. (With some kinds of sorting algorithms, it's typical to ask how many times any two items are compared.)
- Next, to generalize over different inputs to the algorithm, we look for a mathematical function that tells us the number of steps based on the *size* of the input (such as the number of elements in a sequence, for sorting algorithms).

- Finally, because an algorithm might perform differently even on inputs of the same size, we'll ask about its *worst-case performance*.[14] (Some sorting algorithms do more work if the sequence they're given has higher numbers toward the front; the worst case might be a sequence that's in reverse order.)

When we analyze an algorithm, we'll be saying, "If the algorithm faces a choice at any point given its input data, imagine that the input always forces it to choose the option that involves more work." What we end up with is a general way to describe how much work an algorithm does to solve a problem of a given size: its *time complexity*.

To see how this works in practice, we'll use a simple example—the problem we posed for our Turing machine. We have some number of As on a tape, followed by some number of Bs, with blanks on either side. Are there more As than Bs?

Here is a series of snapshots of the tape as the Turing machine does its work on a tape that contains four As and four Bs, eight symbols in all. It starts by erasing an A and then moving all the way to the right; it erases a B and moves all the way back to the left. Gradually, the As and Bs are erased, one by one, until the machines stops and writes an N for "No, there are not more As than Bs" (Fig. 8.7).

How much work has the Turing machine done? It might be easier to see the pattern if we slide each snapshot to the right whenever a B is erased. The series now looks like Figure 8.8.

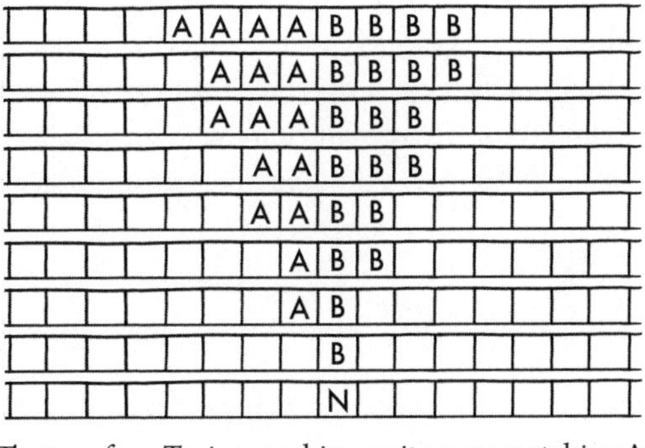

Figure 8.7. The tape for a Turing machine, as it erases matching As and Bs.

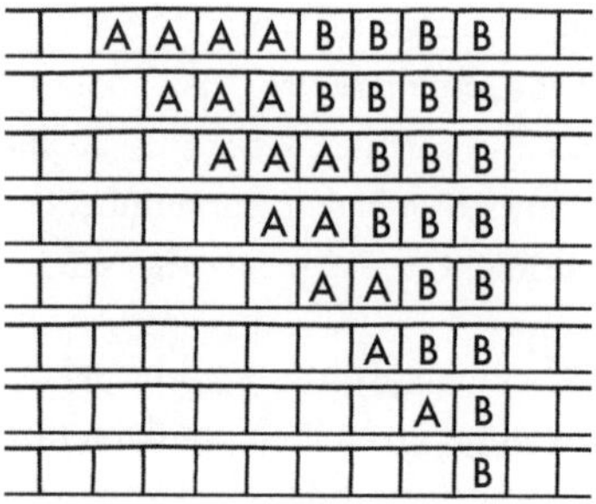

Figure 8.8. The same tape for the Turing machine.

It's a triangle that fills up about half of a square. Each movement over an A or a B remaining on the tape counts as one step, which means that for an input of size 8, the Turing machine is taking about half of 8^2 steps. For an input of size n, the Turing machine would take about $\frac{1}{2}n^2$ steps. There are more mathematically rigorous ways to analyze this algorithm, but the result is the same: it runs in quadratic time.

Is this result important? Not especially, but the general strategy is. We can apply mathematical techniques to analyze algorithms of all kinds: sorting, search, tree and graph traversal, and so forth. We can use computational models other than Turing machines, much closer to real computers, so that our predictions match the performance we will observe.[15]

Through analysis, we can find out something important about an algorithm before it's ever turned into a program—its cost. Algorithm analysis can make a difference in computing. For example, suppose I have a program that's running too slowly, and I know that it's based on a quadratic algorithm. Should I buy a faster computer or look for an algorithm with a lower time complexity? It depends, but in principle, doubling the speed of the algorithm still leaves it running in quadratic time. I might really need an algorithm with a running time that grows at a slower rate.

THE ANALYSIS OF PROBLEMS

There's a different perspective we can take on algorithm analysis. When we learn something about an algorithm, we may also learn something about the problem that the algorithm solves. One of the most important questions we can ask about a problem is whether it is *tractable*.

This is most often a question about whether an algorithm exists that solves any example of the problem in polynomial time—remember the vast difference between polynomial and exponential functions.[16] We call such an algorithm *efficient*. Sorting, for example, is tractable, and the sorting algorithms of Chapter 4 are efficient. The issue of tractability is important enough that we group all known tractable problems together in a single class, called P (for "Polynomial time").

If you're wondering what an intractable problem looks like, here's an example to think about. You're paying at a store counter, and you want to give the cashier exact change. You pull a handful of change out of your pocket and put the coins on the counter: a fifty-cent piece, a quarter, a dime, a nickel, and a penny. Can you combine these coins to add up to a specific amount? This is an example of a problem called *subset sum*. In mathematical terms, it asks, "Given a set of numbers, is there some subset of those numbers that adds up to a specific amount?"

This doesn't seem hard—you make exact change all the time. Let's walk through one way to do it. You line up the coins and systematically push different combinations forward, the same way you might

Figure 8.9. Pushing forward coins to make different amounts of change.

run through the possibilities to open a barrel-style combination lock (Fig. 8.9).

We see four combinations with the nickel and the penny. If you continue with the dime, there are two possibilities, the dime being pushed forward or not, and for each of those two cases there will still be four combinations for the nickel and the penny. That makes eight combinations in all. If you keep going along these lines, you'll discover that each additional coin doubles the number of possible combinations. There are 32 possible combinations for five coins (2^5); you can make 0 cents, 1 cent, 5 cents, 6 cents, and so forth. With two possibilities for each coin, either being pushed forward or not, n coins can be combined in 2^n different ways. (Not all of these combinations might add up to different amounts, but we'll leave that aside.)

What I'm describing is a brute force algorithm that tests all possibilities for solving a subset sum problem. It runs in exponential time in the worst case. Even for a not-very-large number of coins, such as 20, there are 2^{20} different combinations that might produce the exact change we want. We've seen this number before, and we figured it to be over a million. That's a lot of steps to solve a relatively small problem.

We'd much prefer to have an efficient algorithm. We might try an algorithm that would choose one coin at a time to push forward, picking the largest-denomination coins first. Once the algorithm is in the right neighborhood of a solution, it could choose from appropriate smaller coins. This is an example of a greedy approach (remember that for an algorithm, being greedy means being shortsighted), where we try to make as much progress as possible toward a solution with each step.

But imagine being in some country where the coins have denominations 2, 3, and 4, and we have one of each. If you try to add up your coins to reach 5, the greedy approach doesn't work: first you choose the 4, and then you're stuck—being greedy means never revisiting any of your choices. We could try to combine a greedy with a non-greedy approach, but in the end, all of the plausible ideas we have for solving subset sum run in exponential time in the worst case.[17] (We might develop a specialized algorithm to efficiently solve any single example of subset sum, but this wouldn't help us when the next example came along.)

Let's take a different problem. Suppose you're a traveling salesperson, and your region contains the capital cities of five nearby states. If you're trying to figure out the shortest route that visits all the cities, how many different possibilities are there? A mathematical function called *factorial* tells you how many possibilities you have. The factorial of 5, which we write 5!, is $5 \times 4 \times 3 \times 2 \times 1$. That is, in planning a route, you start with five cities to choose from, and once you pick the first city, you have four choices for the second city, and so forth. 5! is 120, which doesn't seem too hard to deal with. You write down all 120 routes, figure out the distances between the cities, do some adding, and pick the shortest route. What if your company expands to cover the entire United States, so that you're now responsible for visiting the capitals of all 50 states? Unfortunately, the factorial function grows exponentially. You have ten times as many cities to visit, but a lot more than ten times as many routes to choose from. 50! is more than 30 million million million million million million million million million million million million. Even if you could harness the processing of all the computers in existence today to solve your problem, it would take longer than the age of the universe to do it. This is the *traveling salesperson problem*, or TSP.

All of this discussion doesn't necessarily mean that subset sum and TSP are intractable problems. We don't know of efficient algorithms to solve them, but perhaps we're just not patient or clever enough. Could we directly prove that these problems are intractable? We'd have to show that any possible algorithm to solve these problems would take more than polynomial time. (We can find such a lower time bound for some problems. For example, finding the highest value in an unsorted sequence can't be done in less than linear time—you have to look at all n elements.) But no one has been able to do this, either. We can't say that subset sum or TSP is easy, by giving an efficient algorithm, but we also can't show that they're definitely hard problems.

Is there anything we *can* say? There is, but it's subtle.

Suppose I give you an example of a subset sum problem, a set of n coins and some target amount, and you tell me a solution, a specific subset of the coins. How long does it take me to check whether your solution is correct?

That's easy. I just add up the denominations of the coins in your solution. In the worst case, this includes all the coins, which still takes no more than $n - 1$ additions. In other words, even if we don't have an efficient algorithm for solving subset sum, we do have an efficient algorithm for checking whether a solution is correct. (We can do something comparable for a specialized version of TSP.) We put all problems that have this property in the class *NP*.[18] ("NP" stands for "Nondeterministic Polynomial time," for historical reasons. Surprisingly, some problems are so hard that even their solutions are hard to check, which means they're not in NP.)

We can think about the difference between P and NP in this way: it's efficient to *find* a correct solution for problems in P, and it's efficient to *check* whether a solution is correct for problems in NP. All problems in P are also in NP, because if we're given a solution to a problem in P, we can check it simply by running an efficient algorithm to generate another solution for comparison. More simply, we can easily solve problems in P, and we can easily check solutions to problems in NP.

This brings us to an important question, perhaps the most important question in all of theoretical computer science: Are there any problems in NP that are not also in P? In other words, does P = NP?

This has been an open question for the past forty years. Let's consider why it's important.[19] Subset sum may appear to be no more than a puzzle, but NP contains thousands of other difficult problems of practical importance. If we had a way to solve TSP efficiently, taxi and delivery companies, military logistics planners, and the makers of in-car GPS devices would all benefit. The knapsack problem involves choosing from a set of objects of different weights with the goal of finding a combination that gets as close as possible to a given weight limit without going over. Efficient algorithms would help shipping companies all over the world. Other such problems are cutting fabric so that waste is minimized, finding the most efficient schedule for a fleet of airplanes, deciding when to schedule exams so that students won't have conflicts, and finding optimal circuit layouts on computer chips. If you've ever tried to draw an organizational chart and had trouble doing it without any lines crossing, it's not necessarily your fault—that problem is also in NP.

There's an enormous range of problems that we don't know how to solve efficiently in general.[20]

The P versus NP question is also interesting from a theoretical standpoint. It turns out that most of the problems in NP that are not known to be in P have an interesting property: in a sense, *they're all the same problem.* The basic idea is that it's possible to efficiently translate one of these problems into another, which means that a solution for one works as a solution for the other.

Here's an analogy. Suppose I hand you a shuffled deck of 53 cards, and I tell you that one card is duplicated. Can you find it? You think for a bit, and you realize that if you first sort the cards, you can then riffle through them to see if any neighboring cards are the same. You've hit upon a *reduction* strategy. You've reduced one problem to another. There may be easier ways to find a duplicated card, but you've discovered finding a duplicate card can be transformed into a sorting problem, which means that the first problem is no harder than the second problem.

In 1971 Stephen Cook proved a remarkable result: any problem in NP can be efficiently reduced to a particular kind of logic problem, called SAT, which is also in NP.[21] As with our duplicate card example, a solution to the SAT problem can be transformed back into a solution to the original problem. This means that SAT is an *NP-complete* problem. It turns out that SAT itself can be reduced to other problems in NP, which makes those problems also NP-complete.

One aspect of NP-completeness is that if we can find an efficient algorithm that solves just one NP-complete problem, we can also efficiently solve *all* NP-complete problems. (Remember that combining polynomials gives us another polynomial, so that an efficient algorithm plus an efficient transformation produces another efficient algorithm.) This would mean P = NP.

On the other hand, if someone develops a proof that one NP-complete problem can't be solved efficiently, then *none* of them can: P ≠ NP.[22] This would be unfortunate, but most computer scientists believe that it's probably the case.

PUSHING THE BOUNDARIES

The two big lessons from the theory of computing are that some problems are (probably) too expensive to solve, and other problems can't be solved at all. In practice, these turn out to be essentially the same thing.

But there are more subtle lessons as well. We know about Turing machines, simple models of computation that can tell us a great deal about even the most powerful computers today. We've discovered what it means to compute something. And for what we can compute, we have a way of thinking about how hard it will be. From a pure knowledge standpoint, these concepts and strategies are as important as any in computing.

The picture I've drawn of the theory of computing may seem slightly pessimistic. That's because it's an incomplete picture. We actually *can* deal with hard problems, even NP-complete problems, if we're willing to settle for approximate solutions rather than perfect ones. After all, the real world doesn't always insist on perfection. We'll return to the solution of hard problems at the end of the next chapter, on artificial intelligence.

FURTHER READING

Most of the technical material in this chapter is based on Michael Sipser's *Introduction to the Theory of Computation* (International Thomson Publishing, 1996), and *Introduction to Automata Theory, Languages, and Computation* (Prentice Hall, 3rd ed., 2007) by John E. Hopcroft, Rajeev Motwani, and Jeffrey D. Ullman. There are also gentler introductions to computer science theory, including David Evans's *Introduction to Computing: Explorations in Language, Logic, and Machines*, a freely available online textbook; David Harel's *Computers Ltd.: What They Really Can't Do* (Oxford, 2000); and Alan P. Parkes's *A Concise Introduction to Languages and Machines* (Springer, 2008), a textbook that successfully "tries not to be too formal."

## Chapter 9

Artificial Intelligence: Being Smart

How is it that we can tell stories, play games, paint pictures, or compose music? Plan for the future and explain what has happened in the past? Learn new concepts? In short, how is it possible to be intelligent?

For many, these are questions about what makes us human, and they've attracted some of the deepest thinkers throughout history, from ancient Greece through the present. *Artificial intelligence*, or AI, proposes answers in terms of computation.

Remarkably, there exist AI systems capable of doing everything I've mentioned above, though not yet with the versatility of human beings. The paintings by Harold Cohen's Aaron system, for example, hang in museums.[1] Some video games construct stories on the fly for players to take part in. The world champions in chess, checkers, backgammon, Othello, and a number of other table games are all computers; some of these systems learn to improve their own play.

Still, hardly anyone would say that we have intelligent computer systems walking among us today—though these accomplishments might have convinced people in the past. Our views about what counts as a demonstration of intelligence have changed over time. As one of my AI professors said, "We used to think playing chess was hard and playing football was easy. Now we know it's the reverse."[2] AI is something of a moving target.

Perhaps performance on isolated, artificial tasks isn't a good measure of intelligence, even if we rely on just that for human IQ testing.

Would the ability to hold an ordinary conversation be a better measure of a computer's intelligence? We might set up question-and-answer sessions, using typed messages, as people do today when they text each other.

Alan Turing devised just such a test for intelligence in 1950, arguing that if a computer could consistently fool people into thinking they're talking to another human being, this would be good evidence for its intelligence.[3] Unfortunately, today's computers are still very far from being able to pass the Turing test, and their failures tell us very little about what they *can* do.

New tests have been proposed to take the place of the Turing test, such as writing a term paper on a given topic, passing a skills test designed for children in the third grade, or fielding a robot soccer team to play against human opponents.[4] Such tests aren't quite as general as the Turing test, but accomplishing these tasks does depend on different intelligent abilities, and even partial success would give us insight into the limitations of AI systems and how to improve them.

Artificial intelligence covers an enormous range, as you might expect; intelligence has many facets, few of which are understood completely. Still, at the heart of work on AI are basic concepts that we'll spend this chapter exploring. We'll see how an AI system can solve problems that we'd ordinarily expect to require intelligence.[5] Performance won't match human intelligence, but we should see hints of progress.

ENVIRONMENTS AND AGENTS

Two important abstractions in AI are *environments* and *agents*. Here's a story to illustrate.

> *You wake up early one fine sunny morning. It might be a nice day for a bicycle ride. You walk to the kitchen, still half-asleep. You measure coffee from the canister into the coffee machine, run water from the tap into a pitcher, and pour it in. Five minutes later the machine beeps. You pour your first cup of coffee and start to wake up.*

Making coffee is a simple task, at least as I've described it. Partly it's because you don't have too many steps to follow. Another part is the environment itself. You're not making coffee onboard a ship in a storm, where you'd have to deal with dynamic, continuous changes when you're pouring water, or people rushing about, or the power going out unexpectedly, or not being able to figure out how to use the coffee maker.

Similar (though less dramatic) factors are at work in your kitchen, but you can largely ignore them. I've described a simple *task environment* for making coffee.[6] It's discrete; each of your actions puts the environment in a different state. It's *static*, in that the environment doesn't change significantly except through your actions. Your actions have predictable results (the environment is *deterministic*) and all the information you need to make coffee is available to you (the environment is *observable*). And you're acting alone.

The concept of a task environment helps us understand why some problems are hard or easy for a computer to solve. For example, chess is "easy" because it's discrete, with pieces on squares; it's static, changing only when the players make a move; it's observable. It's not *that* easy, though, because the opponent player may make unpredictable moves, and the number of possible outcomes of a game is enormous. Football, in contrast, is dynamic rather than static, continuous rather than discrete (a fraction of an inch can make the difference between a successful play and a failure, as can a fraction of a second), and not fully observable (sometimes other players and even the ball aren't visible). All of these features make football a richer and possibly a more subtle task environment than chess—though I imagine that no one but a computer scientist, or perhaps an avid football fan, would make this argument.

Still, task environments are abstractions; my description of coffee making strips away most of the complexity of a real, physical environment. But that's appropriate: after all, the physical environment is literally infinite, extending beyond your kitchen to include the rest of the world, the solar system, and the entire universe. You might even be aware of some distant parts of the real environment, if you've turned on the radio to hear international news, or if you notice the sun shining in through the window. But it's not relevant to the task of making coffee. In general, when we describe a task environment, we restrict it to what's plausible and relevant for a set of tasks.

Now for you, the agent. Agents perceive their environment through *sensors* (the five senses, in your case) and produce changes in the environment through *actuators* (things that can take action, such as your hands and feet). Agents interpret their input to generate appropriate output, often by making decisions. We can divide agents into categories by how well they're able to deal with different kinds of complexity in their environment.

My story imagines you to be following a set of fixed rules in your half-asleep condition. You're essentially a *simple reflex* or *stimulus-response* agent. Simple reflex agents base every action on what can be seen or otherwise sensed immediately in the environment. "No fresh coffee → Open coffee canister..." These agents are not very intelligent, but for many tasks intelligence isn't needed to do the right thing. Insects and other animals with limited cognitive abilities are very successful reflex agents (successful as species, and in an evolutionary sense), and it's enough for you to make coffee in the morning.[7]

But let's imagine a change in the story:

Standing in front of the coffee machine, you remember that you'd used the last of the coffee in the canister yesterday morning. You go to the cupboard, pull out another bag, pour it into the canister, and then continue making coffee.

You've made a decision based not just on what you can see in front of you but on what you remember. You carry information about the world, a model, inside your head, which tells you that there's no coffee in the canister even before you open it. You're a *model-based reflex agent*. You're still acting on reflex, but those reflexes draw on a wider range of information. "No fresh coffee *and* no coffee in canister → Fetch coffee from cupboard..." Model-based reflex agents tend to work well in the same routine environments as simple reflex agents, but they're more capable because they don't need to see (or be told) everything explicitly. Here's another change to the story that introduces some unpredictability:

> *You place an empty pitcher in the sink and push the tap. It breaks off in your hand. Fortunately, the water stays turned off. You head to another room to find a different faucet. You'll deal with the repair after you make coffee.*

Reflex agents have practical limitations. It's possible to imagine a reflex agent, simple or model-based, with a preprogrammed response for every situation, but it's harder to conceive of the foresight and effort needed to build that agent in the first place.

You probably don't have an automatic response when the tap breaks off in your hand; it has never happened to you before. Instead, you reason about the actions available to you, and you choose a course of action that should reach your eventual goal of having coffee. You've become a *goal-based agent*.

One last change:

> *None of the faucets seem to work. "When it rains, it pours," you think. "But no water." Earlier you saw a jug of distilled water in the cupboard, and you also have some bottled water in the refrigerator. You make coffee with the distilled water; it's much cheaper.*

You're now a *utility-based agent*. Utility-based agents, like goal-based agents, can reason toward goals, but they have an advantage when faced with different ways to achieve a goal. They take the approach that has the highest utility. Utility might be a dollar cost, but it could also be something much more abstract, such as personal satisfaction. For example, the bottled water might have been a gift to you, and you'd like to tell the giver that you enjoyed it even though you never drink bottled water. In that case you might have turned the bottled water into coffee despite the expense.

We can find examples of these different kinds of agents working in all the different possible variations of task environments. A task environment influences the appropriate design of an agent, but it doesn't completely determine the design. For example, while we might think that more intelligence is always better, it may come at a cost of storage or processing time that's too high for some unpredictable environments. ("Water spraying from broken tap → Turn off valve under sink" is probably better than "Consider the implications of an inch of water covering the kitchen floor...")

Thinking about the relationship between agents and task environments becomes especially important if we're considering novel tasks in artificial environments. For example, we might be interested in agents for an online multiplayer game or a complex interactive simulation. If we understand the task environment, we'll have a better idea about what an agent needs to be successful in it.

INSIDE AN AGENT: REPRESENTING PROBLEMS AND DECIDING WHAT TO DO

Let's consider a goal-based agent, to see how it might solve problems in a simple task environment. We'll adopt a historically important approach, now described as *classical AI*. The basics of classical AI can be found in the work of Allen Newell and Herbert Simon. Newell was working at the RAND Corporation in 1952 when he met Simon, a professor at the Carnegie Institute of Technology (which later became Carnegie Mellon University).[8] Newell left RAND to earn a Ph.D. under Simon's guidance; their collaboration and friendship continued for the next 40 years. (Coincidentally, I have an indirect relationship to Simon similar to Newell's, through a tree of student–advisor relationships, though the path is longer than a single edge.) Working together, Newell and Simon produced some of the most influential results in the history of AI.

Newell and Simon are perhaps best known for their claim about the nature of intelligence. Imagine a set of tokens, which might be anything from colored strips of paper to specific encoded values in a computer's memory. Call these *symbols*.

These symbols can be arranged physically in different patterns: symbols of different types arranged in a pyramid, for example, or alternating symbols lined up in a row. Any physically possible pattern is allowed. These are *symbol structures;* they can be interpreted as objects.

Now imagine a system that can create new symbols, arrange them in symbol structures, and modify the symbol structures in whatever ways are physically possible. This is a *physical symbol system*. Newell and Simon proposed a hypothesis:

> *A physical symbol system has the necessary and sufficient means for general intelligent action.*

To translate this into more familiar terms, we can think of a physical symbol system as a Turing machine; the Turing machine can compose and manipulate a potentially infinite number of different symbol structures. That is, the physical symbol system hypothesis is a claim that intelligence arises from computation.[9] By this view, all of the agent abilities I described above are based on the symbol manipulations of Turing machines.

The hypothesis has met with controversy.[10] The "necessary" part implies that human intelligence can be modeled with a Turing machine. Not everyone finds that plausible. Is the mind (or perhaps the brain) no more than a machine, no matter how complex? Where is the understanding of meaning that we all experience? Philosophers have gone back and forth on such questions for decades.[11] Computer scientists, on the other hand, may object more pragmatically to the "sufficient" part. For some kinds of problems, such as making sense of visual information, interpretable symbols and their manipulation don't seem to offer the most appropriate solution.

But let's put this controversy aside. The physical symbol system hypothesis has demonstrated its value as a driver for solving a wide range of AI problems. After all, whenever we use logic or mathematics or even language, much of what we're doing is manipulating symbols.

Newell and Simon's hypothesis connects AI to the theory of computing. Newell later went further, to explain how AI systems could come about in practice. Remember Backus's insight that, on top of the hardware level of a computer, we can build a more abstract level with software. The levels are largely modular, so that we don't always have to be concerned with the low-level details of CPU processing if we're writing a program, say, for playing solitaire card games. Newell proposed that AI systems could be designed at an even higher "knowledge level." At the knowledge level we build agents (rather than programs) that deal with knowledge (rather than data structures), by pursuing goals, evaluating utilities, and so forth.[12] Newell's proposal clarifies a widely held view in AI, that intelligence can arise in systems that may have different capabilities at lower levels of detail, and these systems may be computers or human brains—it doesn't matter.

Intelligence is then a matter of building up appropriate abstractions and processing them in the right way. We have two important concepts to help us do this. One is a *problem representation*.[13]

A problem representation is a model, internal to our goal-based agent, of what's known about a problem and how it can be solved.[14] Part of this model comes directly from a task environment: it's the initial state from which the agent works to find a solution to the problem. Another part of the model is the set of actions that can be taken in different states, and a way to identify specific states as goals—the endpoints of problem solving. In our kitchen example, the goal is a state in which *CoffeeReady* is true, and your actions take you toward this goal, step by step.

The other concept important to our construction of intelligence is *search*. We've already encountered search: finding some item in a sequence, a tree, or a graph. In AI, we take a slightly different perspective. AI search is about finding a sequence of actions leading from an initial state to a goal state. That is, finding a goal isn't enough; it also matters how you get there.

The search algorithms we've seen for trees and graphs, such as breadth-first search and depth-first search, are widely used in AI, though we often describe them in terms of visiting "states" rather than "vertices," and applying "actions" rather than traversing "edges." AI search algorithms also have to do more bookkeeping, in order to keep track of paths from an initial state to a goal state, but the essential idea of search remains the same.

AI tends to rely on more sophisticated search algorithms than we've seen so far. It will be easiest to understand how they work with a story.

You're planning a morning bicycle ride to visit your aunt, who lives in a nearby town. It's mostly uphill, but you're feeling energetic. You unfold a local map put out by your local bicycling group. The map is drawn approximately to scale, and it shows a few different routes. The terrain is rougher in some places than others, which makes distances slightly deceiving, but fortunately the map shows typical riding times in minutes between waypoints where you can stop to enjoy the scenery. Can you find the fastest route?

Of course. With only four possible paths to consider, this is an easy problem (Fig. 9.1). But we could imagine a much more complex map, with many more possible routes, and it would be important to search systematically. Breadth-first search is one possibility. This won't be enough, but it will lead us to a better algorithm.

Remember that breadth-first search moves through a tree or a graph one level at a time. Here's a slightly different way of describing how it works:

- Breadth-first search begins with the single location *Start*.
- It checks whether this location is the goal, *Finish*.
- It's not, so the algorithm finds all the vertices connected by an edge to *Start*: *A, B, C,* and *D*.
- It adds these locations to a sequence called the *frontier* of the search, and it continues.
- It takes *A* from the frontier.
- This isn't *Finish* either. From *A*, another vertex *E* can be reached, and so the algorithm adds *E* to the end of the frontier list, giving *B, C, D,* and *E*.

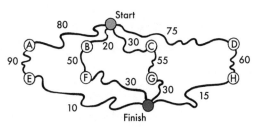

Figure 9.1. A graph of riding times between waypoints.

Breadth-first search continues, working through the frontier one location at a time, checking new locations in the order they were added to the frontier. The effect is to traverse the locations level by level, moving gradually away from *Start* toward *Finish*.

Figure 9.2 shows the progress breadth-first search has made after *B* has been checked. The frontier holds *C*, *D*, *E*, and *F*. The vertices are numbered in the order they were added to the frontier (leaving out *Start*); *C* will be visited next. The light gray vertices have not yet been encountered. When *Finish* is reached along each possible path, we'll add up all the times between the waypoints, and when we've covered all the paths we'll pick the one with the shortest time.

But this is brute force. Intuitively, we should be able to do better than this by paying attention to the total time from *Start* along the path to each location.

If we're looking for the path with the overall shortest time, it makes sense to first look at partial paths with the shortest times. *Uniform cost search* does this in a simple way. It keeps the frontier of its search ordered by the time from *Start* to each location, lowest to highest. ("Cost" here is just time, and we can use a priority queue to keep the frontier in the right order.)

The result is that uniform cost search expands the frontier differently from breadth-first search. The initial visit to *Start* puts *A*, *B*, *C*, and *D* on the frontier, but reordered appropriately. *B* is visited first (20 minutes away), which puts F on the frontier. *C* is visited next (30 minutes away), which puts *G* on the frontier. Next will be *F* (20 + 50 = 70 minutes away).

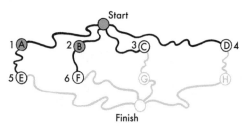

Figure 9.2. Searching the graph with breadth-first search.

Figure 9.3. Searching the graph with uniform cost search.

When *Finish* is taken off the frontier in its turn, the search will have found the path with the shortest time (Fig. 9.3).

Now for something clever. Uniform cost search takes advantage of some but not all of the information we have available. It chooses the fastest paths on each step it takes, but it considers *Finish* only when it appears on the frontier.

What if we also took into account the *remaining* time to be traveled to *Finish*? We don't actually know that time if *Finish* is beyond the frontier, but we can estimate it. For example, we could convert the straight-line distance between a location and *Finish* into an estimated time, ignoring the actual time along the remainder of the path. If our estimates are close enough, then we'll find the same path as uniform cost search, but we'll do less work because we'll be considering the total time instead of just how much time we've taken so far. (Imagine a situation in which all the locations on the frontier are the same time from *Start*, but one is much closer to *Finish* than the others; uniform cost search has no way of deciding that one is better than another.)

This new algorithm is called *A* search*.[15] ("A*" is pronounced "A star." Nils J. Nilsson, one of the inventors of the algorithm, explains that the A part of A* is the name of the algorithm, and the star part means that the algorithm finds shortest paths.) A* first visits *B*, which is 20 minutes away from *Start*; let's imagine that our estimate is 60 minutes left to go, giving 80 minutes total. *F* is visited next: 70 minutes away plus an estimated 20 minutes to go gives 100 minutes. At this point *Finish* is added to the frontier (Fig. 9.4).

The intuition is that a good search algorithm will expand the frontier of the search more directly toward a solution, wasting as little effort

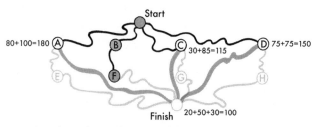

Figure 9.4. Searching the graph with A* search.

as possible on less-promising paths. A* search is an informed search algorithm, in contrast to breadth-first, depth-first, and uniform cost search. It makes choices based on information that's not explicit in the tree or graph it's searching. Those choices are informed by a *heuristic*, a rule-of-thumb estimate of some value that can steer the search in a good direction. In our example, the heuristic is the straight-line distance to estimate the actual time remaining along a path.

The idea of a search frontier has an important implication. From the perspective of a search algorithm, the frontier separates what's known from what's not yet known. We can even say that what's beyond the frontier doesn't yet exist for the algorithm. This means that we don't have to think of a search algorithm as exploring some predefined set of possibilities, such as the locations on your map. Instead, a search algorithm can *generate* hypothetical states reached by actions, essentially by asking "What if?" questions. Those states don't need to exist in advance.

In other words, we're not limited to searching through a tree or graph that represents a fixed set of locations or other items. We can search for solutions to *any* problem that can be represented as a set of states and actions. A search algorithm can even explore an infinitely large space of states, because the number of states inside the frontier will always remain finite.

If we pull back to see the bigger picture, we find a general strategy for deciding how to act. An AI system is given a problem representation, which includes where it starts and what its goals are. It then searches for a sequence of actions that will reach one of those goals. This strategy is an essential part of intelligence, and it's more general than it might seem, because deciding how to act encompasses a great deal more than taking physical actions, as we'll see.

INSIDE AN AGENT: REASONING TO CONCLUSIONS

Intelligent people can reason about what they know. At an abstract level, reasoning can also be thought of as deciding whether to accept some statement as being true.

> *Your bicycle ride brings you to your aunt's house just before noon. She's a collector of books, coins, stamps, and other paraphernalia that you've always enjoyed looking at. After lunch, your aunt tells you, "I've decided to give you an item from one of my collections for your birthday. But you must guess what it is and where it is located in the house. I'll give you hints."*
>
> *"Thank you!" you say. "I'll guess it's either a book, a coin, or a stamp."*
>
> *"That's right. But it's not a stamp."*

We'll turn your aunt's guessing game into *propositional logic* to do a specialized form of reasoning.

Logic isn't quite a game, but there are similarities in that logic has its own vocabulary and rules that may not quite match real life. In logic, we start with propositions about the world that can be true or false. "You will receive a gift," which I'll abbreviate "*Gift*," is true in the context of our story.

The *complement* of a proposition inverts whether it's true or false, using "not." A complemented proposition is also a proposition. If "*Gift*" is true, then its complement "not *Gift*" is false; if "not *Gift*" is true, then its complement "*Gift*" is false.

Propositions can be combined with logical connectives: "and," "or," and "if-then." (A logical "if-then" expresses a relationship between propositions; it's not a decision-making "if-then" as in programming.) For example, we might say, "Your gift will be a book, a coin, or a stamp" ("*Book* or *Coin* or *Stamp*"), or "You have an aunt and you own a bicycle"

("*Aunt* and *Bicycle*"), or "If you receive a gift, you'll be happy" ("if *Gift* then *Happy*"). We'll limit our attention to *clauses*—propositions chained together with "or."

By the rules of logic, a clause is true if one or more of the propositions it contains is true, and it's false only when *all* of its propositions are false.

You've been told that "*Book* or *Coin* or *Stamp*" is true, which means that one or more of "*Book*," "*Coin*," and "*Stamp*" must be true. We treat a proposition standing alone as a special case of a clause.

Our reasoning process will involve using a *knowledge base* of clauses to derive new clauses. The most important thing about this process is that each rule we apply is *truth-preserving*. A truth-preserving rule combines two clauses in the knowledge base to generate a new clause, such that the new clause is true in all the possible situations that the original clauses are true. It's impossible by definition to reason from a true set of clauses to a false clause through truth-preserving rules.[16]

In our story, you have a knowledge base of just two clauses:

Book or *Coin* or *Stamp.*
not *Stamp.*

You derive the obvious conclusion:

Book or *Coin.*

You've applied a rule of logic: the *resolution rule*. From two clauses, one containing a proposition and the other its complement, you've generated a new clause that leaves out both. (It's a little bit like canceling terms in algebra; if you know that $x + y = 10 + y$, then you know $x = 10$.) This is just a small piece of everyday logic, but for computing and intelligence building, it turns out to be more powerful than it seems.

> "*I'll give you a hint,*" *continues your aunt.* "*Either the gift is in the library, or it is not a book.*"
>   *You puzzle over this for a minute.* "*Do you mean, if it's a book it's in the library?*"
>   "*Exactly.*"

"It would have been easier to just say what you mean," you say, with a bit of exasperation.

"That's part of the game," she says.

Your aunt has given you another clause for your knowledge base:

Library or not *Book*.

The "logic" of the resolution rule is that if you have two clauses, one clause containing some proposition and the clause containing the complementary proposition, there's a way for both clauses to be true—we simply don't say anything about the proposition in conflict. (If we say the proposition is true, that will make the second clause false; if we say the proposition is false, that will make the first clause false.)

In other words, we can combine the two clauses, leaving out the proposition about which they disagree, to form a new clause. From "*Library* or not *Book*" and "*Book* or *Coin*" we derive this:

Library or *Coin*.

Does this help you to figure out your gift and its location? It might, if you later find out "not *Coin*" or "not *Library*." "*Library* or *Coin*" is a logically valid conclusion, given your knowledge base.

Because the resolution rule is truth-preserving, we know that if the information in your knowledge base is true, there's no way that this conclusion can be false.

Of course, you probably aren't very often asked to play guessing games like this. Fortunately, we can apply resolution in slightly more realistic examples of reasoning.

Suppose I know this about you:

You often ride your bike, but only on days when the weather is nice. Whenever you ride, you wear a helmet. Wearing your helmet always messes up your hair beyond easy repair, but you like to be presentable: you never arrive at work with messy hair, and you never go out on dinner dates with messy hair.

The resolution rule works on clauses, but there's not an "or" to be seen in this example. The relevant information, though, can be expressed with other logical connectives, in particular "and" and "if-then."

This means we'll have to do some logical gymnastics to translate the statements in my description into the right form.

Fortunately, your aunt has shown us how this can be done. The basic concept is *logical equivalence*. Two statements (English sentences or clauses) are considered logically equivalent if the one is true whenever the other is true, and false whenever the other is false. For example, "*Stamp*" and "not not *Stamp*" (a double negation) are logically equivalent.

More complex statements are trickier to handle, in that they may require a few steps to translate. Take "you only ride on days when the weather is nice." This is logically equivalent to "If the weather isn't nice, you don't ride," or "If not *NiceOut*, then not *BikeRide*," which in turn is equivalent to the clause "*NiceOut* or not *BikeRide*."

These sorts of translations aren't always obvious, but we can check them by testing all the ways that the propositions in the statements can be true or false, to see whether they match in all cases. Table 9.1 is a *truth table*, and it's one way to see whether statements are equivalent.

Table 9.1 TRUTH TABLE FOR TRANSLATIONS OF "YOU ONLY RIDE ON DAYS WHEN THE WEATHER IS NICE."

NiceOut	BikeRide	You only ride on days when the weather is nice.	If not NiceOut then not BikeRide	NiceOut or not BikeRide
True	True	True	True	True
True	False	True	True	True
False	True	False	False	False
False	False	True	True	True

All three statements have the same meaning in propositional logic. They're all true except when it's not nice out and you ride your bike. If you can turn an English sentence into propositions connected by "and," "or," or "if-then," it's always possible to translate the result into one or more clauses. If we translate all of the relevant information in this example into clauses, we have this knowledge base:

- *NiceOut* or not *BikeRide*.
- *Helmet* or not *BikeRide*.
- not *Work* or not *MessyHair*.
- not *DinnerDate* or not *MessyHair*.
- not *Helmet* or *MessyHair*.

The knowledge base simplifies away a good deal of the real world. For example, you can't just comb your hair after a bike ride so that you no longer have messy hair, and there's no way to handle what you do "often" or exceptions in your usual behavior. Still, it captures some of my description, as a model of the real world.

Let's see how well it works. You call me on your cell phone and tell me you're out on a dinner date. If I wonder whether you rode your bike, should I ask you or figure it out on my own?

I can figure it out with a reasoning technique developed by Alan Robinson called *resolution theorem proving*.[17] The strategy Robinson developed is this: If I want to prove a clause, given a knowledge base, then I add the complement of the clause to the knowledge base and see if I can find a contradiction.

The resolution rule is truth-preserving, which means that if all of the clauses in my knowledge base are true, there's no way I'd be able to apply resolution to produce a false clause. (A false clause, in this case, is simply a clause that contradicts something I know is true.)

The beauty of resolution theorem proving is that if this single rule is used to identify actions for a search algorithm, the search is guaranteed to find a contradiction if one exists.

Here's the line of reasoning in our example, as a diagram that's conventional in logic (Fig. 9.5). Each line shows two clauses that contain a proposition and its complement. They resolve into a new clause.

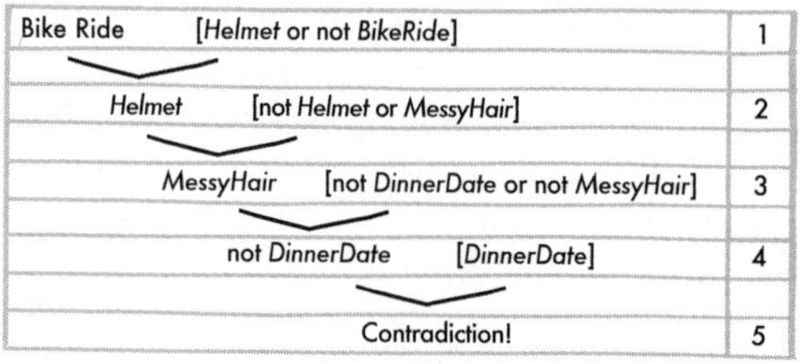

Bike Ride	[Helmet or not BikeRide]	1
Helmet	[not Helmet or MessyHair]	2
MessyHair	[not DinnerDate or not MessyHair]	3
not DinnerDate	[DinnerDate]	4
	Contradiction!	5

Figure 9.5. Using resolution theorem proving to find a contradiction.

In ordinary English, this is what I'm thinking: "I'll assume you rode your bike to dinner (because I suspect otherwise). That means…

1. You wore your helmet.
2. Whenever you wear your helmet, it messes up your hair.
3. I know that you never go out to dinner with messy hair.
4. But you've told me you're at dinner.
5. My assumption must be wrong; you *didn't* ride your bike."

I can do more than prove propositions. If I wonder, "Do you ever ride your bike to a dinner date?" I can make that an assumption: "You definitely ride your bike to dinner dates." I translate the assumption into a clause, add it to my knowledge base, and I reason until I reach a contradiction or not.

This line of reasoning may seem to be a straightforward progression, but it's actually a search problem. In line 5, where I resolve "*MessyHair*" with "not *DinnerDate* or not *MessyHair*," I could instead have tried "not *Work* or not *MessyHair*." This wouldn't have led to a contradiction, but there's no way for me to tell without trying out that possibility. Still, resolution theorem proving can be much faster than building a truth table to find out whether a proposition is true, because it doesn't need to walk through all the possible combinations of true or false for every proposition in its knowledge base.

We could do resolution theorem proving without heuristics, but it turns out that performance can be improved with them. For example, we should prefer to resolve clauses with our original complemented clause, because any solution eventually needs to include that clause. We can also prefer to resolve a clause with a proposition, when possible, because the result is shorter than the original clause. This can lead more quickly to a direct contradiction.

When resolution theorem proving was introduced, there was some hope of discovering that people reasoned in a similar way. It's actually not very common, but we do find examples in real life. In the game Clue (Cluedo, in the UK), for example, everyone starts out with this knowledge base:

Rope or *Candlestick* or *LeadPipe* or...
Library or *Conservatory* or *Ballroom* or...

Each card in your hand contains another clause. For example, if you have a card for Colonel Mustard, then you know "not *Mustard*," and you can create a new, shorter clause for the possible suspects. As you see more cards, you narrow down the possibilities until you reach a conclusion.

All of what I've described in this section, aside from the translation of English into propositional logic, can be done automatically. Given a knowledge base, an AI system can draw conclusions based on a valid reasoning process. Reasoning from what is known is also an essential part of intelligence.

INSIDE AN AGENT: LEARNING FROM EXAMPLES

Our reasoning examples tell us something about the capabilities of an AI system, but there are obvious gaps.

For example, how is the system supposed to know what you think of as "days when the weather is nice"? One approach to this problem is *machine learning*: the system might learn how to identify nice days for bicycle riding by looking at examples.[18]

Suppose you've kept a detailed journal of your bike-riding activities. Each day you write something like "Sunny today, low wind, low humidity—good day for a ride." We can extract this information into a table of examples (Table 9.2), where the headers are *attributes* and each row is a

Table 9.2 EXAMPLES FOR LEARNING WHETHER TO
RIDE ON A GIVEN DAY.

Outlook	Wind	Humidity	RoadSurface	Weekday	Pollen	...	Ride?
sunny	low	low	—	yes	—	...	Ride
not sunny	low	high	—	yes	low	...	Not ride
...	...	...	...	...	...	...	...

set of specific values for those attributes. The first entry in your journal is the first example in Table 9.2. *Ride?* is the *target attribute*. A machine learning algorithm should run through these examples and develop a representation that allows it to process new examples. For a new example, it should accurately predict whether *Ride?* will be "Ride" or "Not ride," based on the values of the other attributes in the example.

We'll use a *decision tree* learning algorithm for this problem. We've seen decision trees earlier, for the game of Twenty Questions. Figure 9.6 shows a decision tree that might be learned in this situation.

Each vertex holds an attribute, and that attribute provides a question to be asked. Suppose we're given a new example: a sunny day on the weekend with low humidity, a low pollen count, and so forth. To ride or not to ride? At the root of this tree, we check the value of *Outlook* in the example (sunny), and we take the left branch. The vertex there tells us to check *Humidity* (low), so we follow the left branch and reach a prediction: Ride.

A decision tree learning algorithm builds such a tree from examples. The algorithm starts with the set of all examples. It chooses one of the attributes and splits the examples into subsets, so that all the examples in each subset have the same value for that attribute. For example, the *Outlook* attribute has two different values, sunny and not sunny. Splitting on *Outlook* produces two subsets, one with all the sunny examples and the other with all the not-sunny examples. The algorithm then repeats, handling each of the subsets in a similar way, but leaving out the attribute that produced the split.

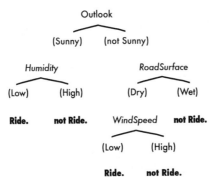

Figure 9.6. A decision tree for deciding when to ride.

This is a specialized form of search, in which each subset of examples is a state and the actions are the choices of an attribute for splitting the examples. It's a divide-and-conquer, greedy search; it never revisits any of the choices it makes. We see the results in the decision tree I've given above.

A critical issue is how to choose the splitting attribute at each step. Imagine that the examples have an equal number of Ride days and Not Ride days. Splitting on *WindSpeed* gives us two smaller sets of examples, but in each set the number of Ride days *still* equals the number of Not Ride days. (They're smaller numbers, of course.)

In contrast, splitting on *Outlook* gives us a much more useful breakdown. For sunny days, we find many more examples of Ride than Not Ride, and the reverse is true for not-sunny days. The intuition is that, for a given set of examples, we choose to split on the attribute that does the best job of predicting the target attribute.[19] In the simplest case, splitting stops when a subset of the examples all have the same predicted value of *Ride?* or no attributes remain.

A decision tree is more than just a hierarchy of tests that lead to a prediction; it can also be viewed as a description of a concept. If we ask, "What's a nice day for bike riding?" we can turn the structure of the decision tree into an answer. "A nice day for riding is when the outlook is sunny and the humidity is low, or when the outlook is not sunny but the road surface is dry and the wind speed is low." We've simply collected the paths in the tree to predictions of Ride.

We now have learning, a third element of intelligence.

BEYOND CLASSICAL AI

The problems and solutions I've described so far give the barest introduction to AI. As you might guess, these simple algorithms sometimes break down.

This happens even with problems that people solve without much thought at all. For example, think about how many facts you know that could be described in propositional logic. Tens of millions or more? Theorem proving is an NP-complete problem, which means that resolution will break down (in the worst case) when trying to handle just a few dozen facts. Decision trees can't find some specialized types of patterns that are obvious to human eyes. Pure search-based approaches to intelligent behavior are sometimes faced with enormous search spaces for which we don't know of good heuristics. On the other hand, the classical approach has produced world-champion chess players, medical diagnosis systems, applications for tax-return preparation and car repair, and an enormous range of other useful systems. But in some cases it's not enough.

Fortunately, AI encompasses much more than the classical approach. Let's consider a different possible path toward intelligence.

Search is one way to find some item in a set by applying actions, but it's not the only way. We can think of some problems in terms of *optimization*. Suppose that we can apply a mathematical function, an *objective function*, to each of the items we consider, to tell us how good the item is as a solution. Then instead of treating the item we're looking for as a goal, we say that we're trying to find the item that has the highest value for the objective function.

Here's a simple example. Suppose that instead of riding your bicycle, you decide to walk to your aunt's house. Remember that your aunt lives on the top of a hill. Is there a way for you to get there without search? One technique for optimization, called *hill climbing*, has you do exactly that. Starting from home, you consider the different directions you could walk. If your objective function is altitude—let's assume you're good at making that judgment—then you can always choose as your next step the one that puts you at the highest altitude. Eventually, after a great many steps, you'll arrive on the top of the hill at your aunt's house.

Hill climbing is easy enough that you could do it blindfolded. There are no long-term goals, just "What do I do next?"

As with search, we have great flexibility in choosing a problem representation to apply optimization. We can do much more than talk about physical locations and altitudes.

Imagine that you're back on your bicycle again, because you've decided that after riding to your aunt's house, you'll visit other destinations in town to run some errands before you return home. If you'd like to find the shortest route, this becomes an example of the traveling salesperson problem. As we saw in the previous chapter, TSP is intractable, which means that solutions for large examples are beyond our practical reach. Say that the town is a labyrinth of curving, intersecting streets, and you have an unreasonably large number of destinations you'd like to visit. On a map, the street intersections and your destinations are the vertices of a graph, and the streets themselves are the edges (Fig. 9.7). How could optimization, in particular hill climbing, work here?

Instead of looking at partial routes and extending them, as we did earlier, we'll start with a *complete* route, constructed at random. We just choose any ordering of all the vertices (your destinations, plus your home as a starting and ending point) and treat the collection of edges between those vertices (the streets connecting your destinations) as the initial route. Our objective function is the distance of the route. We have no way of knowing at this point whether the initial route is good or bad; it might be very long. So we'll try to improve it. We choose two edges,

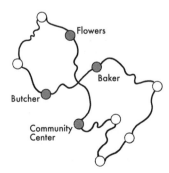

Figure 9.7. A route between several destinations.

say, one that runs from the butcher to the baker, and another than runs between the community center and the flower store. Now we change the route: we run it from the butcher to the community center, and from the flower store to the baker. The new route is still complete; it visits the same destinations but in a different order (Fig. 9.8).

Is the new route longer than the initial one? Then we discard it. Is it shorter? Then we keep it and try to improve it in the same way. We've completed one step in our hill-climbing optimization, with the old route and the new route being the states we've moved between. Gradually we find shorter and shorter routes, and they become harder and harder to improve. We decide to stop, satisfied with the result.

Despite all the randomness, this works surprisingly well. We're still hill climbing.[20] This may not be obvious, but it's an abstract hill we're climbing, each step bringing us to a new state with a better value for our objective function (that is, a route of a shorter distance).

Hill climbing has drawbacks. It never backtracks (it's greedy), which means that if there are ups and downs over the "terrain," it can get stuck at the top of a small hill rather than atop a larger one that would provide a better solution. Other optimization techniques, though, are much more sophisticated. Sometimes optimization can find exact solutions, and it's often robust enough in other cases to find almost-correct, approximate solutions.

Simon gives us a useful way to think about optimization with his idea of *satisficing*, a portmanteau word that combines "satisfy" and "suffice."

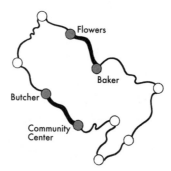

Figure 9.8. Hill climbing to improve the route.

(This was part of the work that earned him the Nobel Prize in Economics in 1978.) Absolutely correct solutions aren't always needed in the real world. Sometimes, especially for intractable problems, a solution that's literally incorrect may nevertheless be satisfactory and sufficient. All of the intractable problems I mentioned in the previous chapter, for example, have algorithms that provide approximate solutions, relying on optimization or search, or a combination of both. (Optimization doesn't "belong" specifically to AI; it's used in all branches of computing, especially theory.) Remember George Box's observation that models are wrong but may still be useful? We can say the same about solutions for real-world problems.

Can you predict tomorrow's weather? Of course, anyone can. Here's one way: Look outside and predict that tomorrow's weather will be just like today's. This works surprisingly well, much better than guessing at random between sunny, cloudy, rainy, snowy, and so forth. We can do better than this, though. Suppose we collect data for a specific location over the course of several years, storing the information in a database, of course. We measure temperature, wind speed, humidity, and various other factors. To predict tomorrow's weather, we query the database for the days that are around the same time of year, and we see which days are most similar to today. We then check what happened *after* those days, and we say, for example, "70% of the time it was sunny on the day after days like today, and 30% of the time it was cloudy." Now imagine that we break up the surface of the Earth into a grid (in simulation, of course) and record information for every cell on the grid. We can do more than predict the weather in specific locations; we can also see how the weather in one location affects the weather in other locations over time. This is a simple example of *computational science*. Computational science is about building models of phenomena in the real world and analyzing what will happen under different conditions. Computational science typically depends on access to enormous amounts of data and processing power, which means close connections to work on databases, high-performance computing (including specialized architectures), and networking. Optimization, search, and theoretical computer science also play a strong role. The most famous example of computational science is the Human Genome Project, which completed a sequence of the human genome in 2003. Computational science has given us insight into particle physics and inorganic chemistry, at a smaller scale, as well as into the evolution of planets, stars, and galaxies, at a much larger scale. It has also told us about global climate change.

Optimization techniques in AI have as long a pedigree as the classical approach. Artificial neural networks, composed of simple computational models of neurons in the brain, learn to recognize patterns through optimization. Biological evolution has inspired genetic algorithms, which work by optimization. Modern robots rely heavily on optimization techniques for identifying and manipulating objects and for navigating through the physical world. It's worth remembering, though, that these techniques don't take us beyond the limitations of Turing machines, even though we're dealing with numbers; we just encode the numbers appropriately.

Even now we've only scratched the surface of AI. But you should have a better idea now about how artificial intelligence is viewed from a computing perspective. We're not looking for a special ingredient that can be added to a computer program to make it smart. An AI system works like any other computer system, processing and transforming information over time. If it seems implausible that this could lead to intelligence, consider how the shuffling of electrical impulses and chemicals through the neurons in your brain enables you to read this book; an intelligent alien or robot forensic scientist, examining a human brain, might be similarly skeptical of the possibility that *we* could be intelligent.[21]

Of course, we are intelligent. We can solve problems in an enormous range of different task environments. In the next chapter we'll look into our own abilities in dealing with computers: human–computer interaction.

FURTHER READING

Nils J. Nilsson's *The Quest for Artificial Intelligence* (Cambridge, 2010) is a fine review of the history of AI. Most of the technical material in this chapter is based on *Artificial Intelligence: A Modern Approach* by Stuart Russell and Peter Norvig (Prentice Hall, 3rd ed., 2010). It's known by its initials: AIMA. I've also relied in part on Thomas Mitchell's *Machine Learning* (McGraw Hill, 1997) and Simon Blackburn's introduction to philosophy, *Think* (Oxford University Press, 1999).

## Chapter 10

Human–Computer Interaction: Thinking About People

Have you ever run into difficulties using a computer? I've never met anyone who hasn't, and it's not just computers. Over the past several years I've collected hundreds of examples of troublesome modern technology. Here are two.

I have an alarm clock by my bedside, a clock radio with several identical buttons in a row on the top (Fig. 10.1). To set the time, I hold down the Hour or Minute button and watch the numbers blink forward. To set the alarm for the next morning, I hold down the Wake button; the display shows me the alarm time and I can change it in the same way as the time of day. The other buttons do what you might expect. The clock is designed in a straightforward, understandable, and even aesthetic way. But that's not enough.

It's easy to change the time on the clock, by pressing a single button. This can be tedious if I'm doing it after a power outage (the numbers only go forward, one hour or minute at a time), but in principle I shouldn't have to worry about this very often. Except... Think about *when* I use the alarm clock. I'm asleep, and the alarm goes off. I reach out to press a button, still half-asleep. Most of the time I hit the Mode button or the Snooze button, either of which is fine, but there's also a good chance that I'll hit the Hour or Minute button, and I'll have accidentally changed the time. This means that every so often I need to reset the time on the clock because it's running fast. This is a minor annoyance, but I can't help thinking, "I bought this alarm clock to tell

Figure 10.1. My clock radio.

me the time and to wake me up in the morning; why can't it be good at both?"

The second example is in my local airport. When returning from a trip, I usually have to pay for parking my car in the airport garage. A row of kiosks is set up to handle this task, and the front of each one looks like the drawing in Figure 10.2.

The labels and some of the instructions were added after the kiosks were installed (the plastic is now peeling a bit). That's a bad indication—people have trouble with the basic design of the machine. The dotted line should help, with numbered instructions, but notice that there's no Step 1; an icon of a parking ticket is shown instead. Step 2 says to press a button for a receipt, with no obvious button nearby. You have to reverse direction, and you'll end up *between* two buttons. There are two Step 3s. Figuring out how to pay for parking might take the average person

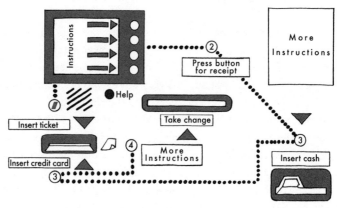

Figure 10.2. A parking kiosk interface.

only an extra half-minute or so, but consider that ten million people pass through this airport every year—all together, that's almost two years of pure wasted time. Small amounts add up.

The modern world is filled with interactive technology poorly designed for human use: curling irons that burn their users, gadgets with impossible-to-find switches sold in impossible-to-open packages, "user-friendly" mobile phones that come with 200-page instruction manuals, and so forth. My own mobile phone once drained its battery by taking 27 pictures of the inside of my pocket.[1] (This was an older phone that I wasn't in the habit of putting in "locked" mode, and something in my pocket repeatedly bumped against the button for the camera. Deleting each picture took six button presses, 162 actions in all.)

I emphasize the "human use" of these products because they *do* generally work, in a sense. They work under carefully controlled conditions when used by knowledgeable, attentive, patient people who never make mistakes. I'm not one of those people. I suspect they're rare.

Sometimes I'm pleased (and surprised) to come across a good design. Every couple of weeks, I fill my car with gas at the self-service station near my house. A small screen asks me, "Would you like to pay inside?" I usually pay at the pump with a credit card, so I press the No button. The screen instructs me to slide my card through the reader, which I do, and then it asks me, "Is this a debit card?" Again I press No. The screen tells me that my card is being authorized, and after a few seconds it instructs me to pick a grade of gasoline and begin pumping. When I put the nozzle back into its slot, the system beeps and asks, "Would you like a receipt?" I am not such an organized person, so I press No, get back into my car, and drive off. Once, when I was in a hurry, I started pumping gas without paying attention to the questions and directions on the screen. This turned out to work perfectly well. Now I no longer wait for the pump to give me instructions and ask questions. I just slide my card and pump my gas. I even feel a little bit of satisfaction that I've figured out the fastest way to get the job done.

I've written about interaction with ordinary technology, rather than specifically with computers, to suggest that designing interactive systems is hard to do right. Designing interactive *computer* systems is even harder to do right. What makes one system good and another frustrating at best? This is one of the core questions in human–computer interaction, or HCI. The issue is *usability*, which has three parts:

- *Effectiveness*—can I use the system to do what needs to be done?
- *Efficiency*—can I do it easily, without too much effort?
- *User satisfaction*—is it something that gives me satisfaction or even enjoyment as I do it?

It's an open question whether well-designed technology can always meet these three criteria (for example, a dental drill may be effective and efficient, but the average patient will not rate it highly for enjoyment), but they are all worthwhile goals.

Following general *design rules* makes it easier to achieve these goals. Two things my favorite gas pump gets right are *New users should find clear directions* and *Expert users should have efficient shortcuts.*

Take my alarm clock or my mobile phone, for contrast. They're badly designed because they break two rules of usability: *It should be easier to do the right thing than the wrong thing,* and *It should be just as easy to recover from mistakes as it is to make them in the first place.*[2] It's not helpful to tell me that I should be more careful when I touch the buttons on my clock, or that I should always lock my phone when I'm not using it. That would be like saying that we don't need guardrails on mountain roads, because people should drive carefully. People inevitably make mistakes, and a good design takes that into account.

Design rules can even be specialized to different tasks and styles of interaction. For example, just like a paper form that you fill out in the doctor's office, an interface for data entry should have clearly aligned labels and boxes for easy reading. Like human bank tellers, bank machines should let people cancel their transactions up to the point that money is exchanged. Like tools and toys, a mobile phone with a touch screen should have relatively large buttons, with space between them, so that you don't accidentally press the wrong button very often.

Designing for usability is the practical side of HCI. On the theoretical side, a general goal of HCI is to understand how people interact with computers, and to develop models that explain and predict the usability of interfaces—even interfaces that haven't yet been built.

Innovations in technology constantly drive the field in new directions. Nowadays HCI considers not only work-related computing (for example, creating a spreadsheet on a laptop) but also people who use computers to play games, to socialize (on Web sites like Facebook), to navigate in their cars, or simply to enrich their everyday lives.

Because of the human element in HCI, the field depends on contributions from psychologists, sociologists, designers, cognitive scientists, and many others aside from computer scientists. But remember that the materials of computing are programs, and the systems we build inevitably reflect their materials.

COMPUTERS AND PEOPLE

Charles Babbage called the people who would use the Analytical Engine "attendants," as if his machine were a rare and exotic beast. In a sense, so were the earliest electronic computers: tremendously demanding of attention, care, and knowledge to keep them productive.

Over the decades, our roles have reversed. We're much more interested today in how computers can attend *us*. This human-centered perspective may seem only natural, but it's actually the result of a long evolution of how we think about computers. A tour through the history of HCI will give us some insight into how this conceptual shift happened and how it continues to drive the field forward.

In 1946, the ENIAC was turned on at the University of Pennsylvania.[3] It was the only general-purpose electronic computer running in the entire world. Six programmers, recruited for their mathematical ability, became the system's main users. The programmers, known today as "the ENIAC women," worked in pairs. They designed their initial programs on paper, and then, because the ENIAC didn't store programs in memory, they'd spend days rewiring the system's plug boards and setting thousands of switches—reconfiguring the ENIAC's hardware to run the new program. The system could then process input data and generate output for weeks (with pauses for almost daily repairs).

Technology improved. It quickly became possible to program comput-ers without rebuilding them, using punch cards that held programs as well as data. By the 1960s, keyboards (in some cases modified typewriters) and video displays (in some cases modified oscilloscope screens) had appeared, and computers could be found in universities, large corporations, and gov-ernment organizations. The era of *interactive computing* had begun.

Interaction was no longer limited to loading a program and waiting for output; with computers fast enough to respond to user input in real time, new kinds of programs could be written. These included the first text editors, the first computer-aided design (CAD) tools, and even the first video games.

A new style of interaction, the *command line interface*, came to dom-inate computing. We can think of a command language as a simplified programming language for common, specialized tasks. For example, in a command language for dealing with the documents on my computer, I might say the equivalent of, "Go to my *Documents* folder, find all of my spreadsheets, and move them to a new subfolder called *Spreadsheets*." Certainly it's easier to type a command and read the computer's response than to rebuild the system (or write a complete program) for each new task, but notice the conceptual shift: we're dynamically controlling a computer on the fly, unlike most ordinary machines, with language.

Language gives us enormous flexibility. For example, we can work with documents by describing them rather than naming them individ-ually. (These are two forms of indirection.) More importantly, we can build up a vocabulary of abstract concepts and procedures for special-ized activities in computing, and when we're interacting with a com-puter, we can think about our goals—what needs to be done—instead of how the internal parts of the computer should behave.

Describing activities in terms of goals, rather than actions, is uni-versal in our everyday lives. For example, I might be filling out a form with my name and other personal information, but depending on the situation, I could be "applying for a credit card," or "signing up for an online service," or "giving my information to human resources at a new company," even if my actions and the information are largely the same. The reverse holds as well: I can accomplish the same goal through differ-ent actions, a flexibility that's often useful.

Command languages do have drawbacks. Even if you know what to do, you have to learn and remember how to express it, as with any foreign language. In my command line example, going to the Documents folder is expressed with the command cd (for "change directory," using the traditional computing term for a folder); creating a new folder is mkdir (for "make directory"); and so forth. The system carries out my commands and then gives me a blank line to enter more commands.

```
% cd ~/Documents; mkdir Spreadsheets; mv
*.xls Spreadsheets
```

Learning a new language by immersion can work if you find yourself in a foreign country, but the environment of a command language doesn't give you the same kind of exposure. In 1964, it was reasonable for Cliff Shaw to write, "The user obviously does not want a message for successful completion [of a command], because it would be so frequent and because it would intrude."[4] This convention is still followed in some of the most popular command languages used today. The interface is built on the assumption that if you've entered a command, you know what happens behind the scenes, and it would be superfluous for the system to give feedback only to confirm your expectations. (Shaw was no novice to programming; he also worked with Newell and Simon to create one of the very first programs in AI.)

Technology continued to improve. In the early 1970s, researchers at Xerox integrated a range of interaction techniques, based on graphics rather than text, into a new computer called the Alto.[5] The Alto demonstrated the first modern graphical user interface, including windows, icons for folders and documents, menus, and a mouse for pointing. (In HCI jargon, these are called "WIMP" interfaces.) The emphasis in graphical user interfaces is on *direct manipulation* of metaphorical objects in a visual environment.

Imagine working in a carpentry shop. Your tools are arranged on a wall above your workbench, with your hardware (nails, screws, and such) organized in bins. As you measure, cut, drill, and fasten, you gradually see your work take shape. If you ever make a mistake, you can usually catch it right away and repair the problem. A direct manipulation interface engages users in a similar way. Users might be looking at a computer screen, reading labels and selecting graphical images with a mouse, but a visually rich and responsive interface can give them the feeling that they're working in a real environment.

This is a valuable illusion. While direct manipulation may seem to take a step backward, giving up some of the flexibility of language, it also has significant advantages. "Put a door in that wall," in an architectural drawing application; "Follow this link to an encyclopedia article," in a World Wide Web browser; "Now I'll kill that monster over there," in a first-person shooter game. Users don't have to give commands to the system; they simply *do* these tasks, acting through the interface.

In a graphical interface, the language in my command line example is translated into a sequence of actions: double-click on a folder icon labeled "Documents" to display the contents; select a menu option, "Make new folder," and type the name "Spreadsheets"; sort the list of documents by their type; select the block of spreadsheet documents; drag them into the new Spreadsheets folder (Fig. 10.3). It takes a bit longer, but if I'm familiar with the visual conventions of the interface, I can more easily figure out how to do it.

Then computing technology really took off. Computer scientist Paul Dourish describes the modern landscape of HCI in terms of *embodied interaction*.[6] Computers haven't remained on our desks or in our laps. They're on street corners and in airports (in banking machines and ticket dispensers); they're in our pockets (smart phones and personal organizers); they're in our purses and backpacks (e-book readers); they're in our living room entertainment centers (games and digital video recorders); they're on and even in our bodies (wearable computers and smart medical devices). We use these computers for an enormous range of purposes beyond "productivity," as with traditional word processing and spreadsheet applications. There's a much stronger emphasis on social interaction through computers, in online communities or simply by sharing photos and videos in email.

We've now reached the present day. Computers have become much more tightly entwined in our everyday living as physical and social beings, which creates opportunities and challenges for HCI. Our lives tend to be complex, and we're all different in some ways. Fortunately, we find some common ideas about the nature of usability even across the

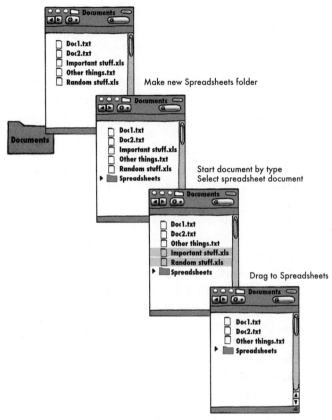

Figure 10.3. Using a graphical user interface to reorganize documents.

wide range of people who use computers, the tasks they perform, and the computers themselves.

USABILITY

A few high-level ideas capture much of what we mean when we say that some application or system is usable.

Let's take a specific example. A friend recommends a new application, something called a life planner. You're skeptical—you've made it this far in your life without advice from a computer—but you decide to give it a try. You've used a computer before, but you don't consider yourself an expert. In what ways do you find this life planner usable?

You learn how to use the application without much trouble. This means more than just starting it up for the first time and being able to do something useful; it means that the more you use the application, the more you find out what you can do with it. You explore the interface and discover a calendar for entering daily events, just as you would in other applications. You can enter monthly and annual events in a similar way. The menu options in the planner are understandable, phrased in everyday language, and when you choose new options, you have some idea about what will happen next.

The application is informative, and not only in the sense that it shows you what your life plan looks like. When you arrange for the planner to send you a reminder of an important event via email, the application walks you through the steps, telling you what you've done and what's left to do in the process. If you make a mistake, the planner explains what went wrong, and you can back up and change it.

The application is efficient, especially after you've become familiar with it. For example, it lets you search for events using a specialized language for describing them, rather than paging through your daily calendar until you see what you're looking for. The language isn't too hard to learn, and the planner shows you examples that you can run to see what happens.

The planner also accommodates your preferences for how to use it. It doesn't force you to do things in only one way. For example, if you're navigating through the monthly views of your schedule, you can click on buttons with the mouse, or you can type the first few letters of the name of the month ("Feb"), or you can type a number (2). When you look at your schedule on your mobile phone, you can scroll rapidly through the months with a swipe of your finger.

Furthermore, the application is flexible. For example, after you've come to use the planner regularly, you wonder whether it can be personalized. You're looking forward to a trip to visit friends in another state, and you've just received a photo from them in email. It turns out that you can arrange for the little graphical icon displayed alongside an event to be replaced by an image that you choose. This takes a bit of work—it doesn't seem to have been foreseen by the designers of the software—but it's possible, and when you've turned the formerly bland interface into one that shows a little bit more of yourself, you're happy with the result.

Learnability, informativeness, flexibility, and so forth: all these contribute to the overall goal of usability in a straightforward way. Take learnability. How could applications be built so that they're easy to learn?

One element is consistency. Different applications on a computer tend to look and behave the same, whether they're for writing reports, drawing pictures, sending email, or browsing the Web. For example, an application running on Windows or a Macintosh will typically create graphical windows, rectangular regions of information on the display. Along the top border of each window you'll see small graphical controls that let you change the window's size or close it completely. The application will offer you different menus of options, including "File" options and "Edit" options. (The ordering of those two labels is always the same.) If you want to open a new document, you'll find that option in the File menu. If you want to "paste" information into an open document (that information might be text, an image, or something else), you'll find the "Paste" option in the Edit menu. Experienced users can bypass the menus by pressing combinations of keys that correspond to specific options: "N" for "New," "O" for "Open," "C" for "Copy." There's consistency across most applications in the way you choose documents to open in an application, the way buttons look and behave, the way you scroll a window to see new information, and so forth.

Consistency makes it easier to learn the basics of a new application, because common actions can be found in familiar places or carried out in familiar ways. Microsoft, Apple, and other software organizations make it easy to follow their conventions by providing a *software development kit*, a "toolkit" of functions and data structures that programmers can use to build new applications.

Remember that a computer's display is an array of millions of pixels; instead of changing pixel colors directly to create windows, buttons, text, and so forth, a programmer relies on the functions in the toolkit, which work at a higher level of abstraction. User input is also managed far above the level of the computer architecture. Instead of thinking about how the CPU should process information from the keyboard or mouse, the programmer can rely on a toolkit function to indicate that a particular button in a window has been pressed.

It's easy to describe applications in terms of consistency and a wide range of other usability properties. How hard could it be to build usable applications?

USABILITY IS HARD

Have you ever scrolled through an alphabetized menu of U.S. states and noticed "Iowa" before "Illinois," or "North Carolina" before "New York," or "Virginia" before "Vermont"? This makes no sense until you realize that the state abbreviation "IA" comes before "IL," "NC" before "NY," and "VA" before "VT."

Or when ordering a product online, you might reach a Web page that instructs you, "Type the numbers exactly as they appear on your credit card." You type in four digits, a space, then another four digits, a space, and so forth. The Web site rejects your card number, perhaps telling you that no spaces are allowed, or even saying only that your card number is invalid. This seems unfair—you've followed the instructions exactly. What's worse is that those spaces make it easier to tell whether you've typed the numbers correctly or not, and the interface makes this more difficult for no apparent reason.

Now multiply these wasted seconds or minutes of your time by millions of people, every day.

In 2007 a Norwegian woman attempted an online transfer of $100,000 to her daughter's bank account, but when she entered the 11-digit account number, she typed an extra 5 in the middle.[7] The banking system silently dropped the *last* digit and transferred the money to a different person, who gambled most of it away before the error was caught. In the financial industry, errors in entering data are notorious.

A so-called "fat finger trade" was responsible for the London stock market losing over $40 billion in value in 2001, due to the action of a single trader; a comparable mistake cost a Tokyo stockbroker $450 million in 2005.

Have you lost money due to usability problems? Perhaps not directly, but probably indirectly.

And yet things could be even worse. I'll use a recent case study of a hospital information system to illustrate. From 2002 to 2004, Ross Koppel and colleagues studied a system for hospital personnel to enter orders for medication and to track when patients receive their medication.[8] The goal was to reduce errors with a system that puts relevant information together and makes it easier to access. We can assume that such a large-scale system would be built using the best software tools available. What could go wrong? Here's a sampling:

- The interface for looking at the information for a specific patient makes it easy to choose the wrong patient. Patient names are listed in alphabetical order for the entire hospital, not grouped by hospital unit. The names are small and crowded together, to show more information on a single screen. Once a patient is selected, his or her details are shown on a new screen that may use a different size and color for the text, and the information doesn't always include the patient's name.
- Seeing all the medications prescribed for a patient can mean looking at up to 20 different screens of information. Doctors and nurses can be uncertain about the medications and dosages for a patient. This makes it possible to enter incorrect, duplicated, or incompatible prescriptions.
- Some kinds of information can't be entered into the system, such as specialized tests to be run before a medication is given. For other kinds of information, the system is *too* flexible. A surgeon performing an operation late in the day might note that the patient should receive some medication "tomorrow at 7:00 am," but this information could be typed into the system much later, by another doctor, even after midnight. The medication would be delayed by a full day.

- Some information is stored in several places, in the system as well as on paper charts and paper records; making sure that all the information is consistent takes extra time.
- Some information is simply confusing: the system might display a drug as being available in 10-milligram doses, leaving it ambiguous whether this is the usual dosage or the units in which the pharmacy stores the drug.

The hospital system also crashes several times a week, leaving doctors and nurses to work without its help.

Supporting patient care in a hospital is more challenging than the tasks carried out by most applications. A hospital environment is typically hectic, with emergencies happening regularly. Information might be needed within seconds, rather than minutes. The relationships between the people are complex. Doctors, nurses, and pharmacists all have different responsibilities and privileges. Some of their interactions happen face to face, while others are through records and messages, such as written treatment orders and prescriptions. But these features of the environment aren't all *that* different from much of our everyday lives.

HOW TO DO IT

Building usable software is difficult but obviously not impossible. In the early 1980s, John Gould and Clayton Lewis asked hundreds of software designers and developers what they do to build a new interactive computer system.[9] Gould and Lewis boiled their responses down into three basic strategies for design: focus on users from the start, test the system with users as it's being built, and change the design to reflect what's learned. These strategies may seem obvious, and yet for subtle reasons, it's easy to overlook them.

First, *focus on users from the start.* Good software developers talk to potential users, watch how similar systems are used, and in general figure out what users do and what they would like to do. Why would anyone skip this step? Finding people who represent your potential users takes time; talking to them takes even longer. Your potential users may not understand the relevant technical issues, and they may find it hard to imagine the future system you're describing. I've tried this on occasion, asking people to describe a new software application they'd most like to have. The requests were generally either for a simple variation on an existing application ("I'd like this application to handle documents created by this other application") or for something impossible ("I want a holodeck, like on *Star Trek*").

All this makes a software developer's life difficult, especially given the temptation to simply write programs. An experienced developer can build a complex interactive system in days, while it might take weeks or longer to work out the details of what users actually need and want. It might be easier to talk with managers and authorized buyers rather than potential users. It's definitely easier for a developer to say, "I already know what I want to build," or "I'll build a system that works well for me; I'm a typical user." These alternative approaches *might* work, but finding out what real users actually need is a much better strategy.

Second, *test the system with users as it's being built.* Good software developers constantly test their work, whether it's a hand-drawn sketch of an interface on a napkin or a nearly completed system. A new application often targets a new problem, or an old problem to be solved in a new way. It's important to test the novel parts of the application and their integration with other parts, as they're developed, so that mistakes don't get locked in place and too expensive to change later in the process.

Why might this process be avoided, then? Testing takes time away from development. You might have involved users at the very beginning, and if they were your clients, they may even have signed off on a requirements document, but that's not enough: users typically can't judge a system until it's in some concrete form. By analogy, have you ever tried to describe a painting or piece of music to a friend, one that you're sure your friend will like? But your friend can't really judge until actually seeing the painting or listening to the music. Acceptance of software systems isn't subject to quite the same range of responses, but it's better in the long run to find out what users like about the system you're building, as you're building it.

The third strategy is *iterative design.* The system should be updated to reflect new information that has been gained. Sometimes testing shows that a new design is needed, based on input from users, and this may mean throwing away a good deal of past work. With interactive software, it's hardly ever possible to get things right the first time, because people and their needs are too complex and unpredictable. But if you plan for a second or third try—or as many as you might need—your work will gradually lead to a usable system, one that's effective and efficient, and that people will find satisfying to use.

THE BIGGER PICTURE

The central theme in HCI is that *people matter*. If we look back on some of the historical developments I've mentioned in this book, we'll see the same theme in all areas of computing.

Early computers, from Babbage's Analytical Engine through the electronic computers of the 1940s and '50s, were designed to take over tasks that people were doing already with pencil and paper or on adding machines. Computers made it easier to solve large, complex problems in science and engineering. But even in the early years computers were targeted at problems of more general interest; in 1952, J. Presper Eckert and John Mauchly, working with a team led by Grace Hopper, used a computer to predict that Dwight Eisenhower would win the U.S. Presidential election (an outcome that surprised many political experts).

By the 1970s, a new world of computing had evolved. Computers with newly powerful operating systems were widely used in large and small companies, in government, and at universities. People could send email to each other through computers connected by the ARPANET, in some cases using wireless satellite communication. Programmers could rely on high-level languages to write sophisticated programs in days or hours instead of weeks. The vision of computers outside the workplace and in everyday life—automated teller machines outside banks, computers in people's homes and children's classrooms—was gradually becoming a reality.

In the modern era, the wants and needs of everyday, nonprofessional computer users drive innovation. In computer architecture and networking we see an emphasis on mobile systems, because people want to carry computers (phones, games, e-book readers, and other networked devices) with them. World Wide Web sites and search engines meet our needs as a library, encyclopedia, community center, auction house, and virtual shopping mall. AI systems, usually working behind the scenes, give us recommendations about what we might like to read or buy, whom we'd want to meet, and what we'd like to do with our leisure time.

Where are we likely to see computing innovations in the future? Look to what people like you and me consider important.

As I hope I've convinced you over the course of this book, the influence can go in the opposite direction as well: ideas that are important in computing can give us a better understanding of how the world works. Sometimes this will be a different way of thinking about the practicalities of day-to-day life. To prepare a meal, do you drive to a farm for your ingredients? No, because you have your refrigerator and a nearby supermarket, a storage hierarchy in which each level acts as a cache for the level below. How much do you need to know about someone's location to send a letter through the mail? Nothing more than a name and an address; the protocols and service layers of the post office handle the rest. How do we get things done on a busy day? We multitask, deciding which tasks to take on based on their priority.

Ideas in computing go beyond practicalities as well. AI gives us new ways to think about hard problems, those that take intelligence to solve. Theoretical abstractions, whether they're high-level models, algorithms and data types, or mathematical models of computation itself, sometimes tell us what we can do (or can't do) in real life. In most of this chapter I've concentrated on the practice of building usable systems, but the long-term goals of interactive computing are much broader.[10] Computers have the potential to help us expand our ways of educating ourselves, of expressing ourselves in art and music, and of interacting with other people. We just have to imagine how to do it.

Think of this book as my attempt to spark such imagination. We've just finished an expedition through the world of computing. If I've properly done my job as your guide, then you've learned not only about computers and what they can do, but also about how the world works and even perhaps something about yourself. I hope you'll decide to go further, to learn more. Have a good trip.

FURTHER READING

Many of the ideas in this chapter can be found in *Designing the User Interface: Strategies for Effective Human-Computer Interaction*, by Ben Shneiderman and Catherine Plaisant (Addison-Wesley, 2009). *The ABCs of HCI*, by Frank E. Ritter, Gordon D. Baxter, and Elizabeth Churchill (Springer, 2013), gives a brief, practical overview of the area. The relationship between HCI and computing concepts is laid out in some detail by Harold Thimbleby in *Press On: Principles of Interaction Programming* (MIT Press, 2007).

ACKNOWLEDGMENTS

This book is dedicated to Luellen Brochu, my best critic for the past 25 years.

I'd like to thank two of my intellectual mentors, Paul Cohen and Mike Webb, for their instruction, guidance, and advice over the years. My other friends, colleagues, and students have also given me invaluable encouragement and advice: Ahmet Babaoglu, Sina Bahram, Arpan Chakraborty, Jon Doyle, John Fels, Mark Guzdial, Christopher Healey, Steffen Heber, KyungWha Hong, Thomas Horton, Dana Lasher, James Lester, Nuno Nunez, Kent Pitman, Frank Ritter, Dario Salvucci, Matt Stallmann, and Mladen Vouk. They may not hold all the views I've expressed in this book, and if there are any mistakes, they're mine alone.

Writing this book first came to mind when I began keeping a blog, the first time I'd written for an audience of nonspecialists in computing. I'd especially like to thank Barry Doyle, Stephen Vaughan, and Denise Montgomery for helping to shape the text.

My friends and family have also supported my writing, though they probably haven't realized it. I've named some of the characters in this book after my nieces and nephews.

Finally, I'd like to thank Joan Bossert, Catharine Carlin, Stefano Imbert, Jennifer Milton, and Nisha Selvaraj for the help and guidance I've received from Oxford University Press.

NOTES

Chapter 1

1. *Most of my friends and colleagues in computer science...* After this point, I'll generally use "computing" as shorthand for "computer science," except where I need to avoid ambiguity. The term "computing" seems to be less intimidating, and it lets me sidestep the question of whether computer science is *really* a science, which has been argued about for more than 40 years.

2. *Computing isn't only (or even mostly) about hardware and software...* A famous statement attributed to Edsger Dijkstra puts this perspective more forcefully: "Computer science is no more about computers than astronomy is about telescopes." This is somewhat controversial, but I think that most computer scientists would agree that the ideas in computing are more important than the technology.

3. *Back in 1963...* I've oversimplified the history of computing; each one of these snippets is part of a larger story. Ivan Sutherland's Ph.D. dissertation is titled *Sketchpad—A Graphical Man-Machine Interface* (MIT Press, 1963). Stanford maintains a Web page showing Douglas Engelbart's entire 1968 demonstration; the videos can be watched online. Tim Berners-Lee's paper, "Information Management: A Proposal," is also online.

4. *...one of today's digital Christmas tree ornaments.* Although the numbers make this comparison correct, the implications don't go far; the Lincoln TX-2 that Sutherland worked on was a general-purpose computer, unlike a digital ornament.

5. *"The purpose of computing is insight, not numbers."* Richard Hamming's aphorism is in the preface to his book *Numerical Methods for Scientists and Engineers* (McGraw-Hill, 1962).

6. ...*the definitions of physics and biology work because we already have good intuitions about those subjects.* Though our intuitions are surprisingly fallible. In physics, for example, Michael McCloskey documents examples of college students whose explanations of falling objects owe more to Aristotle than to Newton ("Naive theories of motion," in *Mental Models*, Dedre Gentner and Albert L. Stevens, eds., Erlbaum, 1983). In biology, belief in creationism is remarkably prevalent, even among educated people.

7. *Peter Denning:* I've simplified the concepts in Denning's "Great Principles in Computing Curricula," a paper that accompanied his invited talk given at the ACM Technical Symposium on Computer Science Education in 2004. In particular, I've used the terms "information management" and "artificial intelligence," which are not as general as Denning's "recollection" and "automation." Denning's framework has also evolved further over the years.

8. *The field of computing...* I'm paraphrasing a definition from the 1967 article "What is computer science?" in *Science*, 157 (1967), pp. 1373–1374, by Allen Newell, Alan Perlis, and Herbert Simon, pioneers in the field. They write, "Computer science is the study of computers." Later, in the same article, they write, "Computer science is the study of phenomena surrounding computers," but argue that this is no different from their first definition. Parts 1 through 4 of Donald Knuth's "Computer science and its relation to mathematics," in *The American Mathematical Monthly*, 81, 4 (1974), pp. 323–343, give further insight.

9. *Any problem in computer science can be solved with another level of indirection.* This was originally attributed to Bruce Lampson, but in his 1993 Turing Award Lecture, Lampson credited David Wheeler with the statement.

10. *This is part of what's sometimes called computational thinking.* Jeanette Wing's Viewpoint article, "Computational thinking," in *Communications of the ACM*, 49, 3 (2006), pp. 33–35, is a good, short introduction to the topic. The *Report of a Workshop on The Scope and Nature of Computational Thinking*, by the Committee for the Workshops on Computational Thinking, National Research Council (National Academy of Sciences, 2009), collects the thoughts of many prominent computer scientists on various aspects of computational thinking. Work in this area has had a strong influence on the ideas developed in this book.

11. *Maxwell's demon and Einstein's elevator are famous thought experiments in physics.* James Clerk Maxwell developed his demon in an examination of the second law of thermodynamics. Albert Einstein used a story about an elevator moving through space to illustrate the idea that gravity bends light.

Chapter 2

1. *We therefore say that computers (and looms) are discrete, rather than continuous, systems...* I'm oversimplifying a bit. I'm describing computers as machines for carrying out abstract computations. If you think about computers at the level of their electronics, they do behave as continuous physical machines. The discrete system view also breaks down if you think about playing a movie or a video game that includes irregular pauses between its states. Still, it's possible to say that the computer is doing what it should—it's just not doing it smoothly or fast enough. States and discrete systems are useful abstractions.

2. *Joseph-Marie Jacquard*: Many of the details of Jacquard's life are taken from *Jacquard's Web*, mentioned in the Further Reading section.

3. *"[A]ccording to the arbitrary fashion of the time..."* The quoted passage is taken from *Biography: or, Third division of "The English encyclopedia,"* edited by Charles Knight (Bradbury, Evans & Co., 1867).

4. *...the raising or lowering of threads is controlled by spring-loaded rods...* My description is taken from T. F. Bell's *Jacquard Weaving and Designing* (Longmans, Green, and Co., 1895).

5. *...computing is the study of abstract models...* Jeff Kramer discusses the importance of abstraction in "Is abstraction the key to computing?" *Communications of the ACM*, 50, 4 (2007), pp. 36–42.

6. *"All models are wrong..."* This is a common paraphrase of a passage in *Empirical Model-Building and Response Surfaces*, by George E. P. Box and Norman R. Draper (Wiley, 1987). Observing that models are approximations, Box and Draper write, "Remember that all models are wrong; the practical question is how wrong do they have to be to not be useful," on p. 78, and "all models are wrong, but some are useful," on p. 424.

7. *"the Jacquard loom is capable of weaving any design..."* This line is taken from *Passages from the Life of a Philosopher*, by Charles Babbage (Longman, Green, Longman, Roberts, and Green, 1864), pp. 116–117.

8. *A great demand for information...* In some areas of computing, data and information are treated differently, with information being data plus some specific interpretation. Throughout this book I use the terms interchangeably.

9. *Analytical Engine processes both numbers and instructions on punch cards.* There were actually three kinds of cards: number cards, operation cards, and variable cards. We'll see the use of variables in Chapter 5.

10. *Now that we know roughly how the Analytical Engine works...* Technical information about the Analytical Engine can be found in "Charles Babbage's analytical engine, 1838," by Alan G. Bromley, in *IEEE Annals of the History of Computing*, 20, 4 (1998), pp. 29–45.

11. *"…there is no finite line of demarcation which limits the powers of the Analytical Engine."* Lovelace was writing about the capabilities of the Analytical Engine for mathematical analysis. I'm quoting from "Sketch of the Analytical Engine invented by Charles Babbage, by L. F. Menabrea, with notes upon the memoir by the translator Ada Augusta, Countess of Lovelace," which can be found online. Lovelace is also historically notable as the daughter of Lord Byron.

12. *"First Draft of a Report on the EDVAC"*…This is a technical report by John von Neumann from the Moore School of Electrical Engineering, University of Pennsylvania (June 30, 1945).

13. *Von Neumann didn't include a diagram*…I've used a diagram from *Computer Architecture and Organization: An Integrated Approach*, by Miles J. Murdocca and Vincent P. Heuring (John Wiley & Sons, 2007).

14. *A modular design*…My account of modularity is based on a definition from Richard Gauthier and Stephen Pont in *Designing Systems Programs, (C)*, (Prentice-Hall, 1970), as quoted by David Parnas in "On the criteria to be used in decomposing systems into modules," *Communications of the ACM*, 15, 12 (1972), pp. 1053–1058.

15. *A group of computer science students in the Netherlands*…Sean Geggie, Mikkel Vester, Anders Nissen, and Martin Have maintain a Web log that describes their construction of a specialized type of computer called a Turing machine.

Chapter 3

1. *A computer's architecture, in general, is the organization of its functional components.* This definition is by Murdocca and Heuring (2007).

2. *The von Neumann architecture gives a good high-level description of a computer*…There are refinements of the von Neumann architecture that we might consider, and even other architectures entirely, but this basic organization is a good place to start.

3. *…the program counter, points to the place in memory where the next instruction should be fetched.* In some CPUs, the program counter stores the location of the current instruction being executed, but this is a small difference.

4. *…Donald Knuth analyzed several hundred programs to answer this question.* Donald Knuth published "An empirical study of FORTRAN programs" in *Software—Practice and Experience*, 1 (1971), pp. 105–133. John Hennessy and David Patterson also contributed influential work in this area. Knuth's multivolume monograph, *The Art of Computer Programming* (3rd ed., Addison-Wesley, 1998), is a classic in the computing literature.

5. *Studies of the behavior of computer programs have shown that when the CPU retrieves data from a given memory location*…By "data" here I mean either data

for a computation or an instruction representing a computation. It's typical for modern computers to maintain a separate data cache and instruction cache (as well as caches for other types of information) for efficiency.

6. ...*a picture of a face.* This is an altered photo of me, taken in 2010, which becomes more obvious if you squint.

7. *David Patterson*... I've paraphrased Patterson's list in his online document, "The Future of Computer Architecture," Version 3, December 2008.

Chapter 4

1. ...*a step-by-step description of actions for solving a problem.* This is an informal definition that we'll revisit in Chapter 8. I'm paraphrasing Michael Sipser's definition, on p. 142 of *Introduction to the Theory of Computation* (International Thomson Publishing, 1996).

2. *Algorithms are models of procedures*...Algorithms support both "control abstraction" (in an algorithm, we can describe what happens next without talking directly about the behavior of the CPU controller) and "procedural abstraction" (if an algorithm has a name, we can refer to it by that name rather than specifying all of its steps).

3. ...*a way of classifying a collection by its type.* I'm following the usage in *Computer Algorithms*, by Sara Baase and Allen Van Gelder (Addison-Wesley, 3rd ed., 1999). Abstract data types are often used to describe individual data items, for example to distinguish numbers from characters, but our focus is on collections. For simplicity, I'm also leaving out the most important theoretical property of an abstract data type—that it is defined in terms of a set of operations that preserve specific mathematical relationships between the items of information stored. Definitions of this kind are concise, but very abstract; their implications aren't always obvious.

4. ...*a few simple abstractions: sequences, trees, and graphs.* There's considerable variation in the naming of abstract data types in the computing literature. A sequence might also be called a "list," a "vector," an "array list," or an "abstract array," for example. More confusingly, sometimes the same term is used for an abstract data type *and* for its low-level representation on a computer—this is problematic because the distinction is important. We'll see more of this distinction in the next chapter. There's also no universally accepted, general way to describe a collection of data organized as an abstract data type as distinct from the type itself. (For example, if I were teaching a class in flower arrangement, I might say that a specific collection of flowers is a bouquet, but I might also talk about a bouquet as a specific kind of arrangement, distinct from other arrangements. We don't have separate words for "a specific bouquet" and "a bouquet as a concept.") The distinction should be clear in context.

5. *A vertex with edges pointing to other vertices is the parent of its children.* For convenience, I'll actually be describing an *ordered tree* in this chapter, in which we can depend on the child vertices of a parent always being in the same order. Further, most of the trees and graphs in this chapter will be *directed*, in that each edge points from one vertex to another. In *undirected* trees and graphs, edges don't have directionality and are drawn as lines without arrowheads.

6. *Dividing 1,200 repeatedly by 2*... Or you could use logarithms, which give the equivalent of repeated divisions or multiplications.

7. C. A. R. Hoare described Quicksort in "Algorithm 63: Partition" and "Algorithm 64: Quicksort," in *Communications of the ACM*, 4, 7 (1961), p. 321. For simplicity, we assume a sequence of unique elements.

8. *Archie has balanced the tree.* The depth of a vertex in a tree is its distance from the root, counting through its ancestors. We can also take the perspective of one of those ancestors, to ask about the longest path to a leaf vertex. That's the *height* of the tree, or the subtree that we get if we consider a particular ancestor a root. In a balanced binary tree, which Archie has produced, the heights of the left and right subtrees differ by zero or one.

9. *For example, imagine being lost in a maze...Depth-first search.* This isn't quite right, though it has the same flavor. In the real world, backtracking to try a different route through a maze means walking back along the way you came. In depth-first search, we can keep a record of the vertices that remain to be visited, which lets us jump back to an earlier point (even if it's far away in the tree from our current location) in a single step.

10. *Jeffrey Travers and Stanley Milgram:* Their work appeared in "An experimental study of the small world problem," *Sociometry*, 32, 4 (1969), pp. 425–443. Milgram is also famous for his experiments on obedience to authority.

11. *It turns out though that graphs of many kinds of relationships in the real world do have the small-world property.* Duncan J. Watts and Steven H. Strogatz describe a number of small-world networks in "Collective dynamics of 'small-world' networks," *Nature*, 393, 6684 (June 1998), pp. 440–442.

12. *In the 1970s psychologists developed a model of concepts in human memory*...The classic reference in psychology is by Allan Collins and Elizabeth Loftus, "A spreading-activation theory of semantic processing," *Psychological Review*, 82, 6 (1975), pp. 407–428. This is based on work by M. Ross Quillian, as described in "Semantic Memory," *Semantic Information Processing*, M. Minsky, ed. (MIT Press, 1968), pp. 227–270.

13. *Relationships between concepts could form a small-world network.* Cognitive scientists Mark Steyvers and Joshua B. Tenenbaum analyzed associations between words, the kinds of relationships found in a thesaurus, and discovered that relationships between words produce a small-world network, as described in "The large-scale structure of semantic networks: Statistical

analyses and a model of semantic growth," *Cognitive Science,* 29 (2005), pp. 41–78.

14. *Instead, we could use a tuple abstract data type.* I'm following the usage of Kurt Mehlhorn and Stefan Näher in *LEDA: A Platform for Combinatorial and Geometric Computing* (Cambridge, 1999).

15. *Encapsulation:* Definitions of encapsulation vary, but one well-known description in the object-oriented software literature is by Alan Snyder, in "Encapsulation and inheritance in object-oriented programming languages," in *Proceedings of the Conference on Object-Oriented Programming Systems, Languages and Applications,* ACM, 1986, pp. 38–45: "A module is encapsulated if clients are restricted by the definition of the programming language to access the module only via its defined external interface."

Chapter 5

1. *Programming means expressing abstractions in a language that a computer can deal with.* Niklaus Wirth's book about programming concepts is titled *Algorithms + Data Structures = Programs* (Prentice Hall, 1976). Wirth expands on this view in the introduction to his book: "*Programs,* after all, are concrete formulations of abstract *algorithms* based on particular representations and structures of *data.*"

2. *In 1954, John Backus...* This material is drawn from two papers by John W. Backus: "Automatic programming: properties and performance of FORTRAN systems I and II," in the *Proceedings of the Symposium on the Mechanisation of Thought Processes,* The National Physical Laboratory, England, pp. 232–255, and "The history of FORTRAN I, II and III," *ACM SIGPLAN Notices—Special Issue: History of Programming Languages conference,* 13, 8 (1978), pp. 165–180. Backus expresses some skepticism in both papers about his work counting toward "mechanization of thought." My earlier observation about the difficulties of programming large systems is also based on Backus's first paper, in which he writes that the original Fortran compiler required 18 person-years of effort to produce a program 25,000 machine instructions long. This is an average of about 7 instructions per person per day. Programmers today work at about the same speed, but they make more progress because each statement in a high-level programming language generally does more work than a given machine instruction. (That is, each high-level statement translates to several machine instructions, as I mention later in the text.)

3. *"I flunked out every year..."* This is from *Out of their Minds: The Lives and Discoveries of 15 Great Computer Scientists,* by Dennis Shasha and Cathy Lazere (Springer, 1998).

4. *In contrast, if you were writing your program in machine language, you'd have to write instructions that look more like this...* For simplicity, I'm ignoring the existence of *assembly language*, which we can think of as an intermediate step between machine language and high-level languages.

5. *Programs can be treated as data.* It's possible to trace this idea to the von Neumann architecture, in which programs and data are stored in memory without a hard separation between the two types of information, or further back in history to the work of Alan Turing, which we'll see in Chapter 8.

6. *...a compiler...* Grace Hopper developed the first compiler in 1952, as described by Denise Gürer in "Pioneering women in computer science," *Communications of the ACM*, 38, (1995), pp. 45–54.

7. *...I'll use the general term translator to encompass them all.* That is, I'll use "translator" to include compilers, interpreters, assemblers, byte-code compilers, source-to-source translators, emulators, virtual machines, and other programs that translate from one language into another.

8. *...a payoff is in the act of creative expression.* This isn't a universal view of programming. For example, Edsger Dijkstra described programming as a difficult branch of applied mathematics, which doesn't rule out creativity but downplays the artistic angle I've described. Still, Paul Graham makes a compelling case for programming as being centrally about inspiration and creativity in his book *Hackers and Painters: Big Ideas from the Computer Age* (O'Reilly, 2004). As for the aesthetics of programming, I'm thinking of Jon Bentley's *Programming Pearls* (Addison-Wesley, 2nd ed., 1999), based on a collection of columns he wrote for *Communications of the ACM*, and of *Beautiful Code: Leading Programmers Explain How They Think* (O'Reilly, 2007), edited by Andy Oram and Greg Wilson.

9. *"It is software that gives form and purpose..."* is in Alan Kay's article "Computer software," which appeared in *Scientific American*, 251, 3 (1984), pp. 41–47.

10. *...simplicity, clarity, and some generality.* You may notice that I haven't included "efficiency" or "correctness" in this list. We'll touch on efficiency in Chapter 8; it's a central topic in computing. Writing programs that we can have some confidence will run correctly is also important. It's a difficult task, both theoretically and in practice, and has been the subject of research on programming languages and in software engineering for decades. Unfortunately there isn't enough space in this book to do more than mention the topic later in this chapter, in connection with error checking.

11. *The first professional programmers in the history of computing...* Their story is told by W. Barkley Fritz in "The women of ENIAC," *IEEE Annals of the History of Computing*, 18, 3 (1996), pp. 13–28. The ENIAC Programmers Project has the goal of bringing their work to greater public attention.

12. *The first step is to make sure we understand the problem*... Some of the specific guidelines I've adopted from *How to Solve It* (Polya, 1957, in the Further Reading section for this chapter) are to draw a picture, check for potentially missing information, introduce appropriate "notations" (our abstractions), and solve a simpler problem than we were given.

13. *Reading through a long algorithm with so-called "go to" statements*... Edsger Dijkstra is famous for a letter to the *Communications of the ACM*, 11, 3 (March 1968), pp. 147–148, titled "Go-to statement considered harmful."

14. *...we'll use "clockwise or not"*... It would be more intuitive to have an input parameter called `direction` and test whether it's clockwise or counterclockwise, but there are good reasons for doing it this way. Using a `direction` parameter, we'd need to test whether direction is clockwise, and then (if it's not) test whether it's counterclockwise, and then (if it's neither) raise a fuss. In programming, binary true/false tests turn out to be simpler to manage than testing between more possibilities.

15. *We'll be using a high-level language called Python*... Guido van Rossum created the Python programming language in 1991. The code in this chapter was originally written in RobotC, a language developed by the Robotics Academy at Carnegie Mellon University. The design, implementation, and testing was done by Kelsey Hawkins while he was a student in computer science at North Carolina State University. I've extended Kelsey's code and rewritten it in Python to make it easier to present. (I haven't tested the Python version of the code on the NXT robot, but the code runs correctly in simulation.) The NXT Python programming project can be found online, hosted on Google Code.

16. *...an equals sign means something more active*... Some computer scientists, notably Niklaus Wirth, who invented the Pascal programming language, believe that this is an unfortunate choice of notation. It would seem more natural if "$x = y$" indicated a test whether x is equal to y rather than meaning "Put y in the memory location referred to by the name x." In Pascal, an assignment is written "$x := y$." It's a tradeoff between clarity (especially for new programmers) and efficiency of typing—assignments are the most common statements in computer programs.

17. *A beacon is a term or feature of a program that carries meaning.* Beacons are a concept used in the computer science subfield of *program comprehension*, the study of strategies for reading and understanding programs. Ruven Brooks defined beacons in "Towards a theory of the comprehension of computer programs," *International Journal of Man-Machine Studies*, 18, 6 (1983), pp. 543–554, as "sets of features that typically indicate the occurrence of certain structures or operations within the code," used by a programmer to refine and test hypotheses about what an unfamiliar program does.

18. *A tuple will do*...I'm actually using a specialization of tuples in Python called namedtuples, based on a suggestion from Jonathan P. Rowe, a computer scientist who attended North Carolina State University.

19. *I've described a somewhat artificial evolution of our program*...The evolution roughly follows a pattern David Parnas describes in "On the criteria to be used in decomposing systems into modules," *Communications of the ACM*, 15, 12 (1972), pp. 1053–1058. Parnas points out that writing a program by concentrating on the steps it carries out doesn't necessarily produce good results. I've nevertheless done this to introduce basic control flow concepts in programming.

Chapter 6

1. *We'll be taking a "systems" view of computing.* Systems thinking can be seen throughout the sciences, in different forms. One of the best books on the topic is in the area of artificial intelligence, but it raises issues that generalize to all of computing: Herbert Simon, *The Sciences of the Artificial* (MIT Press, 3rd ed., 1996). C. H. Waddington's *Tools for Thought: How to Understand and Apply the Latest Scientific Techniques of Problem Solving* (Basic Books, 1977) is also interesting reading.

2. *I'll be describing the kernel of a simple imaginary operating system, designed for a computer with a single CPU*...More specifically, we'll be talking about an operating system that performs preemptive multitasking and demand paging. This should make more sense by the end of this chapter; these are fairly common attributes of an operating system.

3. *The kernel doesn't take up all of memory when it runs; the remainder is left free, but under its management.* The kernel typically reserves the highest portion of memory for its own use as well as the lowest portion, which allows for expansion downward in memory. This level of detail won't concern us.

4. *After some fixed period of time (a time quantum)*...In Chapter 2 I described computers as discrete systems that ignore the continuous passage of time, and yet here we're talking about dealing with time directly. Isn't this a contradiction? Not really. We're breaking up time into discrete blocks, given by the time quantum, and within each block a program still executes instructions step by discrete step.

5. *...driving your car and talking on your cell phone*...The main issue isn't whether your hands are busy with the phone. Marcel Just, Timothy A. Keller, and Jacquelyn Cynkar find that even the apparently simpler task of listening to sentences to judge whether they're true or false pulls cognitive resources (in particular, for spatial processing) away from driving. Their work is described

in "A decrease in brain activation associated with driving when listening to someone speak," *Brain Research, 1205* (2008), pp. 70–80.

6. *Eunice*: I picked the name of this character to suggest an operating system, but Eunice is not Unix. Unix is an operating system developed by Ken Thompson and Dennis Ritchie at Bell Labs in 1969. Descendants and relatives of Unix are still widely used today, and we can see the influence of Thompson and Ritchie's design decisions on all modern operating systems.

7. *The second principle is least privilege.* Jerome H. Saltzer describes the concept in "Protection and the control of information sharing in Multics," *Communications of the ACM*, 17, 7 (July 1974), 388–402.

8. *For an operating system, the question is how blocks of time should be allocated to different processes so that work can be done efficiently.* Scheduling happens at different levels in the operating system; we're concentrating on CPU scheduling here.

9. *If the time quantum is long enough for any process to finish in the time it's given...* This is associated with what's called *batch processing*. For some kinds of tasks (imagine running a weather simulation), we're mainly interested in the results produced by a program rather than interacting with it; we simply let processes run until they finish.

10. *...airports typically follow a first-come, first-served policy when several planes are ready for takeoff.* Patrick Smith outlines some of the complexities of airplane scheduling in his column, "Ask the Pilot," in *Salon* (August 17, 2007), and suggests a priority-based policy based on the number of passengers on each plane.

11. *Perseus and the Witches.* These witches are the Graea of Greek legend, as described in Thomas Bulfinch's *Golden Age of Myth and Legend* (Wordsworth, 1998); similar witches also appear in fairytales and folk stories, such as "The sorceress's head," by Italo Calvino, in *Italian Folktales* (Pantheon, 1980). The Graea share one eye and one tooth, passing it to each other in order to see and eat. This feature—most myths and folktales include comparably macabre elements under the surface—matches the concept of processes that share a computer's resources. The match would be even closer if the Graea shared a single brain that was somehow passed back and forth.

12. *...the entire space gradually gets broken up with free regions scattered irregularly throughout.* This is *external fragmentation* of memory. In the discussion that follows, of breaking up memory into fixed-size frames to be allocated to processes, there's also *internal fragmentation*, when a process doesn't use all of the memory within the last frame it's allocated.

Chapter 7

1. *Vannevar Bush*: Bush's report, *Science: The Endless Frontier* (U.S. Government Printing Office, 1945), can be found in the online documents maintained by the National Science Foundation.
2. *Hypertext*: Ted Nelson coined the term "hypertext" in 1965. He described his vision in "Complex information processing: a file structure for the complex, the changing and the indeterminate," *Proceedings of the 20th ACM National Conference*, pp. 84–100. He is well known for an early computing manifesto, *Computer Lib*, self-published in 1974.
3. *J. C. R. Licklider*: My description merges ideas presented in different papers: "Memorandum for members and affiliates of the intergalactic computer network," by J. C. R. Licklider; "Man-computer symbiosis," by J. C. R. Licklider, in *IRE Transactions on Human Factors in Electronics*, 1 (1960), pp. 4–11; and "The computer as a communication device," by J. C. R. Licklider and R. W. Taylor, in *Science and Technology*, 76, 2 (1968), pp. 21–31.
4. *We can think of an index as a tree . . .* This works only if we don't count being able to access the index from the body of the document and if we have the unlikely situation that no two terms are listed with the same page number. Otherwise, the index is a graph.
5. *They compile your findings with everyone else's in the organization . . .* This is a memex analogy for today's search engines. Ian H. Witten, Marco Gori, and Teresa Numerico give a very good introduction to this area in *Web Dragons: Inside the Myths of Search Engine Technology* (Morgan Kaufmann, 2006).
6. *. . . something that looks very much like today's World Wide Web.* The memex isn't exactly the Web, and the Web isn't the only way to think about hypertext. For example, Bush envisioned people exchanging "trails," or chains of connected documents, while the Web has a strong focus on individual pages. In other plausible models of hypertext, links aren't followed to new documents; a link in one document might be expanded in place to show information from another document.
7. *Bush's article doesn't mention the communication and transportation technology of the time, but I've imagined it to include the pneumatic tubes . . .* My hypothetical extension of the memex is partly inspired by the way U.S. Senator Ted Stevens famously described the Internet in 2006: "the Internet is not something that you just dump something on. It's not a big truck. It's a series of tubes."
8. *Your package moves from one processing center to another . . .* Jeff Blyskal and Marie Hodge explain how mail travels through the New York postal system in "Why your mail is so slow," *New York Magazine* (November 9, 1987), pp. 42–55.
9. *. . . but no one looks inside.* This is an oversimplification. For security or filtering, it's sometimes necessary to look inside packages of information, both in real mail systems and on computer systems.

10. ...*snow or rain or gloom of night*... "Neither snow nor rain nor heat nor gloom of night stays these couriers from the swift completion of their appointed rounds." An online document from the U.S. Postal Service, titled "Postal Service Mission and 'Motto'," states that the Postal Service has no official motto, and that the source of this phrase is *The Persian Wars*, by Herodotus.

11. *Changes can be isolated within a layer.* The strict separation of functionality in different layers can be broken if necessary, to improve efficiency.

12. *A protocol is a set of rules*... Kurose and Ross define a protocol in this way in *Computer Networking: A Top-Down Approach* (2010): *A **protocol** defines the format and the order of messages exchanged between two or more communicating entities, as well as the actions taken on the transmission and/or receipt of a message or other event.*

13. ...*telephones and fax machines, which have existed since the 1800s.* Alexander Bain invented the facsimile machine in the 1840s, for use with telegraphs, some three decades before the first telephone appeared.

14. *Leonard Kleinrock:* Kleinrock describes his early work in "An early history of the Internet [History of Communications]," *Communications Magazine, IEEE*, 48, 8 (2010), pp. 26–36.

15. *Computers can break up the information they exchange into small messages, or packets.* I'm abusing the terminology of networking by calling packets "messages." Information packaged up for communication over the Internet is described in different ways, depending on the protocol involved. They might be "segments," "datagrams," or "frames," and even the term "message" has a specific technical connotation. I'm using "message" to mean any example of what I've called a "burst of information," including a "packet."

16. *Instead, the capacity of the network can be divided more dynamically over time*... This is conceptually similar to the way a CPU's activities can be divided up between processes over time.

17. *In 1969 it connected four computers*... ARPANET connected the institutions of the major players in network computing at the time: Leonard Kleinrock, at the University of California at Los Angeles; Douglas Engelbart, at Stanford Research Institute in Menlo Park, CA; Glen Culler and Burton Fried, at the University of California at Santa Barbara; and Ivan Sutherland, at the University of Utah. Lawrence G. Roberts, at DARPA, developed a plan for the new network, and a team at Bolt Beranek and Newman, in collaboration with Robert Kahn, put the system in place. Dozens of other researchers made names for themselves throughout the life of the project.

18. ... *"multiple independent networks of rather arbitrary design"* ... This phrase and other information about the history of the Internet are taken from an article by Barry M. Leiner, Vinton G. Cerf, David D. Clark, Robert E. Kahn, Leonard Kleinrock, Daniel C. Lynch, Jon Postel, Larry G. Roberts, and Stephen Wolff, published as "A brief history of the Internet," *ACM SIGCOMM Computer Communication Review*, 39, 5 (2009), pp. 22–31. David D. Clark also gives a

good history of ideas that drove the Internet in "The design philosophy of the DARPA Internet protocols," *SIGCOMM Computer Communication Review*, 18, 4 (1988), pp. 106–114.

19. *They simply keep track of which other routers in their neighborhood they can communicate with*. This isn't necessarily true for all systems on the Internet, but it's a rough approximation.

20. *...the Internet Protocol Suite*. There are other ways to organize the capabilities of a network into layers. In particular, there's the Open Systems Interconnection model, which divides network functionality into layers in a different way. I've given a breakdown of the Internet Protocol Suite into four layers, but some sources identify more—the details won't concern us.

Chapter 8

1. *Calculating Space*: MIT Technical Translation of Konrad Zuse, "Rechnender Raum," *Schriften zur Datenverarbeitung, 1* (Friedr. Vieweg & Sohn, 1969). In this paragraph I've used the phrasing of Jürgen Schmidhuber's article, "A computer scientist's view of life, the universe, and everything," in Christian Freksa, Wilfried Brauer, Matthias Jantzen, and Rüdiger Valk (eds.), *Foundations of Computer Science: Potential—Theory—Cognition, Lecture Notes in Computer Science* (Springer, 1997), pp. 201–208.

2. *This is a finite state machine*. These are also called deterministic finite automata, or DFAs. The "deterministic" part means that you won't see two transitions with the same label coming from the same state. That would mean that the same action in a given state could take you to different destination states, as if reality were branching off into alternate universes every time this happened. Such a machine would be nondeterministic. Nondeterministic machines can be simulated by deterministic machines, surprisingly enough.

3. *As a general model of computation...* State machines can be very useful, though, in more restricted situations. For example, we could build a state machine to model the behavior of a four-way traffic light, where we actually *want* restrictions on the number of states in the system. The state machine's simplicity is an advantage here. If someone asks, "What happens if the traffic signal shows green in opposite directions at the same time?" we can answer that we've designed the state machine not to have a *green/green* state. If someone builds a traffic light to our specification and it occasionally shows *green/green*, we'd say that the hardware is behaving incorrectly, and we could point to our state machine model to explain what it's doing wrong.

4. *Let's try a different approach.* We'll be skipping from state machines directly to Turing machines, from one of the least powerful abstractions of computation to one of the most powerful. There's actually a hierarchy of abstract computational models, each more powerful than the last. Computer scientists study

this hierarchy out of theoretical interest, but there's also a practical angle: it's useful to know, for a given class of problems, the least powerful model that's still capable of handling the class. This gives us an indication of how easy or hard those problems are.

5. *...Alan Turing is the single most important figure...* Turing's paper, "On computable numbers, with an application to the Entscheidungsproblem," *Proceedings of the London Mathematical Society*, 2, 42 (1936), pp. 230–265, can be found online. Turing's contributions to mathematics, to biological modeling, and to the future field of artificial intelligence led to his recognition as a Fellow of the Royal Society. Turing's story is cut sadly and abruptly short after this point. His affair with another man was a crime in 1952 Britain. Two years after his prosecution and conviction he was found dead of cyanide poisoning, with a half-eaten apple by his bed. Turing's remarkable life is described in *Alan Turing: The Enigma*, by Andrew Hodges (Vintage, 1992).

6. *You can imagine it lying on an infinitely long table, if that helps.* Joseph Weizenbaum, in *Computer Power and Human Reason* (W. H. Freeman, 1976), describes an equivalent machine built of black and white stones, playing dice, and a long roll of toilet paper.

7. *David Harel puts it this way...* In *Computers Ltd.*, p. 40.

8. *...an excellent model for what real computers are capable of doing.* I'm skirting the edge of a philosophical debate about the "strong" version of the Church-Turing thesis, which runs along these lines: "Turing machines can compute anything that any possible physical machine can compute." Jack Copeland, in "The Church-Turing thesis," *The Stanford Encyclopedia of Philosophy*, Edward N. Zalta, ed. (Fall, 2008), explains the context of Church's and Turing's work, which dealt with the way that human mathematicians and logicians carry out procedures to produce results, such as proving that a specific equation or logical formula is true. Turing machines give us a formal way to describe such procedures, taking human judgment and intuition out of the picture. This is a good match for what computers are capable of, but a key question is left open: Could some physical machine carry out operations impossible for someone working with pencil and paper, following precise instructions (from a limited set) without making mistakes or applying intuition, even in principle? The existence of such a machine would make a good deal of theory irrelevant to practical computing. Still, our concern isn't with whether computers *are* Turing machines; rather, it's whether Turing machines are good *models* of computers. Computer scientists universally take this to be the case.

9. *...a completely general program that could take any other program...* In terms of algorithms, I'm describing what's called a *universal Turing machine*, one that can emulate the behavior of another Turing machine. We've seen a related idea in Chapter 5, in the concept of translators that can turn a program in one language into a program in another. Here we're talking about a program that can execute another program.

10. `loop-forever()`. We can write this in Python as `while(True):` `pass`, which repeats its body, doing nothing, forever.

11. *The halting problem is just one example of an infinite number of undecidable problems.* This is due to Rice's theorem, by Henry Gordon Rice, in "Classes of Recursively Enumerable Sets and Their Decision Problems," *Transactions of the American Mathematical Society*, 74 (1953), pp. 358–366.

12. *Unless someone comes up with a fundamentally different explanation of what computation…* Turing machines do have some limitations as models of real computers. They carry out computations very slowly—for example, notice that a Turing machine can't jump between different locations on the tape; it has to move over all the in-between locations—but that's not a concern for us. We're interested in what Turing machines can do, rather than how fast they are. They don't handle input and output very well, in the way that we're used to thinking of an interactive system such as a computer game. A Turing machine takes a problem-solving perspective on computing: Given some input, produce some output, then stop. Turing machines are also inappropriate as models for computer programs that are intended to run forever, such as one that checks whether you've received email or updates your clock. (Edward A. Lee touches on this topic in "What's Ahead for Embedded Software?," *IEEE Computer Magazine*, 33, 9 (2000), pp. 18–26.) But these are relatively unimportant objections when we're exploring what computers can't do, algorithmically.

13. *Gödel's Incompleteness Theorem…* I've paraphrased Solomon Feferman, in his online document, "The nature and significance of Gödel's incompleteness theorems," Gödel Centenary Program, Institute for Advanced Study, Princeton. Torkel Franzén's *Gödel's Theorem: An Incomplete Guide to Its Use and Abuse* (A. K. Peters, 2005) is a readable introduction to incompleteness; Douglas Hofstadter also explores the concept in *Gödel, Escher, Bach: An Eternal Golden Braid* (Vintage, 1980).

14. *…we'll ask about its worst-case performance.* We can also analyze algorithms to find their average-case and even best-case performance, but analyzing the worst case is typically easier, and the results are useful. We'd prefer not to be surprised if it's possible for an algorithm to take a very, very long time to finish, even if those cases are rare.

15. *We can use computational models other than Turing machines, much closer to real computers, so that our predictions match the performance we will observe.* The time complexity of an algorithm depends on the model of computation we're using. Algorithmic complexity is often based on a *Random Access Machine*, an abstraction equivalent to a Turing machine. In particular, a RAM model gives us direct access to information stored in memory, as on a real computer, rather than requiring linear traversal as on a Turing machine, and so our

analysis results are more directly applicable. The difference in time complexity compared with a Turing machine will always be polynomial, however, which is meaningful for the discussion later in this chapter.

16. *This is most often a question about whether an algorithm exists...* I'm eliding two subtleties here. First, it's possible to prove that a problem is tractable without identifying an algorithm to solve that problem, but this is relatively uncommon. Second, problems in P, the class mentioned at the end of the paragraph in the text, must be *decision problems*, problems whose solution is either Yes or No. The problems in this chapter can all be converted into decision problems, though the conversion can be complicated.

17. *...all of the plausible ideas we have for solving subset sum run in exponential time...* If you're thinking of a pseudo-polynomial time dynamic programming algorithm to solve subset sum, then you already know more than this book can tell you.

18. *We put all problems that have this property in the class NP...* Strictly speaking, NP (like P) contains decision problems that require Yes/No answers. If you're curious about what "nondeterministic polynomial time" means, here's a brief explanation in the context of choosing coins in the subset sum problem. I've already mentioned nondeterminism in the end note for finite state machines; one way to think about it is that if you're deciding between some number of choices, the universe branches into many new universes, one for each possible choice. Suppose we design an algorithm that goes through the set of coins, one at a time, deciding to push one forward or leave it in place. On each step of this algorithm, the universe branches into two new parallel universes, one in which the algorithm pushes the coin forward, the other in which it's left in place. If the target combination is found, the algorithm returns from whatever universe it's in. To solve subset sum for 20 coins, an ordinary algorithm will take up to a million (2^{20}) steps, but when our new algorithm takes a step, every possible outcome is represented across all of the parallel universes. This parallelism means that the new algorithm finishes in at most 20 steps. This is just a theoretical exercise, because we don't have nondeterministic (quantum) computers to run nondeterministic algorithms, but if a problem can be solved by such a nondeterministic polynomial time algorithm, then it's in the class NP. This definition is equivalent to the one in the text.

19. *Let's consider why it's important.* As an aside, the Clay Mathematics Institute in Cambridge, MA, has offered a $1 million prize to anyone who can definitively answer whether P = NP.

20. *...problems that we don't know how to solve efficiently...* This isn't quite true. Many efficient algorithms can produce approximate solutions for some problems in NP, and often they're good enough for practical use. Further, remember that we've been talking about performance in the worst case.

It can happen that most problems of a given type are easy to solve, with only a few examples being very hard.

21. *...Stephen Cook proved a remarkable result...* The two classic papers are Stephen A. Cook, "The complexity of theorem-proving procedures," *Proceedings of the Third Annual ACM Symposium on the Theory of Computing* (1971), pp. 151–158, and Richard M. Karp, "Reducibility among combinatorial problems," *Proceedings of a Symposium on the Complexity of Computer Computations* (Plenum Press, 1972), pp. 85–103.

22. *On the other hand, if someone develops a proof that one NP-complete problem can't be solved efficiently, then none of them can: P ≠ NP.* For example, suppose you prove that subset sum is impossible to solve efficiently. Why couldn't some other NP-complete problem nevertheless have an efficient solution? But that would mean that an efficient algorithm exists for that other problem, and we could efficiently translate it into an algorithm to solve subset sum (that's the nature of NP-completeness), which results in a contradiction.

Chapter 9

1. *The paintings by Harold Cohen's Aaron system...* Cohen's program, Aaron, is the subject of Pamela McCorduck's book, *Aaron's Code: Meta-Art, Artificial Intelligence, and the Work of Harold Cohen* (W. H. Freeman, 1990).

2. *"We used to think that chess was hard..."* This was during a lunchtime conversation with Robin Popplestone, a professor at the University of Massachusetts who worked in the areas of robotics and programming languages.

3. *Alan Turing devised just such a test in 1950...* Alan Turing's imitation game is described in "Computing machinery and intelligence," *Mind*, 59, 236 (1950), pp. 433–460. The original framing of the Turing Test involved a questioner communicating with a computer and a person, who would compete against each other to be identified as the human being.

4. *New tests have been proposed...* Paul R. Cohen describes these and other grand challenges for AI systems in "If not Turing's test, then what?" *AI Magazine*, 26, 4 (2006), pp. 61–67.

5. *...an AI system...* In popular writing you'll sometimes come across the expression "an AI" or "AIs" rather than "an AI system" or "AI systems," but the former usage is rare in the technical literature.

6. *I've described a simple task environment...* Russell and Norvig (2010) identify additional environment features, including whether what happens in an environment breaks up naturally into episodes that can be treated independently (*episodic* or *sequential*) and whether the "rules" about what can possibly happen in the environment are known in advance (*known* or *unknown*).

7. *Insects and other animals with limited cognitive abilities are very success-ful...* Some animals, in particular some species of birds, are remarkably intelligent, much smarter than reflex agents. Robert W. Shumaker, Kristina R. Walkup, and Benjamin B. Beck catalog the variety of ways animals use tools in *Animal Tool Behavior: The Use and Manufacture of Tools by Animals* (Johns Hopkins University Press, 2011).

8. *Newell was working at the RAND Corporation in 1952...* These details are from Herbert Simon's paper, "Allen Newell," *Biographical Memoirs*, 71 (National Academies Press, 1997), pp. 141–173. The history of AI goes beyond this collaboration, of course. AI, as a field, began with a confer-ence at Dartmouth College in 1956. John McCarthy organized the con-ference with Marvin Minsky, Nathaniel Rochester, and Claude Shannon. Attendees, aside from Newell and Simon, also included Trenchard More, Arthur Samuel, Oliver Selfridge, and Ray Solomonoff, all well-known names in AI.

9. *...the physical symbol system hypothesis...* Allen Newell and Herbert A. Simon propose the hypothesis in "Computer science as empirical inquiry: Symbols and search," *Communications of the ACM*, 19, 3 (1976), pp. 113–126.

10. *The hypothesis has met with controversy.* Nils J. Nilsson summarizes the issues in "The physical symbol system hypothesis: Status and prospects," Max Lungarella, Rolf Pfeifer, Fumiya Iida, and Josh Bongard (eds.), *50 Years of Artificial Intelligence, Lecture Notes In Computer Science*, 4850 (Springer, 2007), pp. 9–17.

11. *Philosophers have gone back and forth on such questions for decades.* The best-known objection to the idea that computer programs can be intelligent is given in John Searle's article, "Minds, Brains and Programs," in *Behavioral and Brain Sciences*, 3, 3 (1980), pp. 417–457. The article is accompanied by several arguments by others against Searle's position.

12. *...the "knowledge level"...* Allen Newell, "The knowledge level: Presidential Address," *AI Magazine*, 2, 2 (1981), pp. 1–20.

13. *One is a problem representation... The other concept is search.* This is a main-stream view of AI, but some subfields place less importance on these abstractions. For example, an influential paper by Rodney Brooks is titled "Intelligence without representation," *Artificial Intelligence*, 47 (1991), pp. 139–160, a possibility that he expands on in the collection *Cambrian Intelligence: The Early History of the New AI* (MIT Press, 1999). In robotics, machine vision, and other areas it's possible to find approaches to problem solving that rely on search only in a very abstract sense.

14. *A problem representation is a model internal to an agent...* In *Changes of Problem Representation: Theory and Experiments* (Springer-Verlag, 2003), Eugene Fink describes a problem representation as "a certain view of a problem and an approach to solving it." He further breaks a problem representation

down into a description of the domain (relevant information about the area in which you're solving problems) and a description of a problem (typically what you're allowed to do to solve the problem, where you start, and what counts as a solution).

15. *This new algorithm is called A* search.* I'm leaving out two subtleties in my description. First, when you're estimating the remaining time, is it better to overestimate or underestimate? It turns out to be better to underestimate as you go. If you overestimate the remaining time from a given vertex, there's the chance that you'll ignore that vertex for a long time—but it might be a shortcut. Second, when A* searches a graph it's not done until the goal vertex is added to the frontier and visited in its turn. Imagine that the last vertex before *Finish* along a specific path estimates the time to be 10 minutes and it actually turns out to be 500 minutes. Other remaining paths may beat that time significantly and need to be explored.

16. *It's impossible to reason from a true set of clauses to a false clause through truth-preserving rules.* Blackburn puts it this way (*Think*, p. 194): "Logic has only one concern...whether there is *no* way that the premises could be true without the conclusion being true."

17. *...a reasoning technique developed by Alan Robinson called resolution theorem proving.* J. Alan Robinson described this approach in "A machine oriented logic based on the resolution principle," *Journal of the Association for Computing Machinery*, 12 (1965), pp. 23–41.

18. *One approach to this problem is machine learning...* Thomas G. Dietterich's article "Machine Learning" gives a good overview of the area, in the *Nature Encyclopedia of Cognitive Science* (Macmillan, 2003).

19. *...we choose to split on the attribute that does the best job of predicting the target attribute...* We're making this decision based on information gain, which is derived from information entropy, a concept developed by Claude Shannon in a paper that established the field of information theory: "A mathematical theory of communication," *Bell System Technical Journal*, 27 (1948), pp. 379–423 and 623–656.

20. *We're still hill climbing.* You may notice a small difference between the two examples I've given. The route optimization example relies on the simplest possible version of hill climbing. The walking example is a variant called *steepest ascent* hill climbing, in which you check all possible steps and choose the best one.

21. *...an intelligent alien or robot forensic scientist, examining a human brain, might be similarly skeptical...* This is a familiar theme in science fiction, as represented by the work of Stanislaw Lem in *The Cyberiad: Fables for the Cybernetic Age* (Seabury Press, 1974) and by Terry Bisson's 1990 short story, "They're made out of meat," *OMNI* Magazine.

Chapter 10

1. *My mobile phone once drained its battery by taking 27 pictures of the inside of my pocket.* Donald Norman's *The Design of Everyday Things* (Doubleday, 1990) is full of similar examples and explanations of everyday technology that fails us.
2. *It should be easier to do the right thing...* and the rules that follow are variations on Ben Shneiderman's eight golden rules of interface design.
3. *In 1946 the ENIAC was turned on...* There's been considerable debate about what should be considered the very first computer (whether general- or special-purpose, whether electronic or not). There are at least half a dozen candidates, some with strong claims, including the Zuse Z3 and Z4 in Germany (electromechanical rather than electronic); the Atanasoff–Berry Computer in Iowa (no longer running in 1946, and special-purpose); and the Colossus Mark 1 and Mark 2 in the UK (special-purpose).
4. *"The user obviously does not want a message for successful completion..."* This is from "JOSS: a designer's view of an experimental on-line computing system," by J. C. Shaw, in *Proceedings of the Fall Joint Computer Conference, Part I* (ACM Press, 1964). JOSS had a much more positive impact on interactive computing than this snippet might suggest. The AI program I mention is the Logic Theorist, which was able to prove a number of theorems in Alfred North Whitehead and Bertrand Russell's *Principia Mathematica*, as described in Allen Newell, J. C. Shaw, and Herbert A. Simon, "Elements of a theory of human problem solving," *Psychological Review*, 65, 3 (1958), pp. 151–166.
5. *A* good overview of interactive computing at this time can be found in an article by Jeff Johnson, Teresa L. Roberts, William Verplank, David C. Smith, Charles H. Irby, Marian Beard, and Kevin Mackey about a descendant of the Alto: "The Xerox Star: A Retrospective," *IEEE Computer*, 22, 9 (1989), pp. 11–26.
6. *Paul Dourish:* My presentation of the history of HCI is similar to Paul Dourish's account in *Where the Action Is: The Foundations of Embodied Interaction* (MIT Press, 2001).
7. *In 2007 a Norwegian woman...* Kai A. Olsen describes the Norwegian banking case in "The $100,000 Keying Error," *IEEE Computer*, 41, 4 (2008), p. 108. The trading errors are described by Malcolm Moore in "Japanese trader makes £22 billion mistake," *The Telegraph* (February 26, 2009).
8. *...Ross Koppel and colleagues studied a system...* My description is taken from Ross Koppel, Joshua P. Metlay, Abigail Cohen, Brian Abaluck, A. Russell Localio, Stephen E. Kimmel, and Brian L. Strom's article, "Role of computerized physician order entry systems in facilitating medication errors," *Journal of the American Medical Association*, 293, 10 (2005), pp. 1197–1203.

9. ...*John Gould and Clayton Lewis asked hundreds of software designers*...John D. Gould and Clayton Lewis published "Designing for usability: Key principles and what designers think" in *Communications of the ACM*, 28, 3 (1985), pp. 300–311.

10. ...*the long-term goals of interactive computing are much broader.* A report edited by Richard Harper, Tom Rodden, Yvonne Rogers, and Abigail Sellen gives a fuller account of this view: *Being Human: Human-Computer Interaction in the Year 2020* (Microsoft Research, 2008).

INDEX